Greenhill Books

With Napoleon's Guns

Colonel Jean-Nicolas-Auguste Noël

With Napoleon's Guns

The Military Memoirs of an Officer of the First Empire

Edited, translated and introduced by Rosemary Brindle

Greenhill Books • London
Stackpole Books • Pennsylvania

Greenhill Books

With Napoleon's Guns is a translation of Jean-Nicolas-Auguste Noël's
Souvenirs militaires d'un officier du premier Empire, 1795–1832,
which was originally published by Berger-Levrault, Paris, in 1895.

With Napoleon's Guns: The Military Memoirs of an Officer of the First Empire

First published 2005 by Greenhill Books/Lionel Leventhal Ltd
Park House, 1 Russell Gardens, London NW11 9NN, England
and
Stackpole Books, 5067 Ritter Road, Mechanicsburg, PA 17055, USA

British Library Cataloguing-in Publication Data
Noël, Jean-Nicolas-Auguste
With Napoleon's guns: the military memoirs of an officer of the First Empire
1. Noël, Jean-Nicolas-Auguste
2. Artillerymen – France – Biography
3. Napoleonic Wars, 1800–1815 – Personal narratives, French
I. Title
940.2'742'092

ISBN 1-85367-642-X

Library of Congress Cataloguing-in Publication Data available

For more information on our books, please visit www.greenhillbooks.com, email
sales@greenhillbooks.com, or telephone us within the UK on 020 8458 6314.
You can also write to us at the above London address.

Typeset by GCS, Leighton Buzzard, Bedfordshire, LU7 1AR
Printed and bound in Great Britain by
Creative Print and Design (Wales), Ebbw Vale

Contents

Illustrations

Calibres, Dimensions and Weights
of French Ordnance

The data in the following table is taken from R. W. Adye's *The Bombardier and Pocket Gunner*, London, 1802. The weights of shot are in the French measure (a French pound being 1.08 of its British equivalent). Other measurements are in the British measure.

	calibre (in)	Brass		Iron	
		length	weight (lb)	length	weight (lb)
36-pdr	6.9	—	—	9 ft 8 in	8,260
24-pdr	6.03	—	—	9 ft 1.5 in	5,712
16-pdr	5.26	—	—	8 ft 4 in	4,872
12-pdr	4.78	6 ft 6 in	1,952.6	8 ft 2 in	2,324
8-pdr	4.18	5 ft 8 in	1,291.7	6ft	1,792
4-pdr	3.315	4 ft 6 in	637.2	—	—

Maps

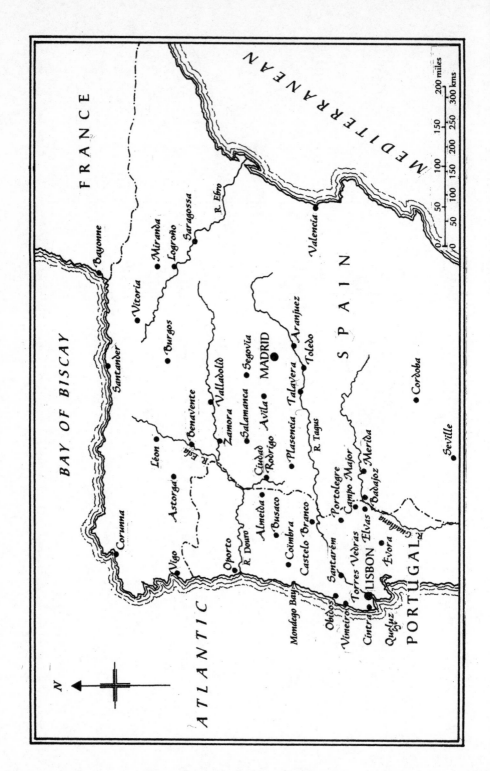

Spain and Portugal, 1809–1811

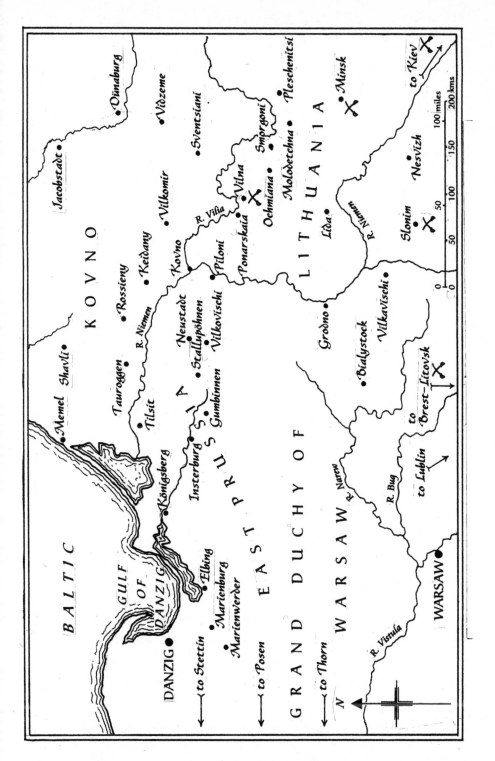

The Russian Campaign, 1812: Marienburg–Kovno–Vilna

Introduction

Jean-Nicolas-Auguste Noël was born in 1778, the year in which Napoleon – then aged nine – was brought by his father from Corsica to be educated in France. Noël's own military education began seventeen years later in 1795 at the artillery school at Châlons, the same year that Napoleon was appointed commander-in-chief in Italy. Napoleon had earned his swift promotion as a reward for having used 'a whiff of grapeshot' to halt two insurgent columns marching on the Tuileries, thereby saving the new constitution of the Republic. About five hundred people were killed by Bonaparte's artillery, using guns that had been seized from the National Guard park and brought to him by a young squadron commander, Murat, who would later become Napoleon's brilliant cavalry commander.

By the time Noël had completed his studies at the artillery school in July 1796 and had been appointed as a second lieutenant in the 8th Regiment of Horse Artillery, General Napoleon Bonaparte had defeated the Austrians at Lodi, entered Milan and was proclaiming himself as the liberator of Italy.

The life of the new second lieutenant of Horse Artillery was to be determined by the young general's ambition and skill for nearly twenty years.

Well before the French Revolution, the artillery of the royal army had been redesigned and standardised by Jean Baptiste Grimbeauval. Napoleon, himself a trained artilleryman, ensured that the artillery under his command continued to evolve and improve, so that it became an arm that could compare with the best in the world. Speed and mobility were the factors upon which his successes relied, and his mobility depended upon the capacity of his guns to keep pace with the infantry, and to manoeuvre so that they could dominate a battlefield.

An important reform was introduced early in Napoleon's consulate: in the past, the royal army had used civilian contractors to move the heavy guns, and the drawbacks implicit in this arrangement were obvious. Civilian contractors could hardly be expected to hurry into danger, or to stay around when it threatened, so they often left the big field pieces on the battlefield where, lacking their drivers and teams of horses, they remained immobilised unless the gunners themselves were able to drag them into

13

new positions. It was not unknown for contractors actually to abandon the guns in positions that inhibited the movement of the rest of the army.

In the year 1800, Napoleon created the *train d'artillerie* (artillery train). At first there were eight *train* battalions, each commanded by a captain, but their numbers grew, as did their efficiency. The personnel consisted of specially trained soldiers who now became responsible, not only for the movement of the guns but also for the training and care of the horses on which mobility was bound to depend. Resupplies, replacement guns, forges and extra caissons were brought up by the artillery park that travelled in the wake of the army. More manageable gun carriages had been introduced to carry the lighter, bronze gun barrels that were now in use, and horses and *train* personnel remained near the guns so that tactical use could be made of fire-power on the field of battle.

This innovative and aggressive use of the artillery demanded a new breed of officer. Young, clever and capable of independent action, they emerged from the training establishments. Many, like Noël, came from the middle classes and were, like him, passionately patriotic and determined to protect France from the foreigners that they perceived to be threatening France and the Revolution. These were the men on whom Napoleon depended to exploit his innovations, to lead the semi-autonomous formations he created; to act with skill and courage in the smoke and confusion of battle as well as to ensure that the guns made their way across Europe from Torres Vedras to Moscow, from Venice to the Channel ports. Their progress was often made under conditions of the utmost hardship, over rivers, mountains and ravines, through war-torn country, ravaged lands laid waste by the passage of successive armies and emptied of food and forage.

Artillery formations and the *train*, slowed by the necessity of negotiating narrow mountain passes and swampy valley bottoms, often found themselves far behind the main army, at the mercy of guerrilla bands and the hostility of a resentful population, and it was at such times that the professionalism and skill of their officers was put to the test.

It was with officers such as the young Noël in mind that the British general, Sir Thomas Picton, was to remark, 'If I had fifty thousand such men as I commanded in Spain, with French officers at their head, I'm damned if I wouldn't march from one end of Europe to the other.'* When his companions objected to this apparently un-patriotic comment, he pointed out that both Marlborough and Wellington had learned the art of war in France, and said that 'nine French officers in ten can command an army, while our fellows, though brave as lions are totally and utterly ignorant of their professions'. These were harsh words, but reflected the exasperation of many senior

* *The Reminiscences and Recollections of Captain Gronow.*

British officers at the shortcomings of some of their subordinates who had not had the advantages of being trained at military academies such as those that were well established in France.

Independence of mind and attention to detail have produced a military memoir of unusual interest in the journal that Colonel Noël kept from the days of his cadetship at Châlons until he retired in 1832. It was not until 1850, in retirement, that he thought to make his memoirs available to his children and grandchildren. As he had no wider public in view, he had no difficulty in allowing himself to be entirely frank in his account of events and in his opinion of the people he encountered. He wrote at the time:

> These are not memoirs that I am writing, but a simple journal of my military duties across Europe and some short accounts of the battles at which I was present. I write of what I saw and of the things that happened around me.
>
> As a soldier I carried out the orders given to me, to the best of my ability, without argument. As I was not party to the secrets of the general staff, I could not allow myself to judge them. Nor is it possible, on campaign, to understand the reasons and difficulties that constrain the Commanding General.

Nevertheless, he took advantage of the opportunity to put on record some account of matters that he had witnessed but which had been incorrectly reported during the intervening years, by individuals who had not had the advantage of first-hand knowledge:

> I add a few memories and remarks suggested by the events. If I sometimes express my own opinions on men and matters, I do it only to put right the assertions of various historians who are more anxious to indulge their prejudices and opinions than to relate the truth.

All who have suffered the irritation of seeing their own actions inaccurately reported may well sympathise with the colonel, and these 'remarks' to which he refers are not the least enlightening part of his writing.

After his death it was his son, Auguste, who decided to prepare the journal for publication. Auguste died before he could achieve his object, but this was finally realised by his son – Noël's grandson – Lucien, in 1895.

The gradual evolution of his opinion of Napoleon is expressed with great honesty in the course of Noël's narrative. An admirer of his commander-in-chief – and no one could have been more appreciative of Napoleon's qualities as a leader in battle and as an administrator – he was not an unquestioning Bonapartist. He was by no means blind to the reverse side of this shining coin. As early as 1802, when the Empire was established, he writes of his doubts about Napoleon's despotic tendencies and his arrogance. Then, as he stood with his detachment, in the cold, waiting for Napoleon's coronation procession to pass by, he felt sympathy with the grumbles of the people, who were kept waiting by their new ruler. He noticed the theatricality of the costumes worn by the Imperial party and wondered at the similarity of the new court to the old Royalist court that had been ousted with so much suffering and bloodshed.

This ability to stand back and observe was not diminished as the years went by. His unwavering patriotism remained as steady as ever, but his humanity and common sense obliged him to see, quite clearly, the disastrous path to which his admired leader was committed. Noël was active at many of the great battles and sieges of the period and, increasingly, it was his love of his country that inspired him. France, rather than Napoleon, became the reason for his service.

The terrible losses by both sides at Wagram, and the chilling sights and sounds of the battlefield after the encounter, clearly appalled Noël far more than the battle itself for, as he remarks, there is too much to do in the heat of the fight to feel either fear or pity at the time. Even more shocking to him seems to have been the wilful extension by Napoleon of the war into Spain and the deposition of the Spanish monarch in favour of Joseph Bonaparte. From this act, which could not by any means be construed as a defensive measure taken to protect his homeland, Noël dates the decline in French fortunes. Up to that point he had felt that the hardships and losses endured by the French armies had been unavoidable in order to repel the foreigner from the fatherland's frontiers. Now, he recognised that an inexcusable war of conquest was fatally draining his country's manpower and wealth. Perhaps he sensed that a vital ingredient needed for victory had been lost – the passion of the soldier who is protecting his own home – and felt, with Tacitus, that 'the man who is prepared to die will always be your master'. But in spite of his doubts and anxiety, his duty was indisputable; it was, as ever, to the legal government of France and to his commander-in-chief.

As the tide of war and death surged across all Europe, Colonel Noël saw the realisation of his most pessimistic fears.

Campaigns in Spain and Portugal were conducted under conditions of the greatest hardship, borne, at first, in the hope that some great battle would see the defeat of the elusive enemy and bring the struggle to an end. Life was particularly hard for the artillery, as it crossed mountain passes so narrow that passage for the field guns had to be hacked out of the rock, and often lagging far behind the army when the ill-armed train was exposed to extreme danger.

It was as the Army of Portugal waited for reinforcement before the impregnable lines of Torres Vedras that Colonel Noël acknowledged the loss of confidence, first in their leaders and then, to some extent, in themselves, that the troops experienced. He saw only too clearly that although his life as an officer was harsh, his men suffered even more, that they had been sustained on their cruel march across the peninsula by the prospect of early victory. Now that the prospect had been snatched from them, indiscipline and brutality became common. Noël never ceased in his admiration of the seasoned, hardy and brave French troops, always attributing their failings to the misery and starvation that they were forced to endure, though he makes it quite clear that the behaviour of some, at least, of the officers left much to be desired. He is frank to question the ability of certain of the higher command and does not hesitate to show his anger at the ostentatious luxury of the lives of some senior officers, whose baggage carts encumbered the line of march.

Even at this stage in his memoirs, while acknowledging the 'recklessness' of Napoleon, the veniality of certain senior officers, the brutal behaviour of some of the marauding French troops, Noël does not seem to question the integrity of his cause. Although he is not blind to the suffering of the natives of the countries that have been overrun and ruined by the passage of armies, as a man of his era he does not ask the moral questions that might trouble a soldier of more modern times. Very occasionally a dangerous tendency towards contempt for his enemy can be discerned – the result, no doubt, of so many years of triumph and victory – and this adds to the bewilderment he so clearly feels when he finds that his Emperor appears to have abandoned his forces in the peninsula to their fate.

Although Colonel Noël had come to query the imperial pretensions of his Emperor, he was not, indeed could not have been, prepared for the terrible disillusionment he felt when, with his disciplined battery of heavy guns, he at last encountered the rabble that was the French army in retreat from Moscow. Not given to hyperbole, his account of the utter breakdown of discipline in the most dreadful circumstances paints an unforgettable and moving picture. He seems to come near to despair when he finds his own officers and men succumbing to the prevailing disorder and melting away into the chaotic crowd. He carries on with typical determination. Although the Emperor has deserted his shattered army and left it under the command of Marshal Murat, an officer completely unsuited to the task, it remains Noël's duty to get his guns safely back to France. He has still to endure the anguish of seeing the wounded abandoned and supplies destroyed so that the disorganised remnants of the army may be withdrawn to a position where a stand can be made.

Thereafter, his journal paints a stoic picture of fighting and falling back, culminating in the terrible two-day Battle of the Nations at Leipzig. His account of that dreadful battlefield is chilling and vivid, as is the story of the subsequent retreat to the Rhine. Muddle, courage, desertions, disease and deaths: he notes them day after day and is even driven at last to admit his own loss of confidence. By this time he has come so far and undergone so much, without apparently losing his belief that his Emperor would at last prevail, that his sudden gloom comes as a shock to the reader.

The last episodes of Noël's memoirs are of peculiar interest. To fears of defeat are added confusion and a growing suspicion of higher command, culminating in the chaos of the defence and final abandonment of Paris. His account of the forlorn attempt to protect the capital, deserted as it was by the Imperial family, and in the absence of the Emperor, illuminates the bravery of the leaders and men in the various doomed pockets of resistance. Suspicions of double-dealing and treachery cloud the final hours before the capitulation.

By this time Noël had survived years of campaigning. If he had been wounded, he has not mentioned it; if he had been among the thousands struck down with fever, he has given no account of it. He has been loyal, dutiful and efficient. That he has observed men and events with an ironic eye has at no time diminished his patriotic commitment to his native land. He has been critical of, but not disloyal to, his superior officers. Now, with Napoleon's departure for Elba, Colonel Noël finds himself confronted with a dilemma that cannot be overcome by courage alone. For years the good of France and of Napoleon had seemed to be identical, but now the only criterion had to be the welfare of France. Noël swears loyalty to the returning Bourbons, hoping for an end to the slaughter and the wastage of his country by war.

There was no wild enthusiasm for the unendearing Louis XVIII, but Napoleon's popularity had waned, and there was an exhausted acceptance of the new regime by the weary population. The period before the Emperor's return was busy with plot and counter-plot that filled minds with ideas of treachery and betrayal. Noël makes quite plain the disenchantment of the army and deplores the debasement of the Légion d'Honneur at the hands of the new rulers. Even so, he remains faithful to his oath to the new king, until that king deserts the country. The stage is set for the last act and another period of confusion, treachery and divided loyalties, when Noël, for the first time in command of a battle, receives his first (and only) wound, ironically at the hand of a fellow countryman, and is taken prisoner.

Where direct comparisons can be made, Noël's narrative is well supported by other writers and his memoirs give a vivid portrait of an era as observed by a thoroughly decent, honest man who viewed the events in which he took part with humour, intelligence and a refreshing absence of self-importance or bigotry. No one could grudge him the long and peaceful retirement that he deserved and enjoyed after the turbulence of his war years.

With Napoleon's Guns

Chapter One

I Begin My Military Career: The First Years in the Service (1795–1799)

The Terror at Saint-Dié. I was born at Saint-Dié, and had barely begun my Latin studies under a tutor at Baccarat, when the great revolution of 1789 began.

I can say nothing of that period except that, among my family and friends, I watched joy and enthusiasm give way to anxiety and terror, to which were added eventually the fear of invasion.

Two events have remained engraved on my memory as a result of The Terror; and they have inspired in me a horror of the violence of the mob and of the persecution that such violence generates. This has been true of almost all regimes. Are not the cut-throats of September 1792 the descendants of the murderers of St Bartholomew? And are the atrocities committed in the Midi in 1815 by the Trestaillon* gangs not similar to the excesses of the revolutionaries?

One night, my uncle – my mother's brother-in-law – a completely harmless man, arrived at our house in search of refuge from denunciation. He was taken to a garden that we owned outside the town and made comfortable in a little cabin, to which everything he needed was taken by night.

In September 1793, when I was on holiday at Saint-Dié, a nobleman who once owned Spitzemberg, a feudal castle of which the ruins can still be seen, was murdered in the streets of the town. He was chased, stoned, insulted, thrown down and trampled underfoot, covered with mud, rubbish and blood then, when he was no more than a corpse, dragged into the gutter. All this was done under the eyes of the authorities who were powerless to restrain such excesses. The descendants of some of the perpetrators of this cowardly murder would hardly be delighted if their names were now divulged; for they had not been the least fanatical in 1815, under the white cockade, against those who had served their country under the tricolour flag.

My studies. In 1793, at the time of the general uprising, I had almost finished my Latin studies at a boarding school in Nancy run by M. Michel, the grandfather of the

---

* This refers to incidents in July and August 1815, when Royalist bands, one of them led by Jacques Dupont, known as Trestaillon, massacred Protestants and Bonapartist soldiers in Nîmes.

21

present notary. I was summoned before the town council in order to be enlisted. But I was only fifteen and the minimum required age was sixteen. Being aware that I should soon have to leave as a soldier, I stopped studying Latin and began the study of mathematics, which I pursued with great enthusiasm and interest.

Many young men of the town were in the same situation as myself. Our professor was M. Spitz, who later became a school inspector and who had previously taught General Druot.*

My admission to the artillery school at Châlons. In February of 1795, a competitive examination was held at Châlons for admission to the artillery school. With two of my comrades, Jacques and Bureau, I went, with our teacher, to the town to sit the examination. The only result of the boasting and pretensions of M. Spitz was to cause the examiner, M. Labbé, to confront us with the most difficult questions. Although still young, M. Spitz wanted to be admitted to the school solely on the performance of his pupils. He was unwilling to submit himself to a public examination that he had previously failed, probably as a result of a natural timidity, for he was well educated. He had presented himself for examination at the same time as an earlier pupil of his, one who later became General Drouot. The latter had been admitted at once whereas his teacher had failed.

On 5 March 1795, all three of us, Jacques, Bureau and I, were admitted to the artillery school.

This time we did not travel by coach, but made our way on foot with our haversacks on our backs.

Our journey was, nevertheless, very cheerful. All three of us had good eyesight, stout legs and some money in our pockets. We saw the future with the hopeful eyes of seventeen-year-olds. However, we were not sorry, after we had passed Bar-le-Duc and before starting to cross the interminable plain of Champagne, to meet a carter who was returning empty to Châlons. He took us up into his cart and we rode with him along the old Roman road that ran to the north of the *route national* and avoided both Saint-Dizier and Vitry.

The artillery school occupied the buildings of the old seminary that is now the school of arts and crafts.

At the school we were paid our wages in *assignats*,† but these had so depreciated in value that they would buy only the occasional good dinner to relieve the school food, which left a lot to be desired. The bread that they gave us was often so undercooked (no doubt so that it would weigh more) that, if it were thrown hard against the wall, it would stick there.

---

* General Antoine, Count Drouot (1774–1847).
† These were banknotes issued during the French Revolution.

Joining the regiment. On 17 July 1796, after spending sixteen months at the school, I was made 2nd lieutenant in the 5th Company of the 8th Regiment of Horse Artillery, which was then stationed in Germany.

Three other pupils from the school were sent to the same regiment: Martin, who was killed at Wagram; Monnot, who died in a lunatic asylum at Maréville, where he had been incarcerated following the murder, in a mad rage, of his own father; and Clément, who became my friend and who died at Limoges in 1815, just at the moment the Army of the Loire was disbanded. He was lieutenant colonel of the 4th Horse Artillery, of which I was then the commander.

My comrades, Jacques and Bureau, left the school at the same time.

Jacques was unlucky. At the first battle in which he fought, one of his legs was shot off by a cannonball. As every man was needed at that time he soon made his way into the ministry of war. The last time I saw him he occupied a delightful sinecure at the Hôtel des Invalides.

Bureau was sent to an armaments factory, where he specialised in this branch of work and became well known. He was a lad of great wit and energy, and very well educated. Later, when we met after we had both retired, he loved to recite the verses of Virgil and the Odes of Horace.

The Army of the Rhine. As communications with the Army of the Rhine in Germany had been disrupted, we were sent to the regimental depôt at Schlestadt.

Not much work was done at the depôt. The garrison officers gathered in the café and, as the junior officer, my job was to refill the tankards. This was no sinecure. I did not enjoy the life.

France, at that time, was at war with Austria, Piedmont and various little Italian princedoms, all subsidised by England.

France had mobilised three armies; that of Sambre-et-Moselle under General Jourdan, Rhin-et-Moselle under General Moreau, and the Army of Italy under General Bonaparte, who was just beginning to be talked about.

It was the Army of Italy, the weakest and worst equipped and the least well disciplined which gave battle first. During the first days of April, without waiting for the snow to melt, General Bonaparte crossed the Apennines, crushed Piedmont within fifteen days, defeated the Austrians, entered Milan in triumph on 15 May and pushed the enemy back beyond the Adige.

The Rhine armies were not so fortunate. They did not cross the river until June in order to advance into Germany. Their general, the Archduke Charles, led the Austrians, who opposed them.

The Army of the Rhine had already reached the upper Danube, when Archduke Charles, leaving a body of his troops on their front, withdrew and, thanks to a skilful march, fell upon General Jourdan, defeated him at Würzburg and forced him back across the Rhine. He then continued along the right bank of the river to attack General Moreau in the rear. Moreau, anticipating this move, fell back on the Black Forest but, before entering it, turned and defeated the over-eager Austrians at Biberach, then carried out a retreat, which is still famous, by way of the gorges of the Val d'Enfer. He reached the Rhine valley at Fribourg-en-Brisgau and recrossed the river at Brisach and at Huningue, with his army intact and confident.

As the army approached the Rhine, Clément, Martin, Monnot and I left for Huningue, reaching it on the same day, 24 October, as our companies were crossing the river on to the left bank.

We camped at Neudorff, near the Rhine. Our guns formed a battery on the dyke, in order to protect the left-hand approaches to the bridgehead.

The captain of the 5th Company, of which I was a 2nd lieutenant, was M. Bourguin, an outstanding officer who had been severely wounded at Biberach, where he was taken prisoner. He was later killed in Calabria.

In his absence, Lieutenant Herbulot commanded the company, and the 2nd lieutenant, M. Rousset, was both ignorant and self-important. The first was a drunk and the second a gambler. Having fallen, at the age of eighteen, into such company, it was only disgust at the one and contempt for the other that saved me from following their bad example.

Huningue. General Abbatucci* was in command at Huningue, where he was killed at the age of twenty-nine [*sic*].

While at Huningue I met General Foy and made his acquaintance. He was a *chef d'escadron* at that time, and still in command of the company with which he had begun the campaign. His company was among the battery at the bridgehead.

Having gone one day, out of curiosity, to the forward posts, I saw a wretched infantryman with a broken leg being carried back supported on muskets. The hanging leg, the flowing blood, the pallor and the cries of the wounded man, gave me a painful shock that I allayed with a glass of brandy at a canteen. I have never, since then, experienced such a painful sensation, for which I am thankful as I was destined to see many similar scenes.

When we were not on duty, we went to Basel, where we were always sure to find good food at the Hôtel Trois Rois or at the Cigogne. We met émigrés in the town, with whom we had a good understanding, for the poor wretches were happy to accept dinner invitations from Republican officers At that time they showed none of the arrogance that they displayed in 1814 and 1815.

* General Jean-Charles Abbatucci (1770–96).

The Austrians contented themselves with attacking the bridgeheads at Kehl and Huningue. They made no attempt to cross the Rhine. Archduke Charles directed his efforts against Kehl, and at last captured it on 9 January 1797. He would have done better to be less stubborn, for it was a poor result, and he should have gone to Italy instead.

We stayed at Neudorff until November. We then left to take up garrison duties at Besançon, where we joined the 3rd and 6th Companies of our regiment, the 8th Horse Artillery.

The Army of Italy. In February 1797, the 3rd, 5th and 6th Companies received the order to leave for Italy. We were overjoyed at the news, for we were inactive with the Army of the Rhine and longed to be in Italy. The exploits of our comrades in that country filled us with envy.

The admirable Italian campaign of 1796 was over. But there was much still to be done.

General Bonaparte and his army of thirty-two thousand men had worked wonders. Within a few months they had crushed Piedmont and put three Austrian armies to flight, each of which was greatly their superior in numbers. Marching by night and fighting by day they had overcome their enemies in a dozen battles and more than fifty skirmishes; they had taken, in killed or wounded, more than a hundred thousand soldiers. Their victories at Rivoli (14 January) and at Favorite two days later, and the capitulation of Mantua had expelled the Austrians from Italy.

However, peace had not been made. Austria was, as ever, subsidised by England, and thanks to the success of Archduke Charles in Germany, was not yet ready to sue for terms. Archduke Charles had finally succeeded in seizing the bridgehead at Huningue. He had left part of his army on guard on the Rhine and, with his best troops, gone to the Tyrol to reorganise and command the fourth army, with which the Austrians planned to confront Bonaparte.

The Directory, for its part, at last decided to send reinforcements to Italy to make good the army's losses. These reinforcements consisted of two divisions taken from the two armies of the Rhine. In January they crossed Mont Cenis in a wild snowstorm. The three companies of the 8th Artillery formed part of the reinforcements, but we did not leave Besançon until 23 February. We travelled through Bourg and Chambéry and, in the depths of winter, we too crossed Mont Cenis, then still covered in snow and ice.

The Italian campaign (1797). We moved down into Italy. Passing through Turin on a Sunday, I saw, on their way to Mass at the castle chapel, the countesses of Provence and Artois, the sisters-in-law of the unhappy Louis XVI. They were not beautiful.

We passed through Turin on 24 March and went into quarters at Monza, a pretty little town with a handsome castle belonging to an archduke.

General Bonaparte had already started his campaign. His army marched off on 10 March, and he found himself for the first time confronted on the Tagliamento by the Archduke Charles, whom he defeated. He immediately pursued the archduke into the Alpes Juliennes, having already skilfully captured from him all the passes that he had tried to defend. The French seized the Tarvis pass and descended into the hereditary lands of the House of Austria. They were at Léoben, twenty-five leagues from Vienna, when their general began to discuss the basis of a final peace treaty.

In undertaking this bold advance across the Alps with a small army, General Bonaparte's objective was Vienna. He relied for success on a diversion being made on the Danube by the armies of the Rhine, one of them still commanded by Moreau and the other by Hoche.[*]

In order to guard his rear, and to restrain the stubborn hostility of the Venetian Republic, he had left an army corps of about ten thousand men under the command of General Kilmaine[†] behind him in Italy. Our companies formed part of this corps.

The Lombards made us very welcome, for we had freed them from the Austrians, and they made common cause with us: the inhabitants of the Cispadane Republic[‡] welcomed us too. This republic had recently been formed by Bonaparte from the duchies of Modena, Romagna and two legations, but apart from Mincio, the population of the states of the Venetian Republic were hostile to us. The people of the towns nearest to Lombardy, nobles, bourgeois, and commoners alike, resented the yoke of the exclusive aristocracy of the *Livre d'Or*,[§] and were well disposed towards the French. Several of these towns, Bergamo and Brescia among others, took advantage of our presence to throw out their Venetian magistrates and proclaim their independence. The countryside around these towns was, on the contrary, devoted to the Venetian aristocracy.

While Venice was powerless we occupied the forts of Bergamo, Brescia and Verona, which had belonged to the republic, for the Venetian senate had permitted the Austrians to establish themselves there and, as we had chased the Austrians out, we filled their place.

Beyond the Adige – and in Verona above all – the citizens and the country folk were hostile to us.

Easter week in Verona. The Venetian Senate, shrewdly political even as it proclaimed its neutrality, had continued to arm itself and to raise levies of Slavs under the pretext of defending its neutrality, but in reality, to prepare for an opportunity to

---

[*] General Louis Lazare Hoche (1768–97).
[†] Irish-born General Charles Edward Saul Jennings Kilmaine (1751–99).
[‡] This was a forerunner of the Cisalpine Republic.
[§] A collection of the signatures of personages who were received officially.

rejoin our enemies. The peasants were armed, and agents of the Senate busied themselves in the countryside inciting the people against us. Our supporters were threatened and lone soldiers were killed.

The fury against us was so great in that part of Italy that, without waiting for an opportunity of the kind that the Venetian Senate would have deemed auspicious, and believing that our army was fully occupied in the Tyrol, mobs of peasants marched on Verona. We were on our guard, but we were not at war, and the gates of the town were left open.

On 15 April, the second Sunday of Easter week, the peasants, taking advantage of the festival, crowded into the town and mingled with the townsfolk and the Slav soldiers who still garrisoned the town, their numbers choking the streets and squares.

At about midday, upon a signal given by blasts on a whistle, this mob fell upon the French, attacked the isolated outposts and murdered the guards. Our sick and wounded, who filled our hospitals, were set upon with daggers and their throats slashed. The bodies of the murdered French were thrown into the river Adige. The murderers spared neither women nor children. Some of the French were able to reach the forts occupied by us. Others sought shelter in the palace of the Venetian magistrate, where he granted them asylum, no doubt in order to preserve the appearance of neutrality should the assault fail, for he did nothing to hinder or calm the rebels.

Once they were masters of the town, the rebels assaulted the forts, their use of cannon in the attack proving that the Venetian soldiers were on their side. They captured one of our forts and murdered the garrison. But they were repulsed from the others in a hail of bullets. They fired on the town as well. The general in command at Verona, although surrounded, was still able to warn General Kilmaine and ask for help.

We left for Verona together with the Lombard legion. Following a battle outside the town against the peasants and the Slavs, we scattered them and as we pursued them we put them to the sword pitilessly. The town was burned. These Veronese people are as cowardly as they are savage and we entered the town unopposed.

Our soldiers were furious. They killed everyone who showed any resistance. They wanted to sack the town and it was only with great difficulty that the pillage was stopped, but it was not possible to save the *mont de piété*.*

The magistrate and the Venetian authorities vanished.

The leaders of the revolt who had been captured were shot, and a heavy tax was imposed on the town. It amounted to a month's pay for the soldiers plus a horse for the mounted officers. I received my horse, but I never obtained my month's pay. Probably not everyone lost out.

* Pawnshop.

The name 'Veronese Easter' was given to these uprisings and massacres.

We stayed at Verona until 8 May, when we left for Mantua, from where, after a few days, we returned to Milan on 4 June.

The Veronese Easter and some other examples of Venetian treachery were the causes of the ultimate fall of the old aristocratic Venetian Republic that was once so rich and powerful.

General Bonaparte was, at that time, at Léoben negotiating terms of the peace treaty with the Austrians. No longer obliged to behave considerately to the Venetian Senate, he abandoned that republic to the Austrians in compensation for Lombardy, which he seized from them. So the Venetians, to their utter despair, became subjects of Austria. Thus they transferred their hatred from the French to the Austrians.

Rivalry between soldiers of the Army of the Rhine and those of the Army of Italy.
The soldiers who came from the Army of the Rhine were unlike those of the Army of Italy. The latter, despite their weariness, were in fine condition and living in a good life. Most of them owned watches and had well-filled purses. They were justly proud of their wealth and of their exploits, and they made rather too much fun of the innocence and poverty of the soldiers from the Rhine, whose smart uniforms and perfect discipline left nothing to be desired. These men were in no mood to tolerate such mockery. So, in the days following our arrival in Italy, quarrels broke out which often degenerated into duels. These were particularly regrettable for we were confronted by real enemies who presented us with daily opportunities to demonstrate our courage.

Shared danger, which was faced at all times with equal gallantry, put an end to this ill feeling. Great rivalry continued to be felt, however, between the Army of Italy and those who remained on the banks of the Rhine, a rivalry that included many of our generals.

The cavalry school at Versailles. On 27 June I was ordered to report to the cavalry school that had just been opened at Versailles. The initial stages of the peace treaty had been signed at Léoben on 18 April and the campaign was over.

I had known almost from the start of my journey that I had been earmarked to join the Horse Artillery formed in Italy for inclusion in the Egyptian expedition. This expedition was not decided upon until later; but we were aware in Italy that, following the signature of the preliminaries of the Léoben peace treaty, General Napoleon was already considering an expedition in the Mediterranean, for we were still at war with England.

Lieutenant Sautereau, who was the same rank as I but had left the school at Châlons after me, took my place while I was at the school at Versailles. We had met before I left Milan, soon after he joined the Army of Italy. One evening, when we had dined together, we surprised, in a side street, three or four scoundrels who were robbing an old man. With one accord we both seized our swords and rushed upon the villains. They fled and we chased them; they nearly got away but a blow on the head that I dealt one of them gave us the upper hand and we took him back to where we had left the old man. He had disappeared. We took our prisoner to the post of the National Milanese guard at the Palace where, instead of thanking us, these Italians believed the assertion made by our prisoner that we had attacked him. They took his side, swore at us and, growing excited, seemed about to get unpleasant. Angered at this behaviour I, in my turn, turned haughty, commanded them to take us to the square and threatened them with severe reprisals if they hurt or detained us. The braggarts grew quiet at once and allowed us to leave. And to think we had just liberated these fellows.

On 27 June 1797, I left the Army of Italy in order to report to the cavalry school at Versailles; on the way, I passed through Besançon, where my regimental depot was located, and also through Saint-Dié and Nancy. From this town as far as Paris the carrier service, leaving from the Place des Dames, took six days on the journey, travelling at a walking pace by day and halting at night.

I reached Versailles on 21 August (4 Fructidor, Year V).

18 Fructidor. We were still governed by the Constitution of Year III. This involved a Directory of five members, holding the executive power and a legislative body composed of two council chambers, les Anciens* and les Cinq-Cents.†

The government was very divided, both in the legislative and the executive bodies. The parties had divided into the 'Patriots', former members of the National Convention who were ardent Republicans, lacking the aggression of the Jacobins and their reactionary tendencies; the 'Constitutionalists' or moderates, who longed above all for power, and upheld the Constitution against all comers, and finally the Royalists, now bolder than ever, who, because they met at Clichy, were known as the *Clichiens*. These last were the most violent. They made no open parade of their beliefs, but, mingling with the Moderates and Constitutionalists, supported any attacks that were made upon the men of whom they wished to be rid.

The majority of the directorate was Patriotic and the minority Constitutionalist. Strangely enough, Director Carnot,‡ previously a member of the Committee of Public Safety, was a Moderate.

---

* The Ancients. This chamber consisted of 250 members, whose minimum age was forty, and was formed to consider the proposals made by the Five Hundred. It selected the first five directors at its meeting on 28 October 1795.

† The Five Hundred. The members of this chamber had to be thirty years of age or over, and were elected for three years to act in concert with the Council of the Ancients.

‡ General Lazare Carnot (1753–1823). Later appointed by Bonaparte to be inspector general of the army, and afterwards minister of war. His influence on the Revolutionary Wars caused him to be known as 'the organiser of victory'.

Apart from the corrupt Barras, the directors were honest men, intelligent, hard-working and devoted to the public welfare, but they lacked a common purpose. Their good intentions were thwarted by the rivalry of their parties.

The recent elections held during Prairial* had increased the opposition in the legislative assembly, creating more adversaries to the majority of the directorate. This systematic opposition, born of hostility, favoured the views of the *Clichiens*. General Pichegru, who had long ago sold himself to the Pretender† and to the English, became one of the Five Hundred, and exerted great influence from that position. He supported the *Clichiens*.

The armies were still openly Republican. That of the Rhine was the more moderate, while that of Italy was more fanatical, but all were inclined to defend the Directory and the Constitution of Year III.

Faced with the threats of the *Clichiens* and the plotting of the Constitutionalists, General Hoche, in command of one of the Rhine armies, ordered twenty thousand men to advance as far as the Constitution allowed – this forbade any army to approach nearer than ten leagues from the capital. General Bonaparte, who was later to overthrow the Directory in the interests of his own ambition, was still a supporter of the Constitution. In a proclamation made at a festival in Milan on the occasion of 14 July, he had made a virulent attack on his enemies. He had even sent an address of loyalty, in the name of the Army of Italy, to the majority in the Directory.

In addition, General Bonaparte had sent General Augereau, an ardent Jacobin and rabble-rouser, to Paris to command the single division that was garrisoned there and was the only one available to support the Directory if it should be attacked.

Matters had reached a point at which the *Clichiens* and the more aggressive of the Constitutionalists decided to vote against the wishes of the Directory. They waited only for the organisation of a National Guard commanded by General Pichegru‡ – who was in a position to select the veterans of Vendémiaire§ – to indict the majority of the Directory.

This majority then decided upon a *coup d'état*. With the co-operation of General Augereau, it was arranged that the Tuileries, where the two councils met, should be surrounded on the night of 17/18 Fructidor.¶ Director Barthélemy was arrested but Carnot contrived to escape. The most hostile and the most influential deputies were seized and taken to the Temple. By five o'clock in the morning, everything was over

---

* Prairial – 20 May to 18 June in the Revolutionary calendar.
† Later Louis XVIII.
‡ General Jean Charles Pichegru (1761–1804).
§ The attempted *coup d'état* by Royalists on 13 Vendémiaire, which was suppressed by troops under Napoleon on the orders of Director Barras. About 600 of the insurgents were killed.
¶ Fructidor – 18 August to 16 September.

without a single drop of blood having been spilled. Parisians rose from their beds without suspecting that a *coup d'état* had taken place.

I arrived at the school at Versailles on 4 Fructidor, and spent the 17th and 18th in Paris, but it was not until the morning of the 18th that I learned what had happened during the night. I can guarantee that the population of Paris remained completely unconcerned by this occurrence and so had, perhaps, avoided a revolution or at least some bloody rioting, for if there had been any opposition to the coup, resistance would certainly have been provoked.

The majority of Parisians and most of the army were still Republican, and the reaction against Jacobinism did not go to the extent of regretting the old order.

On 18 Fructidor three directors called together those of the *Anciens* and of the Five Hundred who had not been arrested, some to the Odéon and the others to the lecture hall of the school of medicine. At the instigation of the directors, and in view of the evidence that was produced to incriminate them in a plot headed by General Pichegru, the deportation of the arrested deputies was decreed, by legislative measure. The most deeply involved, among them Barthélémy, were deported to Sinnamari* in French Guiana, a pestilential spot, where most of them died. General Pichegru escaped from Sinnemari and returned to Europe, to be involved in further conspiracies.

The Councils voted for all the proposed revolutionary laws brought forward by the directors with the same enthusiasm that they would certainly have shown if the *Clichiens* and the Constitutionalists had been the victors, and these same directors were the ones being indicted. It is always the same story – the great ones of the Convention never hesitated to send their best friends to their death to save their own skins; this lot sacrificed their friends to save their positions. In politics this is known as ability.

None of these events much concerned us at the school at Versailles. Politics were little discussed there, and by me not at all. I was not yet twenty years old, and at that age one has too little experience to worry about matters that require a great deal of it. If I speak of 18 Fructidor, it is because I happened to be in Paris on that day, and wish to emphasise the ease with which the *coup d'état* was achieved and the indifference with which the Parisians learned of it.

We at the cavalry school were more concerned with military matters, and those that took place during the twenty months I spent at Versailles just served to break the monotony of our lives. We were in barracks at the old stables, but, apart from our exercises and hours of study, we were free. The riding school, cavalry exercises and instruction in horse management did not take up all our time so we were often able to travel to Paris, and did not fail to do so.

---

* A small port at the mouth of a river in Guiana.

The death of General Hoche: his funeral. A few days after 18 Fructidor, Year V, (4 September 1797) General Hoche died; his health had been poor for a long while. He was widely mourned, and was regretted by everyone, especially at Versailles where his family still lived and where he was well known. This was a great loss to our country, for he was only twenty-nine years old and certainly one of our best generals, being a fine character and a good organiser. Bonaparte might have found that he was ahead of him on 18 Brumaire* or after.

At the time of his death, Hoche was in command of the two armies of the Rhine that were united under the title of the Army of Germany, and were intended for the invasion of England. This followed the disgrace of Moreau that had resulted from his reluctance to hand over the correspondence, seized from the Austrians, which established General Pichegru's treason.

It was widely believed that General Hoche was poisoned, and this is very probable; for, apart from the fact that his illness was never identified, there were many individuals, both at home and abroad, who had a great interest in getting rid of him. Young, tall and strong, he showed no sign of ill health until peace was established in the Vendée, and he died at the moment when he was preparing for the invasion of England. Thus he numbered among his enemies the English, the *Clichiens*, and the aristocracy of the Vendée; since that time it has become clear of what George Cadoudal,† Pichegru, Pitt‡ and others were capable.

At the end of September we were present at the funeral of General Hoche on the Champ de Mars; grief was universal and we were all very aware of our loss. He was loved by the soldiers and his obsequies were impressive.

Bonaparte returns from Italy. Two months later, Paris celebrated the arrival of General Bonaparte, who came to present the treaty of Campo Formio to the directors.

This splendid treaty, which was very much to the advantage of France, would have been even better if the preliminary negotiations at Léoben had not brought to an end the successes of General Hoche in Germany. Everything combined to favour General Bonaparte – the glory that he would have had to share was now his alone. His was the glory of this treaty that guaranteed the independence of northern Italy as far as the Adige, and gave us a border on the Rhine that included Mainz, and the Venetian Isles§ of Greece. It also completed the isolation of England.

---

* This refers to the events of 9 November 1799 which resulted in the dissolution of the Directory and the transfer of power to the Council of Three, one of whom was Napoleon.

† A Chouan chief and Royalist conspirator. A relentless enemy of the Revolution and of Napoleon.

‡ William Pitt, English prime minister.

§ Corfu and the Ionian Isles.

The enthusiasm of the Parisians, who longed for peace, was overwhelming, and a magnificent reception was given to the young general. I am not referring to the official one, for such things are usually much the same. The passion for Bonaparte was even more remarkable because the simplicity of his appearance and dress belied his true merit, and contrasted with the swaggering and triumphant airs of some of his generals, especially that of Augereau, to whom, in his own view, all the credit belonged.

For a long while nothing was spoken of in Paris except the deeds and activities of Bonaparte. He lived very quietly and avoided the crowds. In the cafés and meeting places the conversation was all of him and his way of life; his words were remembered and repeated. Strange folk, the Parisians. It was only a short time since, in the name of liberty, they swept to the scaffold a king who was prepared to make every concession. Yesterday, with cries of 'Death to the foreign tyrants', these proud Republicans bowed before the most humiliating and debasing Terror, yet, behold them today, ready to grovel in front of a new idol. The arms of Paris are truly symbolic – a ship tossed on the waves – but to be more accurate, the waves should be composed of the heads of Parisians. As for me, with the plain common sense of Lorraine, I admired the great deeds performed by Bonaparte, the glory of his armies and the power he brought to France. My fanaticism did not go to the length of concerning myself with what he drank and ate, still less with whether he went to bed with a hairnet or a silk nightcap.

The treaty of Campo Formio ended the war on the continent. Now we were at war only with England. General Bonaparte was appointed to the command of the Army of England. The Directory proposed an expedition, not now against Ireland, but to attack Great Britain. It reckoned without its host:* Bonaparte had other plans.

The Egyptian expedition. It was known in the Army of Italy that its general planned some expedition in the Mediterranean, and it was thought that it would be to Egypt. Not for nothing had he seized the Venetian fleet. We already had the fleet of our Spanish allies. The Italian ports and those of the Greek Venetian Isles were at our disposal. With Egypt we should become masters of the Mediterranean. We could draw nearer to India and threaten England's most important colony.

Nevertheless, all preparations seemed to be in progress for an expedition to England. These measures were undertaken on the Atlantic coast and upon the shores of the Mediterranean, where a section of the Army of Italy would eventually become the left flank of the Army of England.

---

* *Qui compte sans son hôte compte deux fois.* Who reckons without his host must reckon again.

Early in May 1797, General Bonaparte left Paris and, on the 19th embarked at Toulon, with part of the Army of Italy, for an unknown destination.

I should have been with this expedition, but there I was, shut up in a cavalry school.

News of the mysterious expedition was eagerly awaited – and soon arrived.

On its way, on 9 June, the army seized Malta with its capital city* which formerly had been thought to be impregnable. The army landed in Egypt on 1 July and entered Alexandria in force on the 2nd, completely vanquished the Mamelukes at the battle of the Pyramids on the 21st and entered Cairo three days later. In less than one month our army had almost entirely conquered the delta and half of Egypt.

But soon a dreadful rumour was heard. Our fleet had been destroyed by the English off the Egyptian coast.

Admiral Nelson, having searched the Mediterranean for a long while, had at last found our fleet, unwisely moored in Aboukir Bay. He attacked the ships and, within a few hours, had burned many of them.

War against the king of Naples. Now the English were unchallenged in the Mediterranean and in a position to blockade our best general and our best army in Egypt. They had been isolated, but they had now recovered their authority, and found the path clear for the formation of a new coalition against us, one which included Naples, Austria, Russia and the Turkish Empire.

The effect of the disaster at Aboukir was felt at once. The English fleet had suffered and could not stay at sea, but Naples opened its harbours to Nelson and he was received there in triumph.

The queen of Naples was the sister of the unfortunate Marie Antoinette. She felt a blind hatred for the French. Emboldened by the presence of the English, the court of Naples called upon us to evacuate the Papal States, and the king, filled with belligerence, invaded them. He was put to flight at his first encounter with the French. Fleeing, he was compelled to embark in the English fleet together with his court and his treasury. The Parthenopean Republic was proclaimed at Naples.†

Unfortunately we had enemies other than the Neapolitans. Against us there were also the Austrians, the English and the Russians, as well as the Turks, who were shortly to fall upon our Army of Egypt.

The Austrians, as ever, hostile to our Republic, had, since the advent of peace, continued to rearm. They began the new war by causing our negotiators at Rastadt to be murdered, in order to steal their documents.

---

* Valletta.
† This republic survived only a few months.

The Directory became very active and energetic in the face of the problems arising from this situation. Our armies had been greatly reduced during the time of peace and two hundred thousand men were mobilised to reinforce them.

Although much inferior in numbers to our enemies and widely distributed over Holland and Naples, our armies began a campaign without waiting to complete their preparations.

From the end of March, General Jourdan was defeated in Germany by the Archduke Charles, and General Macdonald was defeated at Trebbia in Italy. An Anglo-Russian force invaded Holland. Only General Masséna* held on in Switzerland, drawing his lines back behind the Rhine. There were disturbances in the Vendeé.

The worsening situation in France. Home affairs went from bad to worse. The Directory and the Councils were more divided than ever. Personal and ideological rivalries, which should have vanished in the face of danger to the country, became even more violent. The Directory was blamed for all our reverses. Accusations of treason were heard. The Jacobins grew agitated and reopened their clubs, demanding that the country should be declared to be in danger and that recourse should be had to the revolutionary methods of 1793. The Directory resisted this demand, but was still divided, tired and discredited. The foul Barras, fortune's favourite, was, unfortunately, still a director.

The Directory, popular in the armies at the time of 18 Fructidor, had alienated itself from the generals and the staff by attempting, rightly, to take firm action on abuses and embezzlement.

The good citizens were terrified by the succession of defeats suffered by our armies and by the violence of the factions, especially the Jacobins. The Royalists, since Fructidor, had been quiet. The impotence of the government was also frightening, as was its lack of unity and the chaos of our finances and of our administration. Everyone longed for a strong, united government, capable of restoring order at home and of pushing back the enemies that threatened our frontiers. The absence of the Army of Egypt, and its general, was deplored.

Distance had not caused Bonaparte to be forgotten. On the contrary, this expedition to the Orient increased his fame, and awe was felt at each success. He was perceived as having been sacrificed and the Directory was accused of having sent him into exile in Egypt in order to get rid of him. This was not true, for the Egyptian expedition was his idea alone and was, to some, extent, imposed by him upon the Directory.

* Marshal André Masséna, duke of Rivoli, prince d'Essling (1758–1817).

The rapid formation of the Italian republics, the skilful negotiations carried out in Italy and at Léoben by General Bonaparte, had added the character of an adroit politician and accomplished administrator to his reputation as a brilliant general. His successes in Egypt made him appear to be extraordinary, in fact a saviour. His return was longed for to rid the country of the ungovernable elements within it and to repulse and crush the foreign enemies.

This was what I observed and heard at Versailles, in Paris and everywhere.

My return to the regiment. A duel. Weary of my stay at the cavalry school, which had continued for more than twenty months, and of my inaction, I made many approaches to the minister of war and was finally permitted to return to my regiment, which was then still on garrison duty at Besançon.

I arrived in that town on 22 September 1799, having enjoyed a few days leave that I had spent with my family, and the following day was named as a staff officer. This earned me a sword slash. A lieutenant of the regiment had applied for the position, one for which I had not even thought of asking. He was furious, quarrelled with me and we fought. I was wounded in the thigh. This lieutenant, a hot-tempered individual, was later killed in Spain by the sword of a more skilful adversary than I.

When I reached Besançon everyone was oppressed by the news of the defeat and death of General Joubert.* In August he had been beaten at Novi in Italy by the Austro-Hungarians under the invincible Suvorov.† Moreau, who replaced Joubert, was compelled to withdraw beyond the Apennines, and the Midi was threatened with invasion. The population was apprehensive and, to judge from what was said about the Russians, their appearance, their size and their savagery, they seemed to be veritable ogres.

The disaster at Aboukir Bay brought immediate and unwelcome complications, but an unexpected victory quickly improved matters and bought us a welcome respite. The Russians and Austrians had been completely defeated at Zurich by General Masséna. The terrible Suvorov who, according to the general opinion, was not one of the brightest individuals, instead of following up his success in Italy against a much weakened French army, set off for Switzerland, where, together with the Austrians, he intended to fall upon Masséna. Masséna, having been warned of this, attacked. Suvorov, trapped in the mountains and surrounded by Lecourbe's soldiers and hunted and harassed on all sides, managed to escape only with difficulty, doubtless swearing, though belatedly, that he would never be caught there again. Nothing was heard of him afterwards.‡ At the same time, we heard that General Brune,§ by a series of

* General Barthélemy Catherine Joubert (1769–99).
† Field Marshal Alexander Vasilievitch Suvorov, Count Suvorov-Rimnisky, prince of Italijisky (1729–1800).
‡ Suvorov fell from favour when he returned to Russia, and died in 1800.
§ Marshal Guillaume Marie Anne Brune (1763–1815).

skilful manoeuvres, had compelled an Anglo-Russian army that had invaded Holland to re-embark.

The battle of Zurich brought the 1799 campaign to an end, happily for the armies in Switzerland and in Holland, but less fortunately for the army in Italy. Following the defeat at Novi the remnants of our army in the Apennines were in the most dreadful state.

In their letters, our comrades told us that the troops were short of everything, even of ammunition. They received no pay and no food, and the starving soldiers were begging at the roadside. The treasury was empty, taxes were not collected and, even in France, we were paid only intermittently.

Bonaparte returns from Egypt. During October we learned at Besançon that General Bonaparte had returned from Egypt. He had landed at Fréjus and left at once for Paris. The troops and the people were overjoyed.

General Bonaparte was acclaimed in Provence, in Dauphiné and in Lyon. Bells were rung and bonfires lit when he passed through. At Lyon, to avoid an outburst of joy that might give offence to the Directory, as well as delaying his journey, he left the Bourgogne road and set off on the Bourbonnais road.

I knew enough of the sentiments of the Parisians to be sure that he would be received with the same enthusiasm in the capital; it was not necessary to be a prophet to foresee what would happen then.

Regardless of what might be thought of a commanding general who had abandoned his army, it was indisputable that General Bonaparte's return from Egypt was regarded as a fortunate and desirable event, except by the militant Royalists and the ultra-Jacobins.

There may be various opinions as to his own motives for returning. General Bonaparte did not know what was happening in France until after his fine victory at Aboukir; he could have known neither of our victory at Zurich nor of our success in Holland. Our situation, both at home and abroad, must have appeared to him to be extremely precarious. If his reason for returning had been to help our country, and to confront the very real danger of being overcome by the English, his conduct is worthy of praise. If, on the other hand, he had abandoned an army no longer capable of being of use to him, in order to seize an opportunity to advance his own ambition, then he would have deserved to be brought before a court martial.

The one thing that was certain was that our victorious army in Egypt, even if it were not demoralised or discouraged, was blockaded, exhausted and anxious to return to France. However, the popular view was that it could still remain in Egypt, and General Bonaparte was of the same opinion. Since his return he had been concerned to send the army reinforcements, and from this, unless one is blinded by prejudice, it may be concluded, that he had not abandoned the army in Egypt because it was of no further use to him, but because he believed that his presence would be more beneficial to the country and, doubtless, to his own ambitions, if he were in France. Did not this man, who was imbued with a strong sense of his own destiny, also wish to play a greater part in a larger theatre?

18 Brumaire. An event foreseen by all and wished for by many followed quickly upon the arrival of Bonaparte in Paris. The news of 18 Brumaire surprised no one. The Directory was overthrown and a provisional government proclaimed. Executive power was placed in the hands of Bonaparte, as First Consul. The other consuls were named as Sieyès and Roger Duclos. Together with the consuls, two commissions, each of twenty-five members, were to hold legislative power and were charged jointly with the task of preparing a new constitution.

18 Brumaire was a powerful blow delivered by the army with the support of various politicians. It provided a dreadful precedent, but one that was supported and ratified by public opinion. Very few of our revolutions have not been achieved by force and surprise.

Experience had exposed the defects of the Constitution of Year III, principally the failure of the executive to agree within itself, and this had resulted in a paralysis that halted the implementation of sensible proposals, so rendering the Directory harsh and impotent. It is a pity that the constitution could not have been revised legally, but in France we do not revise, we overthrow.

The despotic nature of the Empire has caused 18 Brumaire to be regretted. Yet it is necessary to distinguish between the Consulate and the Empire. The one drew us back from anarchy and gave us order and distinction; the other, as a result of an insane blindness and despotism, delivered us into the hands of the foreigner. It was the beneficial effect of the Consulate that increased Bonaparte's popularity and so allowed him to proclaim himself Emperor.

A few days after 18 Brumaire, the regiment left Besançon and took up garrison duties at Montélimar, where we arrived on 20 December. As we made our way across Franche-Comté, Bourgogne, Lyonnais and Dauphiné, I was able, by talking to my hosts each day, to obtain a good idea of the prevailing opinion on the *coup d'état*, held by the ordinary inhabitants of these places. The fall of the Directory was welcomed everywhere, and great hopes were expressed of Bonaparte.

Chapter Two

Ten Years in France and Italy (1799–1809)

Garrison duties at Montélimar. The Society of Jesus. We were joined by the 3rd and 5th Companies while we were at Montélimar, when the Army of Italy retreated after the defeat at Novi. These two companies, and any men who were available from the depôt, were frequently employed to escort the mail-coaches, travellers and their carriages. The whole countryside was infested with bands of vagabonds and deserters – a variety of Chouans* who went under the name 'Societies of Jesus'. They robbed and pillaged the mail and stripped travellers of their possessions under the political pretext of opposing the government.

We often chased these bandits into the mountains, but were never successful. Our forays were always carried out on horseback, but the mountain paths were difficult and we were continually compelled to dismount and, walking in single file, lead our horses by their bridles Our watchful quarry, familiar with the terrain, always evaded us. We never caught a single one, and these useless efforts wearied men and horses alike.

The provisional government gave us no cause to regret the end of the Directory, and it began its work by repealing those revolutionary laws that had become abhorrent, notably the law of hostages† and the progressive forced loan.‡ Order succeeded anarchy in tax-collection as well as in administration, and confidence was reborn. The population of Dauphiné admitted that they were happier, and gave the First Consul the credit for the improvements.

The new constitution was promulgated on 15 December 1799. The three consuls were Bonaparte, Cambacérès§ and Lebrun. There were now a Senate, a Tribunal and a Council of State.

---

* A name given, during the Revolution, to all Royalist insurrectionists in the west of France. It was taken from the nickname of one of their leaders – Jean Chouan – one of the four Cottereau brothers.

† A law passed in 1794 that decreed that hostages could be taken from among the relatives of émigrés if there was unrest in an particular area.

‡ A form of income tax introduced in 1793 to finance military expansion, it bore particularly heavily upon the relatives of émigrés and upon the wealthy.

§ Jean Jacques Régis Cambacérès, duke of Parma (1753–1824), an astute statesman who had been appointed Second Consul following Brumaire.

As soon as the Jacobins were defeated, the Vendée grew calm. One fact proved Bonaparte's popularity beyond doubt: as supreme military commander he did not hesitate to take part of the garrison from Paris in order to reinforce the troops sent into Brittany, where they compelled the Chouan bands, commanded by the over-famous Georges Cadoudal, to lay down their arms. At last we were free of civil war.

France needed peace in order to recover. The government needed peace too, and General Bonaparte did what his victories alone enabled him to do in order to achieve it. He sought it directly from the sovereigns of England and Austria. Both refused him, believing that we were more exhausted than we actually were.

I belong to no party and my only wish is for the greatness and prosperity of our country, so I feel that I am able to speak quite impartially of the events of that time. I do this to make clear the effect they had on those about me and, doubtless, on all of France, so that the growing popularity of Bonaparte may be understood. As for military actions in which I played only a secondary and distant part, involving weaponry, equipment and the training of recruits, I shall write of the sequence of the events which were important in our history simply for the information of my children for whom I intend this journal.

The attention of the First Consul was not monopolised by domestic affairs. As Austria and England were determined to continue the war, preparations to this end were carried on throughout the winter.

The Austrian army in Italy took the offensive in the spring and, after 5 April, pushed our numerically inferior Army of Liguria, at that time under the command of Masséna, back from the Apennines. They cut this army in two, driving one half beyond the Var and throwing the remainder back on to Genoa.

General Moreau* was commanding the excellent Army of the Rhine. He crossed the river at the end of April, defeated the Austrians and pushed them back as far as the Danube.

General Bonaparte, who had been thought to be in Paris engrossed in domestic matters, had secretly put together a third army composed of dispersed troops. With great skill he arranged for this army to converge on the upper Rhône valley.

Our regiment left Montélimar on 6 April and first went into barracks at Tullins, a town in a very prosperous region that was known as the 'kidney of Dauphiné'; then, on 15 May we moved to garrison Grenoble.

The Italian campaign (1800). General Bonaparte waited for the success of the Army of the Rhône before starting his campaign. He was impatient to move as quickly as possible to the help of Masséna who was suffering great hardship in Genoa, where he lacked essential supplies. Having previously eaten bread made of beans and oats, he

* General Jean Victor Moreau (1763–1813).

was now reduced to bread made of starch and linseed meal, and the soldiers, population and prisoners were rationed to a few ounces of bread each day.

General Bonaparte left Paris on 6 May, joined the various corps concentrated in the upper Rhône valley and, despite enormous difficulties, led them over the Alps through the Saint Bernard pass. He marched down into Lombardy in the rear of the Austrians who were still held up before Genoa by the stubborn resistance of Suchet's[*] troops and, above all, by those of Masséna. He took Milan, seized the arsenals of the Austrians and, encountering them near to Alessandria, defeated them on the Marengo plain, thanks to the intervention of General Desaix,[†] who paid for the victory with his life. He then forced them to retreat finally from Lombardy and to ask for an armistice.

In Grenoble, alarming rumours had begun to be heard of the Army of Italy, so our joy at learning of the victory of Marengo was all the greater. We had hoped to be called upon to leave Grenoble and go to Italy, but to our great regret we were passed over.

In Germany, General Moreau conquered all of Bavaria and, after the victory at Hochstett, the Austrians were also compelled to sue for an armistice.

Peace seemed imminent, but nothing of the sort happened, and it took another winter campaign in Italy and in Germany, with Moreau's magnificent victory at Hohenlinden[‡] in order to overcome the Austrian resistance. Peace was at last signed at Lunéville.[§]

France had never before been so great and powerful. Peace was everywhere acclaimed with joy and, I can safely assert, the name of Bonaparte was everywhere blessed. If only he had stopped there, for the sake of his own glory, his happiness and ours!

For us, peace entailed garrison duties at Grenoble, Besançon and Metz.

We are sent to Italy. On 21 January, the 7th and 8th Regiments of Horse Artillery were disbanded and incorporated in the other six Horse Artillery regiments. Our 8th Regiment was divided up between the 1st, 3rd and 4th, and I continued as staff officer in the 1st.

The 1st and 4th Regiments were garrisoned at Piacenza in Italy. I left Metz with four companies of the 8th in order to join these two regiments. We were forty-four days on the march passing over Mount Cenis. Between Alessandria and Tortona we

---

[*] Marshal Louis Gabriel Suchet, duke of Albufera (1770–1826).
[†] The gallant General Louis Charles Desaix (1768–1800) was killed on the battlefield of Marengo on 14 June 1800.
[‡] Battle of Hohenlinden, 3 December 1800.
[§] Peace of Lunéville. 8 February 1801.

crossed the great Marengo plain, where scattered human remains were still to be seen. Piedmont had been reunited with France following the treaty of Lunéville, and had been divided into departments. Alessandria was the administrative centre of the Department of Marengo.

Piacenza was a big and handsome town of about thirty thousand souls. The population seemed to be composed mainly of nobles and priests. There were few of the middle-class. There were fifty-two parishes, ninety-four churches, twenty monasteries and twenty-two nunneries. A fortified rampart, in a poor state of repair, surrounded the city and served as a promenade. The château could have been defended and the ducal palace and the main street, the Corso, were very fine. All things considered, it was a fine, attractive town in which to be garrisoned. Piacenza had played its part in the wars that had divided the Italian republics in the Middle Ages, and Hannibal had defeated the Romans near by.

Colonel d'Anthoüard[*] commanded the 1st Regiment of Horse Artillery, in which the *chef d'escadron* was Paul-Louis Courier,[†] the distinguished Hellenist, who later became well known as a pamphleteer.

In my capacity as staff officer, the colonel appointed me to teach this officer (Courier) the theory of cavalry manoeuvres. It was a hopeless undertaking, for I could not make him understand the first elements of the subject, and always found him absorbed in his books. He was quite unique; he rode with a simple quilted blanket in lieu of a saddle, was far from soldierly, was a mediocre officer, but otherwise was a delightful man and free from the slightest hint of pedantry.

He left for Rome one day, and did not return, being replaced by one Duchaud, who had been Napoleon's orderly officer and of whom it was said that Napoleon had wanted to be rid. Duchaud was a very handsome man and, it was rumoured, was the lover, or one of the lovers, of Princess Pauline.[‡]

While I was at Piacenza, Colonel d'Anthoüard appointed me, together with my friend Monnot, to draft the instruction manual of horse artillery manoeuvres, and he then had our manuscript printed for the use of the regiment. Later, and slightly modified, these instructions served as the basis for those adopted by the entire corps.

For the instruction of non-commissioned officers, I drew up a training manual on the use of the cannon, which included rules for the disposal of men killed or wounded, etc. This was especially useful as the regiment was composed of companies and of officers who came from different corps, so that there was no uniformity in the

---

[*] Colonel Charles-Nicolas d'Anthoüard de Vraincourt (1773–1852).
[†] Paul-Louis Courier (1772–1825), a French author of pamphlets against the Restoration and of *Lettres écrits de France et d'Italie*.
[‡] Pauline Bonaparte, later Princess Borghese (1780–1825), Napoleon's second sister.

regulations and, as a staff officer, I was continually involved in disputes on this subject with other officers.

On 29 October 1803 I was promoted to captain, second-class, and attached to the armaments factory at Liège.

At the request of my colonel I remained with the regiment in my new rank and continued to perform the duties of a staff officer.

The Empire is established. The plebiscite. Our victories had brought us peace. The treaty of Lunéville with Austria had been followed on 25 March 1802 by the treaty of Amiens, with England. Order, peace and tranquillity reigned in France. The benefits resulting from the genius of the First Consul were ever more appreciated, as they followed years of trouble and anarchy. The plots and terrorist attacks, in which Moreau, one of the best-loved and most skilled of its generals, was involved were viewed with anger by the army. These attacks, even as they threatened Bonaparte's life, served to increase his popularity. What was really wanted was a stable constitution, one that would guarantee the continuation of the current state of affairs. The very people who, only a few years before, had shouted 'Death to the Tyrants!' now turned their thoughts towards a monarchy. This shift in public opinion was skilfully exploited; there were petitions, prayers and so forth, demanding an empire. It took little persuasion to overcome the Republican sentiments of General Bonaparte. Out of respect for the principle of national sovereignty, the matter, though it had been decided in advance, was put to the vote. Everyone knows how much a popular ratification of a *fait accompli* is worth. The convinced, the self-interested, the half-hearted and the timid, who together make up the majority, will always endorse a proposal.

Colonel d'Anthoüard called the officers of the regiment together. He told us the situation without any attempt to bring pressure to bear on us. He seemed to say, as Paul-Louis Courier has written: 'It is a fact, what does it matter what we call it? Roast or boiled – what difference does it make?'

The commanding officer, in his letter that was published long afterwards, gave an accurate account of our meeting. 'To be Bonaparte and to make oneself a Sovereign! Caesar did not adopt an outworn title, but made his own name into a yet higher honour.'

There was unrest and discontent in the artillery. As soldiers, we all had the utmost admiration for General Bonaparte and the most complete confidence in his abilities. His early exploit at Toulon had been the work of a master. When only a humble artillery commander he had, by the positioning of a few pieces of ordnance, secured the surrender of a place that was not even completely surrounded and was defended by a garrison numerically superior to its attackers. His Italian campaign had instantly shown him to be the greatest commander of the period. In spite of this we were doubtful of his character as a whole, and of his despotic tendencies. We feared his ambition and that unrestrained power could only increase his arrogance. He desired absolute power only in order to throw off all the constraints that still bound him as First Consul. Why was he not content with this title, under which he had achieved many good things? Our history had shown us clearly how absolute power leads to abuse. Why, having suffered a bloody revolution, were we to return so quickly to the past?

In the event, the regiment registered a good number of negative votes in the plebiscite. When the Empire was proclaimed, a coronation, or rather a consecration, was arranged for 2 December. Every regiment was to be represented there by a detachment under the command of a colonel, so that the Imperial flag could, later, be received from the hands of the new Emperor.

The consecration. On 19 December I was one of a detachment of the 1st Horse Artillery that left Piacenza to go to Paris. We reached Melun on 1 November, and stayed there until the 27th. That was the day on which the detachments proceeded to Paris. I was billeted with M. Carion Nizas in the Faubourg du Roule.

Great preparations were made for the consecration. All the papers were full of descriptions of it. It would be useless for me to fill up my journal with copies of the newspapers; all I intend to do is to write down impressions of the general public, not the official reports.

First of all, on 2 December, at the time of the consecration, our new Emperor kept us waiting for a long while. He did not begin his career as a monarch by observing the motto of Louis XIV: 'Punctuality is the politeness of princes'. It was hard to wait in the bitter cold for the arrival of a newly crowned sovereign. Such was the burden of the remarks I heard made behind me by the Parisian crowd.

Being lined up with my detachment, successively in various places along the route of the procession on its way back to Notre Dame, I was in a position to note that very little enthusiasm was shown, in spite of what was written in the official reports. I am certain that the cries of 'Long live the Emperor!' near where I was standing were uttered by only a few of the public and by the urchins who ran alongside the procession beyond the troops who lined the route.

All in all the ceremony was very fine. The luxury, the wealth, the pomp and the organisation all were excellent; only the costumes were a little theatrical.

My place in the ranks gave me a perfect view of Napoleon and Josephine* in their magnificent glass-sided coach; the Emperor was wearing a plumed cap on his head. I had preferred the simplicity of the First Consul. Was all this pomp really needed to win the love and admiration of a people he had saved from anarchy and the attacks of foreign enemies?

* Empress Josephine, formerly de Beauharnais (1763–1814).

Might not all this display, to inaugurate the rule of a democratic monarch raised up by the people, foreshadow a court with all the old abuses, and awaken fears of a return to the *ancien régime,* but this time with upstarts in place of the old nobility. New coins were being minted with '*Napoleon Empereur*' on one side and '*République Française*' on the other. Which side was wrong?

On 4 December, the Eagles were distributed. Detachments of all the regiments in the army, together with that of the National Guard, paraded on the Champ de Mars. The Emperor was seated on a throne in front of the military academy. Each detachment advanced to the foot of the throne to receive, and swear to defend, the eagle that would in future surmount its flag. Although so many oaths have been violated, yet the army must, in justice, be acknowledged to have kept this one.

After taking part in numerous parades, the army detachments left Paris on 20 January 1805.

My marriage. I was granted permission to leave Paris from 12 January in order to go to Nancy for my wedding.

A new coach service had just begun between the two cities which, as the name 'Rapidity' indicated, was able to complete the journey much more quickly than before. I left Paris on the 12th. At Claye a bolt broke and, as we left Épernay, a wheel collapsed. Finally the vehicle reached Nancy on the 16th, twenty-four hours late. These coaches were not destined to be a success.

I was married on 12 February. Colonel d'Anthoüard was present at the wedding and then left for Paris.

My wife and I left for Italy on 4 March. The colonel met us at Lyon, and we travelled together to Piacenza, which we reached on the 21st. I took a young servant with me from Saint-Dié and he was with me through all my campaigns until we were finally disbanded. He served me very well.

The establishment of the Kingdom of Italy. A coronation at Milan. As France was now a monarchy, Lombardy could no longer remain a republic. This was explained to the Italians, and they were promised that they would have an independent monarchy when peace became general. Meanwhile a decree was promulgated in the Senate whereby the Cisalpine Republic became the Kingdom of Italy, of which Napoleon was declared king. He chose Prince Eugène de Beauharnais* as viceroy.

As great splendour had been thought necessary for a coronation at Notre-Dame, it was considered equally necessary in Italy. All of Milan was made ready for the celebration of this occasion.

---

* Eugène de Beauharnais (1781–1824), the son of Napoleon's wife, Josephine, by her first husband, General Alexandre de Beauharnais (guillotined in 1794).

Napoleon reached Italy at the end of April; he travelled by way of Turin, now only the administrative centre of the region, and arrived at Alessandria on 5 May when he assembled all his troops on the Marengo plain. We were made to perform manoeuvres that recalled the episodes of that famous battle, and were watched by the inhabitants and by others who had hurried there from every direction. Then Napoleon laid the first stone of a memorial in honour of the soldiers who had been killed on that celebrated day.

Work was at once begun which would make Alessandria one of the most strongly fortified places in Europe.

Napoleon left Alessandria and went to Milan, passing through Pavia on his way.

The coronation took place in Milan cathedral on 26 May with the utmost pomp and magnificence imaginable. The Emperor had crowned himself at Notre-Dame and, in the cathedral at Milan, the new king of Italy placed the iron crown of the old kings of Lombardy on his own head. The ceremony was perfectly organised and was admired by all, especially by the Italians. Napoleon then presented Prince Eugène to the states as their viceroy.

The prince's court was set up. The Milanese were far from indifferent to the profits they might enjoy from this, and it helped them to forget that their ruler was a foreigner. The celebrations and parades continued.

At the end of the month a military training area was organised at Sainte-Euphémie near Brescia and I was sent to it on 31 May, staying until 16 June. Although the continent was at peace the troops had little rest, and there were endless exercises and manoeuvres. As well as the 1st and 4th Horse Artillery Regiments, the 2nd Foot Artillery were also garrisoned at Piacenza, where a firing range was opened for practice and manoeuvres. This was a very pleasant garrison, thanks to its nearness to Milan. We took part in all the capital's festivals, balls and cavalcades.

To judge from appearances, the new subjects of the new king of Italy were in a state of euphoria. Everywhere, in his continual travels, Napoleon was rapturously acclaimed. Guards of honour and festivals were organised in every town he visited. These journeys, these celebrations, these receptions and reviews, together with the administration of the new kingdom and its finances, together with the organisation of his army, combined to absorb his attention. We knew that he was also busy with the preparation of a great expedition against England. He worked far into every night; couriers came and went ceaselessly. On 7 July he suddenly left Turin for Paris, travelling incognito and leaving Empress Josephine in Italy.

The camp at Boulogne. On 14 July, at the Invalides, he inaugurated the Order of the Legion of Honour, and there was a distribution of the decoration. On the 15th – his birthday – he awarded the star to the officers and troops who had been awarded that military honour.

Since the breakdown of the treaty of Amiens we were again at war with England. On the coast, the Emperor began to make elaborate preparations to transport the army, now encamped around Boulogne, across the sea to England.

These preparations must have frightened the English, for their army, good as it was, would not have been able to resist ours once we had crossed the Channel.

Their government was skilful, selfish if you like, even perfidious, but careful of its own interests and, in order to save itself from invasion, brought together a third coalition against us which included the Swedes, the Russians, the Austrians and the Neapolitans. There was no doubt that a continental war would deflect Napoleon from a sea-borne expedition against England. I often hear England reproached with having caused others to suffer the same peril as that with which it was itself menaced, but this seems to me to be unjust. So much the worse for those who permitted themselves to be caught up in England's intrigues, and who, like Austria, for the third time in a few years exposed themselves to Napoleon's blows.

Resumption of the war in Germany. Our Grande Armée was on the Channel coast and the new coalition thought the time favourable to attack us. In their impatience, the Austrians did not wait for the arrival of the Russians before invading our ally, Bavaria, and with an army of sixty thousand men, occupied Ulm on the Danube. General Mack,* in command of this army, believed that Napoleon, who had already crossed the Rhine, was still in France, whereas he had by now passed to the north of the Black Forest and the Swabian Alps, crossed the Danube below Ulm, separated the Austrians from the Russians and forced them to lay down their arms.

This news was received with joy when it reached us in Italy. What a magnificent start to a campaign that had hardly begun! The Army of Italy was, at that time, under the command of Masséna, while Archduke Charles† commanded that of Austria.

As soon as Masséna learned of the defeat at Ulm, he forced the passage of the Adige at Verona and attacked the Austrians in their entrenched positions at Caldiero. Archduke Charles retreated from Italy in order to protect Austria and retired on Frioul. Masséna followed him.

At the battle of Caldiero, Colonel Demanet of the 2nd Foot Artillery, at that time garrisoned with us at Piacenza, was wounded in the hand and died of tetanus there.

The rapidity of the Austrian retreat from Italy left us with nothing of importance to do in this glorious campaign, which was brought to an end in Moravia on 2 December by the victory of Austerlitz and the subsequent peace of Presbourg.

While at Piacenza we had been, at all times, prepared for action.

Towards the end of the year, the peasants in the Apennines rose, and threatened the town. The citadel was armed and made ready to give them a hot reception. General

* General Karl Mack (1752–1828).
† Field Marshal Charles, archduke of Austria, third son of Emperor Leopold II.

Junot* was responsible for their dispersal. I had been extremely anxious. My wife was about to give birth and, if there was an attack and I was ordered to the citadel, I did not know if I should have the time to take her there. My terror was all the greater as the rabble in the town was menacing and I knew, from what had happened at Verona, of what they were capable.

It was at this time that Colonel d'Anthoüard was appointed aide-de-camp to Prince Eugène and replaced by Colonel Prost.[†]

We join the Army of Naples. The Neapolitan court, although it had signed a treaty of neutrality with France, joined the enemy coalition. Believing our Grande Armée to be fully occupied in Germany, Naples appealed to the Russians and the English.

When Masséna had pursued Archduke Charles as far as Hungary, he returned to Italy and, in February 1806, marched upon Naples. The very fact of his approach caused the Russians and English to re-embark. The Neapolitan court fled to Sicily and Joseph Bonaparte was appointed lieutenant general of the Kingdom of Naples until he could be proclaimed king.

Napoleon had begun by giving the duchy of Lucca to his elder sister Elisa, Joseph was to have Naples, and Holland was given to Louis. Murat[‡] received the Grand Duchy of Berg, while waiting to become king of Naples, at the time that Joseph was made king of Spain and Jérôme, king of Westphalia.

Our victories and the greatness of France were no longer enough to satisfy Napoleon's ambition. His arrogance demanded new satisfactions, as did the pretensions of this family of insatiable parvenus. New kingdoms had to be carved for them from the conquests bought with our blood.

Even as he destroyed the framework of the old Germanic empire, he applied himself to creating, around his new empire, a network of vassal kingdoms, princedoms, duchies and earldoms for his relatives, for the generals, and for people who, like himself, had sprung from our revolution. The future was to show whether these titles, honours and wealth had combined to elevate the characters of men who had hitherto served their country with devotion and self-sacrifice.

The army that had invaded Naples included the colonel of the 1st Horse Artillery and several companies of that regiment. After the victory, the entire regiment was attached to the Army of Naples and we left Piacenza on 3 April to garrison Sainte-Marie-de-Capone.

---

* General Jean Andoche Junot, duke of Abrantes (1771–1813).
† Colonel Ambroise Prost (1776–1840).
‡ Marshal Joachim Murat, prince and king of Naples (1767–1815).

At that time of year (3 April to 14 May) our journey across Italy was delightful. There was great friendship between the officers, many of whom were married. The wives followed the column in coaches. A pleasant spot was chosen where luncheon was enjoyed together, and the best lodgings were reserved for married officers.

We travelled through Parma, a well-populated and beautiful city that contained the Farnese Palace. The citizens were courteous and there were numerous French families there, drawn there by the previous duke, who had been a pupil of Condillac.*

We also passed through the ancient town of Reggio with its fine porticos and magnificent houses and gardens. The road from Modena to Bologna was long and tedious. Bologna, a busy city, is in a fine position and boasts handsome buildings and beautiful churches. There are two towers there, one of which leans over about eight or nine feet. The bishop gave us permission to see, in the convent of Saint Catherine, the body of the saint, which was black but well preserved. Visitors were allowed to kiss the phial that contained the sweat that the saint had shed during her lifetime. It smelled pleasant.

As we went through Florence, a pretty little town, we felt ill-disposed towards the inhabitants, for we knew they were hostile to us. We had not forgotten that in 1799, after the surrender of Ancona,† they had wanted to massacre the French garrison as it passed through their town and the Austrians had been unable to enforce the terms of surrender.

Césena is in a beautiful place, and fine wine is grown there. Wheat is stored in grain silos built beneath the cobblestones of the roads; I do not know whether this is the reason for the abundance and excellence of the bread that is eaten there.

Rimini is a fine old town on the Adriatic that boasts a busy harbour. It is said that Caesar stood upon the pedestal in the grass-market to address his troops before crossing the Rubicon.

The pleasant highway followed the coast as far as the important port of Ancona. This ancient city, with its triumphal arches, is built on the western side of a mountain that slopes down to the sea. The roads of the town are unattractive, being both narrow and steep but, from its large, though rather shallow harbour, the town looks charming. The triumphal arch is well preserved, but the theatre is a dog kennel.

The road to Loretto is mountainous, and the view from the hilltop town is splendid. The lodging that Joseph and Mary occupied in Judaea is in the middle of the church, encased in marble. The steps leading up to it bear the deep imprints of the knees of countless pilgrims. The infant Jesus' bowl is to be seen there, and there is a

---

* Étienne Bonnot de Condillac (1715–1780), author and philosopher.
† This refers to the surrender of the French garrison at Ancona to Austrian, Russian and Turkish forces following a siege that ended in November 1799. The garrison was granted the honours of war and allowed free passage back to France.

good trade in the rosaries that are blessed in it. The story of the manner in which the house was carried from Judaea to Loretto is written in every language on the pictures shown in the church. The lodging was borne by angels from Judaea to Dalmatia, but, as brigands were over-running the country, the angels carried it on into Macedonia to a field owned by two brothers. These two quarrelled over the ownership of the house, so it was taken up again and came to rest, at last, in Loretto. Between Loretto and Recanati, the views are superb; there can be few landscapes more lovely and fertile than that between Ancona and Tolentino.

Tolentino is a dirty little town at the head of the valley through which one travels across the Apennines to reach Foligno, where there is a delightful little theatre, undoubtedly the most elegant in Italy. The arms of Saint Nicolas of Tolentino are to be found in the church.

Spoleto, Terni and Otricoli are villages on the heights above the Tiber; the famous falls of Mamora are near Narni.

On 1 May we reached Civita Castellana (previously known as Veii). It stood on a steep escarpment, and was in such a strong position that the Romans had been tempted to make it the headquarters of their republic.

We reached Rome on 2 May and remained there until the 6th. There were too many things to see there in such a short time.

Only tombs and ruins were to be seen in the wild country between Rome and Albano.

Velletri is a big town in a fine situation on the heights.

On 7 May, reaching the Pontine Marshes, we took a direct road across the mountain, which from Sermonda and Piperno took us to Terracine. At the foot of the mountain the road became so bad that we were forced to abandon our carts, spend the night at Sermoneta on the heights, and then collect them again the following day to follow the Apennine road across the Pontine Marshes.

This swampy, desolate countryside, ravaged by malaria and thickly covered in vegetation, could become very fertile if it were made healthier. It seems that this was the case in the time of the Volscians but all efforts to render it less unwholesome since then have failed.

The Pontine Marshes must, at one time, have been a gulf. They stretch at the feet of the Lepini mountains and are divided from the sea by a series of dunes. The water flowing down the mountains, added to the rainfall – heavy in that part of the country – has no outlet and stagnates, giving off a foul miasma that poisons the air. The plain is very low so that there are few purifying outlets to the sea.

Terracine, at the tip of the Pontine Marshes, is a poor, dirty town, at the end of a range that forms a promontory. The area called the Marina would be beautiful if the buildings, which had been begun and abandoned, should ever be finished.

Mola is a suburb of Gaeta on the coast. The French were besieging the town, and on the next day, we followed the coast as far as the bridge of boats that crossed the Garigliano near its mouth, where our journey was enlivened by shots fired from English gunboats.

At last, on 14 May, we reached Sainte-Marie-de-Capua, where we were to be garrisoned. We had been forty-two days on the march from Piacenza and had covered the most picturesque part of Italy; we had marched by the Adriatic, seen Latinium and crossed the malarial countryside.

Sainte-Marie-de-Capua had been built on the ruins of ancient Capua, in a rich and populous countryside. There was no danger that the pleasures it offered were likely to enfeeble the courage of our soldiers. It was a town of some twelve thousand souls and contained twelve tanneries. Everyone there was employed; there was neither an aristocracy nor a rich middle class, and the inhabitants did not seem to enjoy themselves more than was usual elsewhere; they had, in fact, earned the reputation of being disagreeable. However, we ourselves had nothing to complain about. Among the ruins of ancient Capua there was a fine triumphal arcade of two arches that was well preserved, as well as one of the largest amphitheatres in Italy, but this latter was daily despoiled by the theft of stones.

We made sightseeing expeditions to the famous royal castle of Caserta, and the superb gardens adorned with statues that surrounded it

From 1 to 4 June we travelled for pleasure to Naples. Vesuvius was erupting and, so that we could enjoy the magnificent spectacle to the full, we had ourselves taken by night out into the bay. I have never seen anything so impressive; it is quite impossible to describe such things. We also travelled to Pompeii, Bäia, Solfataro, Sorrento, etc. I enjoyed the surroundings of Naples far more than my stay in Rome. Nature, when beautiful, never wearies me, but I confess that the works of man grow tedious after a while.

The siege and capture of Gaeta. In spite of the rapid conquest of the Kingdom of Naples, peace was not entirely restored there. One of the princes of Hesse, with some troops, had retreated into Gaeta and, with the help of the English fleet, defended it energetically.

Elsewhere, the English had disembarked in the Gulf of Saint-Euphémia and stirred up the ever-restless Calabrians. The war in that area was difficult, dangerous and wearisome. The Calabrians, a fierce people, massacred our prisoners after torturing them.

The siege of Gaeta also posed great difficulties. The town was built at the end of a rocky promontory, which provided only a narrow means of access. As well as its very strong position, it had well-built defensive works that presented several lines of fire. The English fleet added its firepower, so that the position that could previously be attacked from only one side was now inaccessible from three sides. As a result, it was impossible to surround Gaeta completely and the town was continually resupplied from the sea.

Early in July, I received an order from General Dulauloy,[*] commander-in-chief of the artillery of the Army of Naples, to proceed to Gaeta for attachment to the besieger's artillery park. I arrived there at ten in the morning. The approach road had been skilfully built by engineer officers and it was long and dangerous. As the soil of the isthmus was sandy on the surface and rocky beneath, it had been necessary to cut trenches into the rock and cover them with sandbags.

Marshal Masséna was the commanding officer of the troops there.

On the evening of my arrival, the officers of the staff were determined that an attack should be launched; as it was not they who would mount it, they were not too concerned to find out if the breach was practicable. Not only was this not the case but, in addition, the batteries destined to protect the assault were incapable of doing so.

We spent the whole night repairing the batteries, but it was not until dawn that they were capable of firing. Throughout the night the enemy kept up a continual musketry fire upon us, so that we were forced to abandon one breach battery in front of the trench, about fifty yards from the top of the covered way. This battery was not in communication with the trench, so reaching it and working there had to be achieved out in the open.

Our batteries continued to fire throughout the night of the 11th/12th until eight in the morning, when a negotiator was sent to demand the surrender of the town. Negotiations were carried on unsuccessfully until eight in the evening, when firing started again.

Lively firing continued throughout the following days, only being interrupted by the arrival of ammunition transports, and by the replacement of unserviceable guns, particularly those in which the touch-hole had widened.

An attempt was made to install a breaching battery trained on the citadel, but this proved to be impossible as it was too greatly exposed to musket fire from the town and from the gunners. Every effort to silence the fire from the town was in vain, the enemy was always able to replace the guns that were put out of action; he even increased the number of his batteries.

It was decided, during the night of the 16th/17th that a breaching battery had to be positioned in the trench itself, and on the night of the 17th/18th I was ordered to arm it with six 24-pound guns. Conveying these cannon through the trenches was slow and difficult. The gun carriages sank to the hubs in the sandy soil. I ordered strong beams to be placed in the path of the gun carriages. Many were wrecked, but at last I was able, by the morning of the 18th, to have several of them in position.

* General Charles-François Dulauloy, Count Randon (1764–1832).

We were so close to the enemy that, in order to avoid attracting his attention, all this work was carried out in silence. I had an inexperienced young lieutenant under my command and he was so enthusiastic that he was continually shouting and rushing about to encourage the working party, and so earned us several cannon and musket shots. My remarks and the sarcastic comments of the gunners failed to shut him up.

Two breaches were opened and efforts were directed to making them practicable. During the night, while we were repairing our batteries, the enemy cleared the bottom of these breaches and established a strongpoint behind the bigger one. The army called for an assault. It would be murderous for, in addition to obstacles both natural and artificial, the enemy did not seem to be at all disheartened.

On the 18th at three o'clock in the afternoon, a white flag was flown over the larger breach and a negotiator was taken to general headquarters. Firing stopped for a moment; French, English and Neapolitans began to chatter. No order to cease fire was received, so we started firing again. Only one battery responded. The white flag flying above the larger breach was carried away by one of our shots.

At last, the order to cease firing and stop work was received. The French took possession of Gaeta the same day, and the Neapolitans sailed for Sicily in English ships, having sworn not to take up arms against the new king of Naples again.

Gaeta had held out for a long while. It had been blockaded from February 1806 when the French, under General Reynier* (who lacked the supplies necessary to attack it) marched into the Kingdom of Naples, until it finally surrendered to Marshal Masséna on 18 July. The siege had been difficult in many ways, and we had often lacked the materials we needed.

Powder had to be brought from Pésaro on the Adriatic. Such a long journey, at that time of the year, damaged the barrels so that the powder leaked out along the way. In the streets of Mola I have seen children, carrying a coal in their hands as they followed the carts, trying to set fire to the train of gunpowder leaking on to the road. It is amazing that, throughout the siege, there was not a single accident, or rather disaster, caused by these children or by sparks from the wheels as they travelled the burning hot road.

In our army we had a battalion of negroes,† courageous and determined men, who were convinced that they could best help their badly wounded comrades by ending their lives. Projectiles were so scarce that, in order to obtain them, a premium of three *carlins*‡ was paid for a cannon-ball or shell fired by the enemy. The negroes ran after the balls, at the risk of their lives. They watched the shells as they flew past,

---

* General Jean-Louis-Ébénezer, Count Reynier (1771–1814).

† These were members of the 'Pionniers Noirs', formed in 1803 from black soldiers enlisted in Egypt or French Caribbean possessions. They were transferred in 1806 to the service of the king of Naples as the Royal African Regiment.

‡ An Italian coin.

repeating 'Three *carlins*, three *carlins*!' and when the shell exploded they yelled, 'Bugger the *carlins*.'

We also had some Neapolitans with us as auxiliary troops; they were appalling soldiers and quite merciless.

The depot for ammunition and supplies of all kinds was in a huge tomb that we called the Round Tower. Fortunately this tower was vaulted because, knowing the use to which it was being put, the English kept it under continual bombardment. The ammunition storerooms opened off a passage which ran all round the tower; one of these rooms contained gunpowder.

The officer in charge of the explosives and of the guard of this tower had been wounded in the head by the explosion of a bomb, and I was ordered to take his place. One day, when we were engaged in putting a convoy of powder barrels into storage, I noticed that one of the barrels was broken. I went into the tower to assure myself that every precaution had been taken, and saw a candle fixed to the wall immediately above the broken barrel. If the candle, or even a single spark from it, had fallen, the whole tower could have blown up, together with provisions for the entire army. I felt so shaken that I could not even be sure that my hand was steady enough to move the candle. I called the guard and told him to do it. I felt that only a person so blind to danger that he could place a lighted candle above a broken barrel of gunpowder would have a steady enough hand to remove it.

Contempt for danger is, doubtless, creditable, but only when the threat is to oneself alone, and when it achieves some purpose. In this instance our supplies and everyone working in the tower, as well as the troops camped nearby, were uselessly endangered. I had that guard demoted, for he had been guilty of other mistakes. On 19 July, the day after the surrender, we disarmed our batteries, of which there had been nineteen, and on the 22nd I returned to my regiment.

Once Gaeta had been taken, Marshal Masséna returned with his troops to rejoin General Reynier in Calabria. There he forced the English to re-embark and he subdued the entire country, so that the Kingdom of Naples was at peace, as was the rest of Italy.

The regiment was too overcrowded at Sainte-Marie-de-Capua and, on 4 January 1807, left to take up garrison duties at Aversa, which was barely four leagues from the capital, Naples. Aversa was an important town of some 20,000 inhabitants that had been founded by early Norman adventurers. I have seldom seen a barracks better appointed than the one we occupied. The lodgings reserved for officers were each provided with a kitchen and stove. The stables were vaulted.

We spent the winter very happily in this wealthy and beautifully cultivated countryside, enjoying the pleasant climate. Every Sunday our regiment provided a detachment for a parade that was inspected by the king of Naples, and we took part in all the festivals that were held in the town. Uniform was compulsory at such festivals, and we had no wish to wear anything else, but we were allowed to embellish it. This led, in the case of the Horse Artillery, to the addition of red morocco leather boots with gold tassels and nankeen breeches with gold braid on them.

While our life passed so easily and pleasantly, the Grande Armée was fighting and, after having avenged Rossbach* at Jena and at Auerstadt, went on to attack the Russians in Poland, having previously, within a single month, utterly crushed the Prussian army.

We ourselves, beneath the Neapolitan skies, celebrated the victories of Eylau and Friedland that had been so dearly won by our comrades and finally, at last, the peace of Tilsit that ended the war.

At Tilsit the autocrat of all the Russias together with the elected representative of the French people divided the continent of Europe between them and swore eternal friendship.

Return to North Italy. After eighteen months spent in the pleasant countryside around Naples our regiment was recalled to the Army of Italy and, on 18 November 1807, we left Aversa for Verona.

Our return journey to the north followed exactly the same path as the one we had taken in May 1806 as far as Reggio, where we turned towards Verona, passing through Mantua on the way. This journey was less pleasant in November, partly because of the weather, but also because we were in charge, as far as Mantua, of a party of five hundred galley slaves or rebels, who were to be incorporated into the Neapolitan regiments that were garrisoning that town. A company of *sbires*† was attached to us to guard them until we were over the Apennines. They were handcuffed during the day with *poucettes*‡ and, at night they were shut up in churches or in sheds. The order was given that any of them who attempted to escape should be shot. When we reached the Pontine Marshes near Trepanti, an escape attempt was discovered in time. The major commanding the column gave them a warning, but they took no notice and, at Fogliano, having broken through the wall of the place where they were locked up, were surprised only at the moment of their attempted escape. Threatened with death, they named one of their number as the ringleader. He was shot by the *sbires* at the roadside.

These scoundrels, who had been completely equipped when they left Naples, managed, although they were watched, to sell their possessions so that, when they reached Mantua, they had only their shirts beneath their overcoats. Like our soldiers,

* Scene of a French defeat at the hands of Frederick II in 1757.
† A pejorative term for police, similar to 'copper'.
‡ A means of restraining prisoners by tying their thumbs together.

they were entitled to subsistence rations; when they were late in arriving at a halting place and too lazy to make soup, they would sell their rations in order to buy cheese. The major, to make sure that they were not swindled in these sales, arranged with the suppliers to give them food that was ready to eat instead of meat. As one man, they asked for cheese. As a result they crossed Italy from Naples to Mantua for forty days living on nothing but bread and cheese.

The Neapolitan regiments into which these bandits were incorporated became part of the army that went into Catalonia in 1808. What atrocities they must have committed there, perpetrating horrors that were to be blamed on our soldiers.

At Verona there was garrison duty and the usual routine.

In June we learned, in turn, of the happenings at Bayonne,* of the proclamation of Joseph as king of Spain and of the uprising in that country. This news had an appalling effect. Apart from fanatics, to whom Napoleon was infallibility incarnate, there was universal condemnation. The Italians were careful of what they said in front of us; but I had been in the country for six years and understood and spoke their language, and judging from the conversations and comments that I overheard, I concluded that Napoleon's reputation was damaged in their eyes as well as in the eyes of the army.

To follow Tilsit with Bayonne! Having done such great things, to sink to the politics of Machiavelli! To drag the king of Spain and his son to Bayonne so as to consolidate their alliance with France, then to lay hands on them, force them to yield up the crown of Spain like some rich sinecure, intern them in France and then to place the crown on the head of his brother Joseph, was a despicable act. The Spanish had no intention of permitting themselves to be so disposed of and they rose up in protest.

It was not that the king of Spain was particularly attractive. He was a degenerate Bourbon like his relation the king of Naples, to whom he was very similar. Both were mediocre individuals, narrow-minded and mean. One thought only of hunting, the other of fishing, both were ruled and deceived by their wives. If they followed different policies it was because the lover of one was English and so was hostile to us, and the lover of the other was Spanish and had a personal interest in being of use to us. So we were right to throw out the king of Naples, but why remove from the Spanish a sovereign who had remained our faithful ally?

Joseph, now proclaimed king of Spain, was replaced at Naples by Murat, who, it was said, was not happy about it; he was hard to please. It was a considerable promotion for him.

---

* Charles IV and Prince Ferdinand of Spain were induced by Napoleon to surrender the throne of Spain to him at Bayonne in April 1808.

A leave spent in France. My thoughts. As we were at peace with Italy, leave was granted at the end of the year, and I had no difficulty in obtaining a six-months holiday. My wife and I, with our daughter, left Verona on 27 November to go to Lorraine, which we reached on 21 December. We made this long journey in a *voiturin*, which provided a comfortable way to travel and see the countryside. The *voiturin* was like one of our *fiacres*, with room for four in it, covering between ten and twelve leagues a day, usually at a walking pace. One paid in advance, and everything was included in the cost, food and lodging. I had never been to Switzerland and was determined to visit the country, in spite of the time of year. We travelled by way of Milan, Turin, Mount Cenis, Chambéry, Geneva, Lausanne, Soleure, Basel, Colmar and Saint-Dié.

When I arrived in Lorraine, I was struck by the alteration in the atmosphere. Our soldiers, returning from Germany, had been received with joy and the Emperor had been everywhere acclaimed with as much enthusiasm as if a final peace had been achieved.

Until that time our wars had always been provoked by others. As First Consul, Bonaparte had, following 18 Brumaire, vainly sought peace with England and Austria; in 1805, the formation of the third coalition had interrupted the Emperor's preparations for the invasion of England and he had been compelled to undertake the Austerlitz campaign. The disloyalty of Prussia and the persistent enmity of Russia had led to Jena and to the Polish campaign.

Then, at last, there was peace, a glorious and advantageous peace – except with England, but that country no longer had a foothold on the continent. Yet, suddenly, the disgusting trickery at Bayonne stirred up our former allies, the Spanish, against us and once again opened the continent to the English. The indignation and anger caused by these events was the responsibility of Napoleon alone. He was about to impose an endless war upon France in order to satisfy his arrogance and the ambition of his family. The anger was all the greater and more widespread in that this wretched war was unlucky from the start, it imposed new sacrifices upon us, and the conscription of 1809 and 1810 brought deep despair to families. Everywhere it was said that our children were being made into cannon fodder. It had indeed been cruel to find that we had overthrown a king only to replace him with a tyrant.

Soon, other consequences of Napoleon's disgraceful conduct became apparent. The indignation of Europe was aroused against him, and England again had an excuse to intrigue against us. We were exhausted by the Spanish war, and Austria seized the opportunity to avenge herself for all her defeats, relying on the exasperation felt by Germany at the creation of the Kingdom of Westphalia and the Confederation of the Rhine. These creations had damaged German interests, reanimated its patriotism and silenced its rivalries. Counting, too, on the anger of the Tsar, Austria began to rearm and prepare for war.

Napoleon was not easily deceived and, while in Spain, he kept his eye on everything that went on in Europe, ensuring that he was well informed. He anticipated the coming war and returned to Paris, where he, in his turn, began his preparations.

Relations between France and Austria were so strained that war broke out without any declaration. There were several fights at outposts and finally, on 10 April, the Austrians, hoping to surprise us, crossed the frontier of our ally, Bavaria. The feelings of the Germans, both the allied and the neutral, had been so stirred up against us that it was said that, at the smallest setback, every state beyond the Rhine would rebel. We had learned this from the reports of our neighbours in Alsace and Baden.

I return to the army. As war was imminent, I left my wife and daughter with her family and left for Italy on 3 April. As ever, I crossed Mount Cenis – for the seventh time in the past year – and reached Milan on the 18th. The commander-in-chief of the artillery in the Army of Italy, General Sorbier,* was still in the town and I went to see him. He reproached me, but kindly, with being late, rather in regret that I had not been with the corps when the regiment began the campaign. He invited me to dinner and, after the meal, offered me the provisional command of the 4th Company, in place of Captain Paris, who had fallen seriously ill. I accepted gratefully, and a few days later, the general confirmed me in my new position, and left for Verona.

At last I was about to take part in real warfare.

I had left school thirteen years ago. Throughout that period France had been at war; her soldiers had fought wonderful campaigns in which I had not taken any direct part. I had fired a few cannon shots at Huningue and, at Verona, had exchanged a considerable number of shots at Gaeta with the English and the Neapolitans, but I had not been present at a single big battle. The campaign that was now beginning would yield nothing in the way of danger and difficulties to those that preceded it, and this time I should take my part, although as only a plain junior captain at the head of a light artillery company.

---

* General Jean-Barthélmot, Count Sorbier (1762–1827). A companion of Bonaparte at Valencia, he became a general in 1797. An artilleryman, he took part in the campaigns of 1805, 1809 and 1812, leaving the army after Waterloo.

Chapter Three

Campaigning in Italy and Germany (1809)

The battle of Sacile. This campaign of the Army of Italy was not begun with seventy thousand troops as is usually supposed, but with barely fifty thousand, and this figure does not include the ten thousand men of the Army of Naples who did not arrive until after the first battle.

The army was under the command of Prince Eugène, so young and brave and so well loved and admired. He had fought battles before but had never previously been in command. Commanders-in-chief require so many and such varied qualities that, although great leaders had indeed emerged from our revolution, they were the exception rather than the rule; the spontaneous emergence of leadership qualities is rare.

Archduke John,* who commanded the Austrians, had scarcely any more experience than Prince Eugène. On 10 April, the same day as their offensive in Germany, the Austrians, without any declaration of war, burst out of Carinthia and the Tyrol and surprised and overran or pushed back our advance posts.

Prince Eugène had not yet concentrated his army, for he had not anticipated this sudden and treacherous attack. Several of his corps were some distance away and he had no option but to fall back, which he did. This retreat, at the beginning of his first command, affronted his courage as well as affecting the mood of his soldiers. So, without waiting for an adequate build-up of troops, and without selecting a favourable position, he turned to face the enemy, attacked them near Sacile and was thrown back. This battle of Sacile was a bloody one and the hasty retreat, in terrible weather, beyond the Piave, caused us many losses.

General Macdonald arrives. Happily, General Macdonald arrived at that moment. He had been in disgrace for some time,† I do not know why, and had been sent to help Prince Eugène with his advice.

---

* Archduke John (1782–1859), son of the Grand Duke of Tuscany, who later became the Emperor Leopold II,

† General (later Marshal) Jacques Étienne Joseph Macdonald had fallen from favour with Napoleon when, in 1804, he publicly defended Moreau against charges of treason.

General Macdonald, in spite of his defeat at Trebbia,[*] had made a favourable impression on the Army of Italy, and the soldiers, who had begun to be discouraged by the weakness shown by their commanding officer, regained confidence, for it is essential, as they say, that malcontents should be strictly disciplined. General Macdonald rejoined the army wearing his old Republican uniform. This gave pleasure to the older soldiers, but was turned to ridicule by some young fools and arrogant officers, of whom there began to be far too many in the army and at headquarters.

As he retreated, several of his divisions joined Prince Eugène, and the withdrawal from Piave was carried out in a more orderly fashion.

After leaving Verona on 23 April, I joined the 4th Company of 1st Light Artillery, of which I was, temporarily, the commanding officer. This company was attached to the Light Cavalry Division under General Sahuc. Prior to the battle of Sacile, this general, in command of the rearguard, had allowed himself to be taken by surprise at Pordenone and suffered heavy casualties there. The 4th Company had been hard pressed at Sacile, losing two of its guns, of which it possessed only four when I joined it.

25 April. At Lonigo, on the river Gua.

26 April. In the evening we bivouacked on the Villa Nuova Bridge.

27 April. The division took up position on the road behind Caldiero. At five in the evening the enemy attacked General Seras's division on the Villa Nuova bridge. This division did not abandon the bridge until the following day, (the 28th) in order to retire into the Caldiero hills.

29 April. There was a general reconnaissance along the whole of the enemy's line, where there appeared to be signs of an Austrian retreat. This became more noticeable on the following day, and was explained by the receipt of news of the Grande Armée's success on the Danube.

1 May. We resumed the offensive, and recaptured our position of the 26th on the Villa Nuova bridge.

2 May. The enemy put up some resistance at Montebello and finally retired upon Vicenza, which it evacuated the same evening. There was skirmishing all day long.

3 May. In Vicenza.

4 May 4. On the Brenta.

5 May. The river was crossed by means of a ford. On the other side, the enemy seemed prepared to resist and the cavalry divisions of Sahuc and Pully were deployed. But only skirmishers were firing all day.

6 May. The enemy crossed the Piave and destroyed the bridges.

7 May. My company left Sahuc's division and joined the advance guard, which was composed of six battalions of light infantry, of the 9th Chasseurs à Cheval, and

[*] June 1799.

was under the command of Général de Brigade Dessaix.* We spent the night on the bank of the river before the village of Lovadina.

The battle of the Piave. The Piave rises in the Italian Tyrol and flows into the Adriatic. It is not a long river, but at this time of the year was a veritable torrent because of the melting snow and the rain. As the bridges had been destroyed, we were obliged to ford the river.

At four in the morning of 9 May the advance guard received the order. I was to follow the leading troops with two cannon. I took command and placed myself at the front, preceded by a young trumpeter, a brave and intelligent boy of fifteen, with whom I had already reconnoitred the ford. The current was so rapid that many of the infantry were swept away and drowned. The precaution had been taken of positioning anchored boats that were manned by sappers who held out poles to the unfortunates as they were swept past, but very few were saved.

The ford was narrow and ran diagonally. This is to say that, after having crossed the current, it was necessary to go downstream between the current and the left bank, and it was this last crossing that was the most dangerous for, if one went slightly to the right, one was suddenly swept off one's feet. This happened to my trumpeter, who had been only the length of a horse in front of me. The poor boy was carried away and drowned before my eyes. At the moment when I felt my horse stagger, I was able to collect him, spur him forward and save myself. The guns followed my course.

When it reached the left bank of the Piave, the infantry formed square with the cavalry on the left. With my four guns, the two others under the command of Lieutenant Morizot having rejoined me, I went forward and to the right, to facilitate the deployment of the troops who were to pass in front of the advance guard.

The enemy who, until then, had revealed only a few skirmishers, now exposed his batteries and these, consisting of twenty-four guns, engulfed our left and front. The shot rained down, bouncing on the stony soil. To the Austrian artillery fire was now added a charge by a large and excellent body of cavalry. A countercharge by our 9th Chasseurs failed, and the situation of the advance guard became critical. Reinforcements were slow to arrive. The waters of the Piave continued to rise and, in order to make the crossing easier, ropes had been stretched across from one bank to the other, so that the troops could cross the river naked, carrying their clothes and equipment above their heads.

This was the first serious encounter in the open countryside at which I had been present. The heat of the struggle, so much more acute than in a siege, made one forget the danger. Forgeot's company, the 4th Horse, joined the artillery of the advance

* General Joseph-Marie, Count Dessaix. (1764–1834).

guard, and this made it possible for us to withstand the enemy gunfire. Soon we began to run short of ammunition and several of our guns were forced to draw back. I was left with one gun and the 4th Company had only two but this did not prevent us from carrying on the fight until the cavalry, which had finally succeeded in crossing the Piave by another ford, arrived to support us. One brigade of the cavalry deployed to the rear of our artillery, a foolhardy position as it offered the enemy two targets at once; all the shots aimed at us went on into the cavalry ranks, thereby causing quite unnecessary casualties. The general commanding this brigade had his thigh carried away by a shot. At the same time, the horse ridden by my lieutenant, Morizot, was killed under him.

A brilliant charge by the 6th Chasseurs and the 28th Dragoons knocked the enemy off his feet, captured his guns and took prisoners; it swept so far forward that the enemy line was crossed. When this line was re-established, our cavalry returned to re-form on our left, thereby turning the enemy flank. The charge had not achieved all that had been expected, for the advance guard alone could not bring enough pressure to bear. In spite of having suffered a great deal from the guns and from the enemy cavalry, the advance guard nevertheless moved forward. I was there in this new position, with my single gun, under the fire of four of the cannon that had earlier been captured in the charge and since abandoned again. Our advance guard received no support, and could not profit from the gains that the charge had brought us. The enemy had time to re-form.

While this was taking place on the left, the right, under the command of General Macdonald, crossed the river downstream, pushed the enemy back and had established an extended order of battle on the Piave.*

At the same time the main body of the army, having crossed the river, marched upon the Austrians and compelled them to retreat. The battle continued from four in the morning until nightfall.

---

* Extract from a letter written by Colonel de Gonneville, sent to his family after the death of Colonel Noël. At the battle of the Piave, Colonel de Gonneville was an aide-de-camp to General d'Avenay, who was mortally wounded with the advance guard.

> In the course of the unequal battle that took place at eight in the morning, the battery of the light artillery attracted particular attention on account of the bravery and coolness with which, despite many losses, it continued to reply to the unremitting fire of several enemy batteries. Overrun momentarily by a charge of the Austrian cavalry, the gunners and their brave commander did not give up their guns, two of which had been overthrown, so that, as soon as they were able to do so, they began firing again, without having given up any ground at all.
>
> The behaviour of this battery was greatly admired, not only by the advance guard, of which it formed a part, but also by all the army which, massed on the right bank and covering the left bank, were able to witness all the phases of the battle taking place on the latter. The battery was commanded by Colonel Noël, at that time a captain. [This note was included in the original edition of the work.]

The advance guard division bivouacked on the banks of the Piave, upstream of the battlefield.

I have read, in the history of this period, that the advance guard had been thrown back, by the Austrians, into the Piave and that, but for the arrival of General Macdonald, would have been drowned, put to the sword, or captured. It was not so. With the infantry formed into squares, the advance guard continued to hold the enemy at bay. As is always the case, there were some who fled, but the advance guard had been ordered to stand firm against the enemy, and this it did, in spite of great numerical inferiority, until the army had had time to cross the river and attack and defeat the enemy.

We marched towards the Tagliamento on 9 and 10 May and, although the Austrians had destroyed the bridges, we crossed it on the 11th and at about ten o'clock we met up with them, where they were in a good position at San Daniele. I was able to distinguish all the artillery emplacements facing me. At about four o'clock, part of the corps commanded by General Grenier formed up on our right. The enemy was overwhelmed, and one of their regiments, complete with its colonel and its flag, was captured. In the evening our skirmishers, who had advanced too far beyond San Daniele on the road to Osopo, were pushed back. The advance guard bivouacked at the camp at Plaisance that had been burned by the Austrians.

The enemy defended themselves in the market town of Venzano, but the town was violently captured.

Marshal Masséna marched his army corps towards Trieste and Carniola to the aid of Marmont,* who was ordered to march, with 10,000 men, from Dalmatia towards the Danube, in order, like us, to join up with the Imperial army there. We continued to follow Archduke John along the Carinthian road.

As the Austrians had burned or cut all the bridges in their wake, the artillery's progress was delayed, and at Capolara on the 13th we were forced to stop, for the Pietra Tagliata bridge had been burned.

At two o'clock in the afternoon of the 16th I received the order to go to Malborghetto. The bridge at Pietra Tagliata had been rebuilt on the burned piles of the old one. It did not appear to be strong enough for the weight of the artillery, but time was short. I had the guns dismantled, the carriages and the caissons emptied. The guns were securely tied with ropes to beams carried on the shoulders of soldiers positioned at either end. The soldiers also carried the ammunition, the carriages and the caissons across separately, and the horses were led over, one at a time. The whole operation, in which a Neapolitan battalion assisted me, took until nine in the evening and we did not arrive at Malborghetto until two o'clock on the following morning.

---

* Marshal Auguste Frédéric Louis Viesse de Marmont, duke of Ragusa (1774–1852).

The battle of Tarvis. The fort at Malborghetto commanded the route into the Alps and denied access to the artillery. This position had been strongly fortified by the Austrians and they had constructed breastworks, a stockade and a fortified battery half-way up the heights. At the top of the very steep mountain they had built two blockhouses, one at each end of the position; these combined to present a formidable defence.

On the 17th, before daybreak, on a hill about forty metres from the fort, we made ready my company's four cannon and the two guns to be served by the foot artillery; we began to fire at half past nine, just as the attack started. With astonishing verve the infantry attacked from all sides and, in spite of the steep slope, within a quarter of an hour had seized the fort and put the garrison to the sword.

The village of Malborghetto was also seized, enabling the army to continue its advance; only the artillery was delayed.

The Austrians had entrenched themselves beyond Tarvisio in order to defend the pass and the steep banks of the Schlitza; lacking its artillery, our army, confronting them, was powerless to attack. We left Malborghetto at three o'clock as soon as our means of access was cleared and we arrived before Tarvisio at about six o'clock. The enemy believed that we were still held up by the fort. As soon as the artillery arrived the attack began, and the impetus of our troops was such that within an hour the Austrians were in full retreat. We captured sixteen guns from them.

During a review following these battles Prince Eugène commended my company and presented us, as a sign of his satisfaction, with two guns and gun carriages, a howitzer and a 3-pound cannon.

We bivouacked near the battlefield.

As the bridge over the Gail had been burned, the artillery had to cut down trees to widen lanes and force its way forward in order to reach Villach on the 18th. From Villach to Klagenfurt and Marburg the road followed the picturesque valley of the Drava.

On the 20th the advance guard was disbanded and my company went to Pacthod's division.

On the 25th the army met with the corps under General Jellachich* who, after having taken part in the insurrection in the Tyrol, was attempting to rejoin Archduke John at Graz. In spite of the strong position that he occupied he was quickly defeated and a third of his army was taken prisoner, the rest vanishing into the mountains.

At Marburg on the 27th, I learned, from a chance remark, that the general commanding us had requisitioned some horses for the artillery. I had not asked for any and I had a strong suspicion that these horses would be replaced by money, for I was

* General Franz Jellachich von Buzim (1746–1810).

well aware of the transgressions of some of our leaders and their staffs. I went and found our general and asked to be given the requisitioned horses. He dared not refuse me, but his embarrassed replies confirmed my suspicions. In his presence, I ordered my blacksmith to mark the horses with the letter 'A'. They had certainly not original-ly been destined for the use of the army. I could say much more about this general, but he is dead.

At Marburg we left the lovely valley of the Drava and entered that of the Mur, which took us down into Graz, the capital of Styria, which we reached on the 29th.

Graz is a fine, prosperous town dominated by a high fort. Austrians occupied both the town and the fort. On the 30th, as they seemed prepared to defend the town, I received the order to get ready to burn it. I positioned two howitzers on the outskirts, while avoiding the fire of the castle guns. Fortunately, before firing started, the Austrians surrendered to us in order to save the town, and retreated into the fort.

For a long while the Emperor had been in control of Vienna, and had even crossed the Danube, but following the battle of Essling he had been compelled to return to the right bank. With the minutest attention to detail and his usual energy, he planned to recross the river in the face of the army of Archduke Charles which was encamped on the opposite bank.

Archduke John, in his retreat, could no longer hope to reach Vienna; so, having crossed the mountains, with us always at his heels, he turned towards the lower Danube and to Hungary either to rejoin his brother or to obstruct our right wing and impede our crossing of the river. He retired beyond the Raab, a river that rises in Styria and flows into the Danube in Hungary.

Joining the Grande Armée. We arrived in Neustadt over the mountains, a few leagues from Vienna on 4 June, and there we joined the Grande Armée.

The countryside had been opened up to us by the defeats at Pordenone and Sacile on 15 and 16 April. We had taken our revenge at the Piave and, until 4 June, our march through the Tyrolean gorges had been a series of battles and victories. And, if our troops had been, for one moment, demoralised by weak leadership, they had recovered quickly. They bore the fatigue, the privations and dangers of a forty-five-day march through a rebellious countryside with patience, courage and an unselfishness which was all the more praiseworthy in that most of them had no reward to look forward to. I cannot say the same of certain officers who yearned only for rest, and could not endure the slightest discomfort without complaining: but these were the exceptions; almost all the officers, like the troops, accepted their discomfort cheerfully, for they were victorious. In the Tyrol we often spent the night without protection from the driving rain and I felt fortunate to have the shelter of an artillery caisson above my head.

The battle and capture of Raab. After two whole days of rest at Neustadt, we left at midnight on the 6th for Hungary, seeking Archduke John, who was known to be across the river Raab. We passed by Ödemburg at nine in the evening; we did not go into the town but, in the suburbs we seized two warehouses, one of them full of oats and the other of wooden saddles, like those of the hussars.

During our march, a division from the Grand Duchy of Baden, under the command of General Lauriston,[*] and the light cavalry division of General Montbrun[†] had joined the Army of Italy from the Grande Armée.

Cavalry skirmishes warned us of the proximity of the enemy.

On the 13th, two leagues before Raab, these skirmishes developed into a serious battle. Warned of this, we set off at a trot and, after a rapid ride, reached the battle-field. I had my guns loaded, but was unable to fire. The disorder was so great that everything was in confusion. Towards the end I managed, at last, to direct some shot towards the Austrians, who finally retreated. This battle was relatively bloody. I lost a gunnery sergeant and one of my guns was dismounted. We spent the night in a village near the battlefield at the edge of the plain.

When we encountered it on the 14th, the enemy army was in a favourable position on a plateau. The village of Szabadhégy and the Raab were to their right. Their centre was protected by a ravine and a stream and by four hundred men occupying a position in a big farm. The fine Hungarian cavalry was on their left. The troops from Baden were at once confronted by an entrenched encampment covering the Austrian right flank. My division, together with the Italian Guard, formed the reserve.

The enemy was not engaged until just before two o'clock. In succession, the divisions under Seras, Durutte[‡] and Severoli went in to the attack. Our cavalry threw itself determinedly upon the Hungarians and dispersed them with an ease that astonished us. The Austrian hussars put up more of a resistance but were finally thrown back on to the left of their army. There was hard fighting in the centre. When our infantry had, with difficulty, crossed the ravine and the stream, they proceeded to attack the farm, from which they were repelled with losses. They returned to the charge and the sappers broke down the doors with axes. When they forced their way in, nearly all the defenders were killed. The resistance was the same on the plateau to our left, and the village was taken with the bayonet. It was captured, lost and recaptured. The first brigade of our division was ordered to the aid of the infantry on that flank. The Austrians were compelled to abandon their positions and nightfall covered

* General Jacques-Alexandre-Bernard Law (1768–1828). He was one of Napoleon's aides-de-camp, and later became Marquis Lauriston and a marshal of France. He was taken prisoner at Leipzig. He continued to follow Louis XVIII after the return of Napoleon from Elba.
† General Louis-Pierre, Count Montbrun (1770–1812). He was one of the great cavalry commanders of the Empire. He was killed at the battle of Borodino on 7 September 1812.
‡ General Pierre François Joseph Durutte, baron and count (1767–1827).

their retreat. They had fought very well, but the brilliant Hungarian cavalry performed very badly.

The archdukes retreated towards Comorn, where they would, doubtless, recross the Danube.

Our division slept on the battlefield, and kept watch on the town. In order completely to clear the right bank of the Danube and prevent the enemy from returning there, it was necessary for the French to take Raab and destroy the Pressburg bridge. Marshal Davout* was to undertake the latter task, and we were to take the town. The Baden troops under General Lauriston began the siege and the Italian army supported them; this gave us some rest after our hard work.

The siege could not present too much difficulty. There were about twelve thousand souls in the town, which stood on the river of the same name, which was, at that point, divided into several branches. There were no outer defences, and the ramparts were encircled by river and marshy land for three-quarters of their length.

Trenches were dug and, on the 15th, the attack began, with a battery of six howitzers firing on the town from the right bank. Some 12-pounders, which had arrived from Vienna, made it possible to open up a breach.

The garrison capitulated on the 23rd, was taken prisoner and paroled. Our division was billeted in and around the town, where we remained until 1 July.

Raab was quickly put in a state of defence, the ramparts were armed and the town resupplied with provisions and ammunition in case the Austrians attempted to recross the Danube and attack us on this side. To provide a garrison for the town, the weary and the sick of the Army of Italy were left there, including those who would recover quickly after a few days' rest. Count Narbonne,† a minister of war under Louis XVI, was appointed by Napoleon to be the city's governor. He had been in Napoleon's service for only a short time. Once a minister of the king, he had now become the governor of a little German town under the rule of a democratic monarch! What strange times we lived through!

1 July. We leave Raab to rejoin the Grande Armée.

2 July. At Saint Peter.

3 July. At Bouck.

4 July. At Schwechat, a little town by the Danube, that lay opposite the island of Lobau, where we bivouacked together with the Imperial and Royal Guards.

---

* Marshal Louis Nicolas Davout, duke of Auerstadt and prince of Eckmühl (1770–1823).

† Louis Marie Jacques Amalric, count of Narbonne (1755–1813) was a natural son of Louis XV and had been minister of war in 1791–2. He had returned to France under the Consulate and became a general in 1801. He died of typhus during the defence of Torgau in 1813.

Crossing the Danube. Near Ebersdorf, where our operations were based, all the preparations for the crossing of the Danube were made. Here the brave Marshal Lannes* had just died, after having been mortally wounded at the battle of Essling.

The French had been in control of Vienna since 12 May. The main Austrian army, under Archduke Charles, was in position and vigilant on the left bank of the Danube; we could not make an attack until the river had been crossed. The Emperor attempted such a crossing in May. For this daring enterprise, in the face of an army of one hundred and fifty thousand men, he had chosen the spot superbly well. Downstream of Vienna, opposite Ebersdorf, the Danube is divided into two branches by the wooded island of Lobau, which is wider than it is long. The main stream was on our side, so that it was possible to cross it, sheltered by the island from the Austrians. Once on the island, only the narrower branch remained to be traversed, but this was as wide as the Seine in Paris. However, in the course of the battle that followed the crossing, the main bridge had been destroyed, and the French army, deprived of communication and of supplies, was forced to retreat on to Lobau island, over which it retained control.

Since then, two bridges had been firmly established over the wider arm of the river; one had been built by the engineers on piles and the other, on boats, by the artillery, and both of them were defended by strong stockades. Lobau island had been fortified, and a construction site had been set up; in the creeks that intersected the island all the materials that would be needed for the rapid building of more bridges were assembled, as was a supply of boats, pontoons and ferries.

Now everything was ready for the crossing. To deceive the Austrians, the Emperor arranged for a feint attack at the same place where the previous crossing of Danube had been made. During the night of 4/5 July he sent some of the troops of Oudinot's† corps to the area opposite the island and threw three bridges across the narrow branch above the place where it widened into the main stream. This difficult operation was achieved in a few hours without a hitch and with admirable co-ordination. The Austrians, taken by surprise at a spot where they were not strong, were easily pushed back and the crossing began.

In a terrible storm on the same night, the Army of Italy, in its turn, crossed the wide branch of the river, and assembled on the island of Lobau, waiting to cross the narrow stream. Although we were soaked by the rain, we were ordered not to light fires in case they should provide targets for the Austrian artillery. The noise of the thunder mingled with the sound of the heavy guns positioned on Lobau that were firing from all sides into the wretched little town of Enzersdorf in order to dislodge the

---

* Marshal Jean Lannes, duke of Montebello (1769–1809).

† Marshal Nicolas Charles Oudinot, duke of Reggio (1767–1847).

occupying Austrians. Happily, as we were in the month of July, the sun rose early to dry and cheer us. How many of us would not see it set! It was a thought that came unbidden to one's mind.

It was not until the afternoon that my company at last crossed the narrow branch of the Danube by means of a pontoon bridge below Enzersdorf. The weight of the guns and the horses made it sag as much as twelve to twenty inches, which was not very reassuring. Once over the bridge we marched towards Wagram, passing through Enzersdorf, which had now been captured by the troops ahead of us and was engulfed in flames.

As soon as the troops reached the left bank, they deployed across the plain and, wheeling on the left wing that rested on the Danube, occupied the whole width of the Marchfeld plain that stretched from the river to a line parallel with the hills.

Detachments of Austrians, withdrawing towards the hills, were pushed ahead of the army, as it advanced in a line. The army shot them and cut them down with sabres, and seized the villages they overran; Essling and Aspern to the left and Rutzendorf and Raschdorf on the right.

From my own observations at the time, and with the help of my map, I can describe the position of the Austrians.

Their army occupied a line of hills parallel to the Danube, on which were Neusiedel and Wagram. At the bottom of these hills ran the deep and muddy stream of the Russbach. Wagram seemed to be the centre of their line. From that point their right wing curved almost to the Danube, passing through the villages of Gerasdorf and Stebersdorf.

By the evening our army was confronting the enemy army all along the line, with the Army of Italy in the centre, opposite Wagram.

At nightfall the Emperor, hoping no doubt to profit from the presumed confusion of the Austrians, attempted a limited attack on Wagram, with a view to cutting their army in two.

This was unsuccessful and, in the darkness, deceived by their unfamiliar uniforms, the French and the Saxons fired on each other. My division took no part in this unfortunate attack that cost the army several hundred men.

We spent the cold night without any fires. I slept in the shelter of a caisson, rolled in my cloak.

The battle of Wagram. We were up before daybreak on the 6th.

Cannon fire, from the direction of Neusiedel, was heard at four in the morning. The Austrians took the offensive and attacked our right. Firing soon stretched along the entire line from Neusiedel to Wagram. Our artillery replied along the front from the Danube to our extreme left.

Although positioned in the centre and in the second line, I was able, from the start of the action, to counter the enemy batteries on the hills that were doing so much damage to our first line. Our division repulsed the Austrians beyond the Russbach and attacked the village of Baumersdorf, located at the foot of the hills and on the stream itself.

When Baumersdorf had been taken, I was ordered to place my battery in the angle formed by the enemy and facing the village of Aderklau. This was a very exposed situation, for I was vulnerable, on the flank, to the Austrian artillery firing from the plain in front of Wagram. I was forced frequently to change the direction of my guns. First, I would fire on the enemy centre, then, when the batteries of Wagram stopped firing on me, I would fire on them again.

In a battle, at least when one is not part of the general staff, one sees only what is right before one's eyes. Smoke blinds and the struggle is all. I have no idea what happened in places other than Aderklau and Wagram, but on my left I heard a terrible gun battle. It was certainly there that our fate was decided. The Emperor must have been there. I learned afterwards that the Austrians had directed their greatest efforts to breaking through our lines and interposing themselves between us and the Danube; this they had almost achieved near Aspern, but they had been stopped by a hundred cannon rushed to the place on the direct order of the Emperor. The Austrian infantry, shaken and decimated by cannon-shot and musketry, had been pushed back and overwhelmed by General Macdonald. This had decided the result of the battle, and earned the gallant general a marshal's baton.

Our right wing, having crossed the Russbach, climbed the heights and threw the extreme left of the Austrians back from Neusiedel to Wagram. We, in our turn, then attacked this position. I took my guns up on to the plateau, and the village and encampment were taken. The enemy's left wing was clearly in retreat, but it was retiring in very good order in the direction of Brno in Moldavia. We pursued them until nightfall and bivouacked where we were, with the guns ready to fire. No sooner were we settled than an alarming rumour caused us to pick up our arms again, but calm was soon re-established. These rumours are continually arising in wartime, no one knows where they come from, but they can have terrible consequences and certainly have an effect on young, inexperienced troops.

We had won the battle, we were victorious along the whole length of the line and the Austrians were everywhere in retreat, but not in disarray.

Two things, sufficiently strange to merit a mention, occurred near me in the course of the battle. A shell came to rest between the legs of a mounting block on the left side of a draught horse harnessed to a gun. I shouted to the hurriedly dismounting soldier to draw his legs up and lie flat on the horse. Either he was too terrified to obey or he did not hear me, for he jumped off at the very moment the shell exploded and neither he nor the horse was injured.

One of the draught horses of my battery was hit by a small bullet that penetrated between the skin and the flesh all along one flank, without causing any internal damage, but raising a long ridge in its path. There was no veterinarian available, but I knew something about the care of horses and was unwilling for the horse to be abandoned. I myself treated it and succeeded in curing it by applying the usual method of dressing wounds. I put a long pad of tow in the wound every day, and it healed over quickly.

On the 7th we pursued the enemy and bivouacked on the road between Vienna and Brno. We were ordered to retire.

On the 10th I received a letter from General d'Anthoüard, who had been wounded at Wagram; in it he announced my promotion, dated the day before, to *chef d'escadron*. To this news he had added the words 'This is not enough; I hope that you will get the Star.'* Already, after the battle of Raab, Prince Eugène, as he passed near my company, had told me: 'Well, captain, this time we shall get something.' I believed that he was referring to a matter that he had already mentioned to me after the taking of Tarvis hill, namely that he had recommended me for a decoration.

On the same day, the 10th, we crossed the battlefield of the 6th on our way to Siebenbrunn. The villages were filled with wounded. We passed a field hospital near which was a heap of limbs, arms and legs. It is better to see such things after a battle than before.

In the course of the battle of Wagram, many of the wretched wounded had been roasted when the ripening corn had been set on fire. While crossing the battlefield I saw a wounded officer at the roadside; he was lying on the ground, covered by his cloak. I went to him and asked him about his injury. He pulled his cloak aside, revealing a terrible wound. His stomach was ripped open and the lesion was already green. He was beyond hope, and I was not able to have him carried away; but I left my water bottle with him.

An armistice was announced on the 13th. Everyone was delighted. Although it has been said that all that an army longs for is a battle, nothing could be more mistaken. After the weariness, the suffering and the misery that accompanies every campaign, all that soldiers long for is rest.

The division went to the Marsch on the 14th. The artillery went to Augern and general headquarters to Marcheck. We remained there.

On the 20th, going to walk in Vienna, I saw, near the bridges of the isle of Lobau, that there were still putrefying corpses in the water.

We changed our quarters on the 21st. We slept that night in the pleasant town of Pressburg and camped at Brugg in Hungary on the 22nd.

* Of the Légion d'Honneur, a system of honours to reward achievement and loyalty instituted by Napoleon in 1804.

On the 27th I received my nomination as a member of the Légion d'Honneur. It was dated from the 17th.

On 8 August, Captain Paris, having recovered from his long illness, rejoined the company and I handed the command back to him. I left on the same day for the general headquarters of the artillery at Neustadt, to await my new posting.

Neustadt is a charming town, well built and clean, and it lies in a beautiful and fertile plain. There is a cadet school there, and also one for the cavalry. The women are nearly all handsome and the people are good-hearted, like most of the Austrians. We got on very well with them. They fought well in Germany; I speak only of south Germany. Our hosts seldom gave us anything to complain about and, when billeted on them, we found them friendly. It is true that I was never very demanding; it is unfortunate enough for a population to have to endure the presence of invaders, without having to bear harshness and arrogance in addition. Unfortunately, not everyone agreed with me.

I did not have sufficient free time during my stay at Neustadt and in the neighbourhood of Vienna to go often into that beautiful and attractive city in which were to be found pleasures and distractions of every sort.

I was appointed as commander of the artillery of the cavalry division of the 8th Corps under General Junot, duke of Abrantes on 15 August. I was not notified of this until a few days later and it was not until the 23rd that I received the order to join my new corps. It was not without sorrow that I left the 1st Light Horse Artillery and those of my good comrades who still remained.

The Wagram campaign was over, but peace had not been concluded, although it seemed certain that this would soon be signed. The Emperor was still at Schoenbrunn.

The campaign had taken three months; from 10 April, when the Austrians attacked us in Austria and in Italy without declaring war, until 6 July after their utter defeat at Wagram. At the beginning I was a captain of the second grade and now, here I was – a *chef d'escadron* and an officer of the Légion d'Honneur. I was among the lucky ones; I was the most fortunate in the regiment. The artillery had suffered terribly at Wagram and, in the 1st Light Horse, there was no company that had not lost several officers killed and wounded. In war it is not enough to prove your zeal and courage, danger must bring you to the attention of your superiors. I have seen so many officers of great merit remain in low rank in spite of the endless warfare.

The Wagram was the last campaign to prove fortunate for us – everything that followed was ill-fated. And in view of all our Emperor's errors, it must be admitted that our misfortunes were deserved. Up until that time we had resisted hostile coalitions, and fought for our independence, but starting with the war in Spain, we, in our turn, had tried to oppress others and we had been defeated. Napoleon's genius as a commander did not diminish after 1809, neither did the courage and devotion of the

French, but the former was blinded by his good fortune, while we were, at last, exhausted by our endless losses.

Napoleon did not lack warnings. Already, in 1809, with most of his best troops in Spain, the war with Austria took him by surprise, forcing him to scrape the bottom of the barrel and fill his army of Germany with conscripts, even as his enemy's resistance grew stronger.

Everywhere, popular feeling turned against him; there was insurrection in the Tyrol, Germany seethed with anger, and if we suffered a reverse it could be the signal for a general uprising. The Prussian government could not control its people. In spite of the fact that we were at peace with Prussia, whole regiments, under the leadership of Major Schill, fought against us stubbornly, and were joined by numerous partisans.

As a general who had risen to power from a popular revolution Napoleon should have been warned by the anger of these people, just as the difficulties, the sufferings and the dangers endured in the course of the Polish campaign should have shown him the hazard of waging a distant war in the bitter climate of the north. But Jupiter renders blind those he wishes to destroy.

I am sent to Bayreuth. On 23 August I left Vienna to rejoin the 8th Corps of the Army of Germany, which was stationed in the principality of Bayreuth. I travelled post on horseback, with only my servant with me. We travelled through a countryside that we had laid waste and where peace was not yet assured, in as much safety as if we were in France. I slept in the ruined village of Siegharskirchen.

At Saint Palten on the 24th I saw, shut up in a barracks, a group of Austrian prisoners-of-war, guarded by other, armed, prisoners. There was not a single French soldier in the town. On the following day I passed, on the road, another group of prisoners, under the guard of a sergeant of the same nationality. What good nature!

At Melk the road ran along the Danube, following the course of the river on its right bank. The countryside was beautiful and picturesque, well populated and fertile but ravaged by the passage of armies and by battles. My ride, in fine weather, was pleasant and most interesting. I followed the road by which the ever-victorious Grand Armée had travelled to Vienna barely three months ago. As I journeyed by the swift streams rushing from the Alps down to the Danube, where the burned bridges were being rebuilt, and observed the defensive positions offered by the lie of the land, I was impressed by the hard work, the zeal and the devotion of our soldiers that had enabled them to cross the rivers and overcome all the difficulties that had confronted them.

On the 25th I slept at Melk, which is dominated by a magnificent abbey which had been fortified and where Napoleon had established his headquarters.

26th. I reached Amstädten. An agreeable town in a fine position.

27th. Enns is a little town on a hill on the left bank of the Enns whose attractive position is reminiscent of some towns in Italy. The French were building a bridgehead there.

29th. I crossed the Traun to Ebelsberg. This town, which was totally laid waste by the battle of 3 May, was just beginning to recover; several houses had already been rebuilt. When I examined the position I could not understand either how the French had been able to take it and cross the river, or why the Austrians had let them pass. If the passage of the Lodi bridge has astonished every military man who knows the terrain, there is even more reason to be amazed at the success of the French in their attack on the bridge at Ebelsberg.

Masséna, who was in command, had displayed all his energy and the French all their courage, but what was the point of all the effort and the sacrifices made by these brave soldiers when it would have been possible to ford the Traun above Ebelsberg? And in the course of battle on 3 May, a cavalry corps had actually forded it? This is gambling with the lives of men.

Ebelsberg is near the Traun, with steep heights behind it, and is dominated by a fortified castle. A long, wooden bridge has to be crossed in order to reach the town. The Austrians commanded the bridge, the town, the heights and the castle, and they directed their fire down on to the French below. Everything was captured, it is true; but the bridge was so blocked with French dead and wounded that the troops, in order to cross, were forced to throw the bodies of the dead, and all too probably, the wounded as well, down into the river.

I only passed through the fine large town of Linz and went on to Efferding, where I slept at the house of the priest, an excellent man who was most courteous and spoke perfect French.

I reached Bavaria on the 31st. Without being aware of it, I had passed from an enemy country into an allied one; it looked the same, the people were the same, the language and behaviour were the same. There was even the same devastation. The little town of Scharding on the river Inn had been burned to the ground. Passau stands at the convergence of the Inn and the Danube, at a place where both are of the same width. It is a badly built town; ill-paved on uneven ground, and it, too, bears the scars of war.

I followed the right bank of the Danube as far as the old town of Ratisbon, which is large and also ill-built; it is surrounded by a rampart that the late and much mourned duke of Montebello had stormed at the beginning of this campaign. I was still in the town on a Sunday and was very much struck by the self importance of the Bavarian officials who paraded gravely in their embroidered uniforms, their heads held high, swollen with conceit, seeming to command the passers-by: 'Hail me, I am ...'

After Ratisbon, I left the Danube valley to head to the north along another, marshy, valley where the countryside was no longer of interest. By way of Amberg, a fortified town, on 8 September, I reached Bayreuth, the ancient capital of the Margraviate of Bayreuth which was abolished, with so many others, by Napoleon in 1806.

Standing near the source of the river Main, Bayreuth is a fine town, with a castle and a park but it is thinly populated. There are two manor houses that are open to the people of the neighbourhood: Ermitage* and Fantasie.

As soon as I arrived in Bayreuth, I was put in charge of the inspection of all the armament of the cavalry division; this made it necessary for me to travel all over the countryside for a considerable distance. I visited Nuremberg, Gräfenberg, Neustadt, and the pretty little town of Erlingen, where a French colony had established itself since the revocation of the Edict of Nantes,† that event so fateful for France. They had preserved the language of that period, and had their own church and ministers. Everyone in the country was friendly to us. I lodged with a widow in Bayreuth who, with all her family, showed me every care, even kindness.

In the course of my inspection of armaments, I listened to some strange complaints. Dragoon officers complained that their sabres were straight instead of curved. It fell to me, an artillery officer, to inform them that the cavalry of the line was intentionally armed with straight sabres for thrusting, and not for slashing like the sabres of the light cavalry, and that it was this weapon that our enemies feared most in our cavalry charges, for two inches of straight sword in the body of a man would kill him, whereas a blow across the body would only put the enemy out of action for a short time.

Peace was announced at Bayreuth on 18 October and the army corps set out for Mayence.

I remained at Bayreuth, alone apart from a few gunners, to receive the horses that the province was due to supply to the artillery. This task took me until the end of October and I travelled, with the quartermaster, M. Sieyès, all over that part of Bavaria. I saw every horse in the countryside and caused those that seemed to me to be suitable for the army to be marked with an 'A'.

As soon as a number of horses had been collected I sent them off to Mayence under the care of a gunner who was helped by some locally hired men. All these convoys arrived safely at their destination in good condition and without having experienced any trouble although they had crossed a countryside in which there was no longer a single French soldier.

* This can be the name of a secluded country retreat.
† The Edict of Nantes was proclaimed by Henri IV in 1598 to regularise the position of the reformed church in France. The edict protected the right of Calvinists to practise their religion and gave them certain rights and protections. In 1685, Louis XIV revoked the edict, and brutal persecution of Protestants followed which resulted in the flight from France of some 20,000 to 30,000 people, most of them to Switzerland and to the countries across the Rhine.

I left Bayreuth on 2 November to return to France. I went through Bamberg, Würzburg and Frankfurt, three towns in the beautiful and fertile valley of the Main. In the course of this lonely journey of sixty-eight leagues, that took me eight days, I observed the countryside and, when time permitted, I visited anything unusual in the towns while studying the inhabitants. I reached Mayence on the 10th, leaving again on the 12th. I was at Metz on the 14th, and at Nancy on the 15th. I arrived at Saint-Dié on the 22nd.

Notes on the Germans and the Hungarians. The following are the observations I made on the inhabitants of the countries I crossed during the previous campaign.

Practically all the Hungarians wear moustaches, a fashion which only became widespread at home with the creation of the National Guard in 1830. Among us, the military, only certain branches of the army wore moustaches. Everyone wore the Hungarian pelisse, men, women and children, and the men wore hussar boots, with braided breeches and spurs. The national colour was sky-blue. All the older Hungarians could be mistaken for hussars. Everyone rode well, but without much style. The endless plains and marshes of Hungary made the breeding of horses easy, and riding was second nature to the inhabitants. The horses bred there are small and lively, in size like the horses of Lorraine, though I do not mean those bred on the stud farms of the big landowners, which are very handsome.

It is inexpensive and simple to raise an army of cavalry in Hungary. The men are good horsemen and they dress in a military style – one has only to hand them a sabre. Nevertheless, in the last campaign, the Hungarian levies, of which much had been heard, did not do well. Perhaps this might have been because they were not fighting for their country.

The Hungarian peasant is almost a serf and possesses nothing of his own; all belongs to his overlord, who alone has the much vaunted touchy pride and spirit of independence. In the last war uprisings only took place where the Austrian army was present; the magnates of Lower Hungary did nothing.

Most Hungarian villages are clean and orderly. Acacias are often planted in front of the houses and sometimes all along the roads, and this produces a pleasant appearance. Lodgings are as bad in Hungary as in Germany, where the inns are as dirty and ill-kept as they are in Italy, beds being small and narrow with napkins for sheets and mean covers; both the table and the bed linen are filthy, though I have to say that this does not apply to the hotels in the big towns.

Food is highly spiced and served with thin sauces that the Germans scoop up with their knives. Fowls stuffed with herbs, pigeons in honey, roasts with preserves are served, and with this, only a morsel of bread the size of round shot for the whole meal. As also in Italy, the rooms are furnished with taste, the walls and ceilings usually painted. Like the Italians, the Germans shake you by the hand, and are similar in their self-importance, although they are kind and generous. The most junior government employee wears a uniform and thinks himself important, while his wife is always referred to by his title. Whereas, in France, the husband's title is only sometimes accorded to the wife of a marshal, or, occasionally to the wife of a general or a president, in Germany the husband's position is given to the wife of a clerk, a road-mender or an inspector.

I did not regret leaving Germany to return to France, and I am sure that the Germans were no less pleased to see the back of us. I had hoped for a glorious campaign and to be present at a major battle. I had been granted my wishes, but I had seen enough of war, its miseries and its ruins, to make me curse the rulers who, without real necessity, had brought this blight upon peaceful and harmless populations. It would be better for their subjects if crown princes could be shown, not brilliant parades, but field hospitals after a battle. I still loved my career as a soldier, but I should have been happier fighting for our national independence, rather than taking part in wars of conquest.

Chapter Four

My First Spanish Campaign (1809–1810)

I leave for Spain. All the artillery of the entire 8th Corps left Mayence for Paris on 12 November, and I rejoined the corps at the end of my leave on 4 December.

The Emperor and Josephine were divorced on 16 December. Some people approved of this and others did not. Josephine, a true Creole, was frivolous and extravagant, but she was kind and friendly so she was popular and most people were sorry for her. It was said that her behaviour had been very loose in the past, but that her husband had forgiven her and that the real reason for the divorce was his need for an heir, one who would be brought up in his own image. An alliance with one of the oldest ruling families was already being discussed.

We had hardly begun to settle down when, on the 20th, the artillery of the 8th Corps received a sudden order to leave for Spain. We were to sleep that same night at Arpajon and we did not arrive there until very late.

The journey from Paris to the frontier took forty days. It was a pleasant road, in spite of the tedium and our regret at leaving Paris and France. When we passed through the endless village of La Ferté-Senneterre, the officers were invited to the château that belonged to M. de Talleyrand, the ambassador to Switzerland and cousin of the prince of Bénévent. On 1 January 1810, when we were at Châteauroux, the prefect, M. Lecouvreur, invited us to a ball that was held that day. We observed that most of the ladies of Châteauroux are pretty and elegant.

The rivers Isle, Dordogne and Garonne had to be crossed by boat before we reached Bordeaux on 16 January. This presented difficulties for the artillery.

We followed the course of the Garonne as far as Langon, through a beautiful, rich and well-populated countryside. At Langon we came into the Landes* where the soil was sandy, making the progress of the artillery slow and difficult. The gun carriages sank up to their hubs and, in some places, the sand had been covered with logs placed side by side across the track, and this caused endless jolting.

The journey from Saint-Jean-de-Luz to the Bidassoa was beautiful, and the views

* The Landes, a region of south-west France on the Atlantic coast, with a vast, sandy plain in the interior.

were extensive and varied. It was on this road that I first saw people travelling on a *cacolet*. This consisted of a double seat fixed to a pack-saddle on the back of a mule, donkey or horse. The two passengers rode, one on each side, with their backs to each other, and any weight discrepancy was balanced by the addition of stones. This was a gentle way to travel, particularly suitable for the sick, and was often used to trans-port the wounded, where their recovery depended on swift treatment.

From the frontier to Astorga. On 31 January we crossed the Bidassoa and entered Spain, but we felt no eagerness. This war was not to our taste, and was extremely unpopular. Everyone grumbled, but everyone marched. We were on our way to fight the Spanish, who had been our most faithful allies, in order to impose an unwanted foreign ruler upon them; we, who had risen against coalitions that had attempted to meddle in our own affairs. In a ruined country that had, quite reasonably, risen up against us we were being forced to fight for the ambition and arrogance of one family, and not for the advancement of France or for our own glory. We were to be mutilated, slaughtered or condemned to rot in English prison ships. What a miser-able policy it was that had thrown the Spanish and the Portuguese into the arms of England, and had excited the anger of the civilised world while, at the same time, exhausting us.

The trickery at Bayonne had stirred Spain up against us and we had been fighting in that country for two years, successfully, in spite of a few reverses, but still with no good outcome. Napoleon saw, by what happened there, that it is easier to win a battle than to subdue a population determined to defend its independence. The Spaniards did not fight well in open country; they could be beaten but they did not surrender.

At the beginning of the war, in 1808, Napoleon had had to intervene to give the campaign a sense of direction. He had returned his brother, Joseph, to the throne in Madrid, from which he had fled. He had subdued the north of Spain and, after a dis-astrous retreat in which it was demonstrated that English soldiers were less resistant to fatigue and privation than ours, had compelled an English army to re-embark at Corunna.

However, events in Germany called him away and, since he had left Spain, our leaders had lacked vigour and direction. Our various army corps were acting inde-pendently and our generals were divided by their rivalries.

When we crossed into Spain we forced our march so that we did not to arrive at Irun at the same time as two thousand dragoons who, like ourselves, were on their way to reinforce the French army there.

The country we crossed was beautiful, mountainous and picturesque; above Irun the view extended as far as the sea, where the mouth of the Bidassoa was surrounded by sandbanks, with Andaye on the right bank and Fontarabie on the left.

As soon as the Bidassoa was crossed everything changed; the dress, the behaviour of the people, their customs, and their dwellings. The houses were without windows, having only a tiny opening in the shutters; the men all dressed in the same way: coats, hats, breeches, and brown woollen stockings. The farm carts were small, pulled along by oxen, the two wheels turning with the axle and making a piercing and unpleasant noise. Everything about these Spaniards was depressing. However, the country was beautiful, fertile and cultivated in spite of being mountainous. The roads were well maintained and there was industry and security.

The mountains that bordered our route between Irun and Vitoria were full of guer- rillas but, as we marched in a troop, they did not show themselves. Moreover, nothing in the behaviour of the people up to this time supported what we had been told of the hatred felt for us by the Spaniards. As we came into a village, the women, the girls and the children rushed up to sell us bread, wine, cider and apples, and if we did not find inns as good as those in France, at least the innkeepers were kindly and the men were not hostile.

On 4 February we reached Vitoria, a fairly large town but badly built. It stands on a fertile plain where there are several villages. From a distance the town looked very fine. Leaving Vitoria, we marched down the valley of the Ebro, with its vine-covered banks, and crossed the river at Miranda, following it as far as Logroño, an ugly little town, as if we were heading towards Saragossa. Three days after reaching Logroño, we returned up the river Ebro and took the road to Burgos. On the 11th we arrived at Haro at the junction of the Ebro and the Tiron; this was a town surrounded by three high mountains that dominated the countryside and, as they were fortified, rendered the position impregnable. There were the ruins of a Moorish castle on one mountain top.

Santo Domingo is a little town where, for six centuries, a variety of white fowl has been carefully bred in the church, as the result of a miracle. In the thirteenth century, a Frenchman named Dominique, in the course of a pilgrimage with his mother, was accused of having stolen a vase and was taken before the alcayde,* who was, at that moment, sitting down to dine. The mother protested the innocence of her son, but the disbelieving alcayde replied that it would be as difficult for her son to prove his innocence as for the fowl being served to him to crow. At once the fowl began to crow. To preserve the memory of this miracle, the progeny of this fowl is still cared for. The saint was named Santo Domingo della Gallina.†

The country was mountainous all the way to Burgos, the road following the course of a narrow gorge and protected by a fort occupied by the French. I was curious

* A town mayor.
† Saint Domingo of the Chicken.

enough to climb up to it. The mountain on which it was perched was so steep that, from the road passing directly below, one had little to fear from its fifty heavy guns. On the contrary, it would have been possible to defend the road quite easily by rolling boulders down on to it. In the fort I saw a sort of little mortar, a calibre of about twelve [*sic*], which was only fourteen inches long at the most; a wooden lever regulated the elevation on the breechblock near the gun sight. These guns were mounted on wheeled carriages, making for ease of transport. I was told that they had a very long range. In the defence of a position such as this they would be of great use, and the fact that they fired hollow projectiles was indeed their great advantage. These mortars could be positioned anywhere, firing into places inaccessible to heavier guns.

Burgos could be seen from the fort. On the 15th we reached Burgos; this is the capital of Old Castile, a big, dirty, unsavoury town, poor and decadent. Part of it is built on the side of a mountain dominated by the ruins of a castle and part on the banks of the Arlenzon, which is crossed by two bridges. There are fine old buildings in Burgos, and these include a handsome square with arcades, and a statue of Charles III, but, above all, there is a lovely cathedral remarkable for the elegance of its architecture and the delicacy of its sculpture. There are several relicts in the cathedral, among them, so it is said, the ashes of Cid Campéador.*

Two days after our arrival in Burgos, all the artillery and transport of the 8th Corps was sent into quarters in the various surrounding villages until the 22nd, and was then recalled to Burgos. The country was very fertile, producing a great quantity of oats, but our horses preferred barley.

On the 22nd I took over command of the artillery of the 1st Division under General Clausel† and we left for Benavente.

25th. At Torquemada, which had been burned by the French.

26th. Palencia. A town of seven thousand to eight thousand inhabitants, who, having kept themselves clear of the troubles, had not suffered much as a result of the war. It is an industrial town.

28th. Ampadia. This little town contained a museum of very rare old weaponry. In July 1808 the French had burned the town.

1 March. Median de Rio Seco. On 14 July 1808, eighteen thousand French under the command of Marshal Bessières had defeated forty thousand Spanish and killed ten thousand of them.

3rd. At Benavente. We stayed here until the 21st. By now we had left Old Castile and were in the kingdom of León. We had already noticed the difference; the country

---

* El Cid; born Rodrigo Diaz de Vivar [1043–99]. A Spanish soldier who was a champion of Christianity against the Moors and became the ruler of Valencia.
† Marshal Bertrand Clausel [1772–1842].

around Vitoria was beautiful, picturesque and fertile and the inhabitants were lively, considerate and hard-working, while the Castilians were sluggish and lazy and their land was barren and poverty-stricken. The disparity became even greater in the Benevente countryside. The wonderful weather that we had enjoyed on our arrival in Spain had been followed, since Burgos, by cold and snow. Nevertheless, in our quarters near this town, we had been relatively comfortable and the surroundings had not been completely devastated. Even in the smallest villages, our hosts offered us excellent chocolate in the morning. At León it was no longer the same and, at Benavente, our accommodation was poor. Supplies grew scarce and as the weather grew colder, we could find no shelter from the icy wind. Continual and pointless moves grated on our nerves and boredom increased. Our state of uncertainty began to be oppressive. We had no idea what was to be done with us, or in which direction we were to be sent; were we destined for Galicia, Portugal, Extremadura or Andalusia, and which enemy should we face, the English, the Portuguese or the Spanish? This is the sort of thing that happens during a campaign, but not usually for so long nor in such conditions.

On 6 March, Mardi Gras, all the artillery officers of Clausel's division met in my quarters to celebrate. My servant, Souillé, a resourceful lad, had been instructed to obtain the festive delicacies. He was able only to serve us soup and a piece of bacon cooked with rice. We tried to delude ourselves; we all told stories of past festivities that we had enjoyed and the fine wines we had drunk, but quite soon the cold and depression gained on us, and we found nothing better to do than go to bed.

We should not have grumbled when we saw how our unfortunate soldiers were so badly lodged and so malnourished.

On 21 March we received the order to march off to besiege Astorga, a fortified town in León that was still in Spanish hands. We were delighted to leave our miserable quarters in Benevente.

The Spanish revolt was led by provincial juntas,* under the direction of a central junta that met in Seville.

On the 19th of the previous November, the main Spanish army advancing from Andalusia towards Madrid had been defeated by the French at the battle of Ocana, after which the central junta had retreated to Cadiz under the protection of the English fleet. The English in their turn had withdrawn into Portugal.

King Joseph, profiting from the victory at Ocana and the help that Napoleon was able to send him after the peace of Vienna, crossed the mountains of the Sierra Morena, invaded La Mancha and Andalusia and besieged Cadiz and Badajoz.

Despite these successes, which could have restored the prestige of King Joseph, Napoleon, in March, relieved his brother of the overall command of military

---

* Junta (Spanish council or meeting), a group of political or military leaders forming a council, particularly in the aftermath of a *coup d'état* or revolution, when there is no legal government.

operations, so that these could be controlled from Paris. Only a weak army with which to protect his capital was left under the direction of King Joseph. Marshal Soult[*] retained the command of the army operating in Andalusia; while a third army, of Portugal, was composed of the 8th Corps under General Junot, the 6th Corps under Marshal Ney,[†] and General Reynier's 2nd Corps, all under the supreme command of Marshal Masséna.

It was while waiting for the formation of this latter army that our division, the 1st of the 8th Corps, was sent to besiege Astorga. If, as its name indicated, our army was intended to invade Portugal, then fortified positions held by the enemy could not be permitted to remain in our rear.

The siege of Astorga. The road between Benevente and Astorga was passable, but the English in the course of their precipitate retreat to Corunna had cut the bridges over the rivers.

We reached the town on the 22nd, and began the siege on the same day.

Astorga was situated on a plateau, with steep slopes on the north, the east and in the centre. To the west the plateau, level with the town, stretched down to a ravine; the town walls were high and terraced, and the towers flanking them were not prominent enough to threaten attackers in the flank. There was an old castle at the southern angle that dominated the valley and commanded the plateau on which the district of Retebia was situated. Two other districts, those of Saint Andre and Portare, lay to the east and to the south. The Spaniards had fortified Retebia and burned the other two districts.

The garrison of the town was four thousand strong.

The various positions were captured, one after another, so that the enemy was forced back into the town and we established ourselves on the plateau. On the 24th two bodies of foot artillery from the 8th and the Berg Regiment,[‡] came to reinforce my artillery, which consisted only of one company of the 6th Horse Artillery. I at once sent detachments out into the villages to obtain tools and wood suitable for building defences and for the manufacture of *gabions* and *saucissons*[§]. On the 25th all my workshops were busy.

Surrounding Astorga and on the banks of the Orbigo there were several villages that, from a distance, looked beautiful, as they all did in the west of Spain; however,

---

* Marshal Nicolas Jean-de-Dieu Soult (1769–1851).
† Marshal Michel Ney, prince of Moscow, duke of Elchingen (1769–1815).
‡ In 1809, Napoleon annexed the Grand Duchy of Berg and acquired a light-horse regiment consisting for the most part of Germans.
§ Cylindrical baskets, often made out of interlacing tree branches and filled with earth and stones, and long thin bundles of brushwood, used primarily to protect gun and other vulnerable positions.

as one came closer, all was poverty, misery and there were few inhabitants. Those who were to be found there were indolent and their way of life was careless; they did not, however, lack bread, wine, meat and cattle fodder.

The artillery was quartered in the village of Barientes, on the left bank of the Tuerto. I lodged with the priest, a good man who was not at all fanatical, and I was very comfortable with him. In my rare free moments we went out hunting together, with ferrets, and we caught some very fine rabbits.

At night on the 30th we obtained a foothold on the extreme left of the plateau, having expelled the Spaniards from it. At eleven o'clock in the morning, the enemy made a sortie here, bursting out of the Retebia district, and they overran our position, but, in less than half an hour, and although the enemy was a battalion strong and had two cannon, he was pushed back by a few companies of infantry. The position was then fortified to support the attacks that would be made from that side.

During the night of 1 April, I succeeded in positioning a mobile battery trained on the parts of the plateau menaced by such sorties. On the same night the convent of Saint Dominique in the Portare district was seized, and this was followed by the capture of the ruins of the entire area.

On the following nights, I ordered the batteries between the Galicia and Benevente roads to begin firing. This had no purpose other than to keep the enemy busy and deceive him as to the actual point from which an attack would be made.

The night of 6/7 April was occupied in using *gabions* to build a redan* on the heights in front of the convent of Saint Dominique, in order to protect the flank of a parallel† that was to be opened and in beginning the construction of two batteries, one of them opposite the town and overlooking the attack, and the other slightly to the right.

Artillery supplies for the siege should have left Valladolid on the 8th. There was a delay, but in spite of this, the engineers opened a trench and, throughout the hours of darkness, pushed the works forward so that the parallel could be established near the town. The trench started in a small depression where the engineers and the artillery had their depots, and, with six zig-zags,‡ reached the parallel which was one hundred and thirty *toises*§ distant.

On the night of the 12th/13th the parallel was opened and, on the night of the 13th/14th, a breaching battery was established. As this was near the town and too exposed to gunfire, it was impossible to continue the work on the 16th. The bad weather, snow, rain and stormy winds combined to hinder the work. The trench was

* An arrow-shaped embankment, part of a fortification.
† Siege trenches running parallel to the fortification under attack.
‡ Trenches used to approach and supply the parallels.
§ About 800 feet.

so full of water that it could not be made deeper to provide protection from the gunfire coming from the town, and it became impossible to work in the open during the hours of daylight. As a result, and also because of the unwillingness of the workers from the line, my breaching battery could not be completed until the night of the 19th/20th. The 8th Corps consisted, in part, of provisional regiments[*] that were composed of new recruits who were still unaccustomed either to fire or to fatigue. These foot soldiers arrived late at the trenches and at the batteries, and left again early in the morning.

The siege park[†] arrived on the 15th.

On the 17th the duke of Abrantes arrived, with General Foucher,[‡] who was in command of the artillery of the 8th Corps. After inspecting the works, General Foucher approved the placement of all my batteries. These batteries were completed in the course of the following nights, I armed them and the work continued until the 20th when, at dawn, firing began from all the emplacements.

No. 1 battery fired towards the Retebia district and the shot ricocheted[§] towards the front under attack.

No. 2 battery, which consisted of howitzers, raked the front overlooking the attack.

No. 3, which was the breaching battery, had been placed in the parallel, and consisted of 24- and 16-pound guns that were intended to open the breach, howitzers to clear the breach and to fire nearer to the town and, finally, two 12-pounders that were to engage a fortified house that was occupied by the enemy and in a position to threaten our attacking column. The Spaniards had killed many of us from the crenells in the wall of this house.

Battery No. 4 was intended to harass the enemy to the rear of the breach.

On the 20th, the enemy returned our fire fiercely. His guns were well served.

On the following night we repaired our badly damaged batteries.

At dawn, I noticed that the besieged had changed the position of their guns and had opened three embrasures in the centre of the front in order to avoid the fire of No. 4 battery. I responded by altering my positions as well. I used the 12-pounder to flatten the parapets and brought my howitzers up to fire as closely as possible on to the town and behind the breach.

---

[*] Provisional regiments, formed to counteract the strain placed on the army by the French occupation of Spain, often consisted of squadrons detached from existing regiments with the addition of raw recruits to bring them up to strength.

[†] This would include the heavy guns and specialist equipment and ammunition needed to mount a siege.

[‡] General Louis-François, Baron Foucher de Careil (1762–1835), was one of the greatest artillery commanders of the Grand Armée.

[§] A method of firing supposed to have been invented by Marshal de Vauban, in which the cannon is charged with only enough powder to carry the shot to the face of the defence works under attack. The shot so discharged rolls and bounds, killing and maiming everything in its path, causing a great deal of damage.

Firing began again on the 21st, as heavily as before, and at five o'clock increased sharply. At half-past five the duke of Abrantes ordered the assault. He had been in the trenches since the firing began.

Elite companies from the Irish Battalion* and from the 67th Line Regiment threw themselves into the breach, led by their officers in a hailstorm of bullets. The rear of the breach was very high and steep, and the defenders had cleared away gaps to the right and left of it and put traverses on the ramparts. Our soldiers, their momentum checked, suffered terribly, but they got into the town, nevertheless, and established themselves in a house that backed on to the ramparts. The rest of the attacking column sheltered beneath the breach, where the enemy could not see them.

In the course of the night, by means of a *double sape volante* [double flying trench] we connected our arms depot with the breach, and the artillery positioned its siege guns to counter the threats that were most dangerous to us. This night proved as murderous to the engineers as the day had been to the artillery.

At half-past four on the morning of the 22nd when firing started again, the defenders sent out a negotiator and surrendered unconditionally. At midday, the garrison left the town and laid down their arms; they were taken prisoner and sent to France. At three o'clock we entered Astorga.

The Spaniards, poor soldiers in open country, had, in the defence of this town, shown the same courage and determination as the defenders of all the places which we had been obliged to capture from them by force, for they had never capitulated.

The artillery of the town, especially the mortars, had been well positioned. The officers in their specialist branches were far superior to those in other branches.

Throughout the siege there was perfect harmony between the engineers and the artillery. Chef de Bataillon Valazé, who was attached to the staff of the duke of Abrantes, commanded the engineers. He was promoted to colonel. I was commanding the artillery until the arrival of General Foucher and I was made an officer of the Légion d'Honneur. I had not expected, so soon, to receive an honour which the Emperor did not distribute lavishly. I had only been a member of the legion since 9 July 1809 – barely ten months ago. My family in Lorraine knew of this award before I myself learned of it.

I moved into Astorga, leaving my kindly priest at Barientes with regret. He was a learned man and knew a great deal about the history of the neighbourhood. We had begun to have discussions for I had been in Spain for more than three months and had started to understand and to speak the language – this was quite easy for a French-speaker who also understood Italian. We had always avoided contentious subjects, for he could hardly love us and I had no wish to upset him.

* An Irish Legion had been formed in 1803. In 1809, it was thrown open to recruits of all nations and renamed the Irish Regiment.

He had told me that Astorga – the town we were besieging – had been founded and occupied for a long while by a Roman legion; that the first uprisings and the first successes of the Spanish against the Moors had taken place in León, and that the Saracens had ruled Spain for nearly seven hundred years. He blamed the decadence of his country, one that had been so powerful and prosperous in the sixteenth century, on the discovery and conquest of America. He said that the huge amount of gold brought into Spain at that time had made the population lazy and had drawn the best and bravest of them away into the New World.

While I was with the priest, I was struck by an incident that would be trivial if it did not have a bearing on the harsh relationship we had with the Spaniards. It is for this reason that I recount it here.

In the house of the priest of Barientes we lacked for nothing. Food was abundant, although not varied. Tired of game, the sight of herds of horned beasts in the mountains made me wish to see a dish of veal on our table. It was impossible for the soldiers to catch these animals, who fled before them and which they could not chase into the hills for fear of guerrillas.

Leaving the courtyard one morning to go to the trenches, I found a calf tied to the gate. It had appeared there during the night. Doubtless the priest had told the herdsmen that he had a French officer staying with him of whom he had a good opinion, and who wished to eat some veal. And these Spaniards, fierce though they were, wished to respect the good wishes of their priest, and so had brought the calf to me in the night. This was certainly an unusual occurrence in the course of that war.

The Spaniards loathed us, and what could be more natural? We were waging a wicked war upon them and they were defending their country against the invader. But they were cruel; they mutilated and slaughtered our wounded and our prisoners. This was what infuriated our soldiers and made them retaliate. What is so odd about politics is the illogicality of its outcome. In 1810 we were fighting the Spanish who were supporting their king; ten years later we were fighting them in order to impose on them the same king, whom they no longer wanted because, ungrateful for the sacrifices made by his people, he had broken his promises.

From Astorga to Ciudad Rodrigo. On 26 April the division left Astorga and headed towards Léon. The country we passed through was well cultivated, and there were numerous villages. It was also well wooded, which was unusual in Spain. Spain looked quite different when, instead of the immense, bare plains and rocky hillsides, one saw trees and greenery. It appeared that the peasants were destroying the trees because they provided shelter from raptors for the small birds that ate their crops.

27th. At León. This town lies between two rivers. The surroundings of León, which are thickly wooded, mainly with elm trees, presented a pleasant contrast as one left Old Castile and Benavente, and gave a cheerful impression. The town had many attractions, it was well built and surrounded by old and imposing walls and the main square had fine arcades and a majestic cathedral. There was less misery to be seen there and the people were cleaner and better dressed. It was said that we were particularly loathed in this place.

The weather was bad, it rained nearly all the time we were at León and, although it was May, we were forced to find ways to warm ourselves. It is said that León is the chamber-pot of Spain, having ten months of winter and two months of hell.

In spite of the dreadful weather, a stay in a town like León was restful after the exhaustion of the siege of Astorga, and we all, officers and soldiers alike, were happy to spend twenty-six days there.

We left León on 23 May, in order to return to Benavente. On our way we passed through the lovely valley of the Esla and then on to Zamora, a very charming town with many attractions. The countryside was rich and fertile. Zamora is on the Douro, a river that rises in Old Castile, flows through narrow gorges in the Portuguese mountains and into the sea at Oporto.

Our division had been detached to the north to lay siege to Astorga, and had gone as far as Léon in order to subdue the country and to rid it of guerrillas – of whom we saw no trace. During this period, the Army of Portugal had been concentrated in the vicinity of Salamanca, where the 6th Corps was already stationed and where our commander-in-chief, Marshal Masséna, had just arrived. General Reynier's corps was still in Extremadura.

After crossing the Douro on the 29th, the division went into camp at Villamayor, about four leagues* from Salamanca. From this encampment I went on horseback, accompanied by only one gunner, through the wooded countryside to Salamanca, where the headquarters of the 8th Corps was stationed. There was much talk of guerrillas, but I had never seen any and no longer believed in their existence.

Salamanca is quite a large town, famous for its university but, as it is built on uneven ground, the streets are steep; they are also badly paved and very dirty, like those of all Spanish cities. The town stands on the banks of the Tormes, which is spanned by a magnificent bridge, built, so the locals say, by Trajan. The cathedral is superb and the frontage of the university is immense. There are many fine buildings of the sixteenth and seventeenth centuries to be seen here, more elegant and less heavy than those that I had previously seen in Spain. The main square is similar to our Palais Royal.

Convents take up a third of the town; everything is reckoned in twenty-fives here; twenty-five monasteries, twenty-five nunneries, twenty-five parishes, etc.

* League, about 4 kilometres.

The surroundings of the place are varied and pleasant and offer delightful walks and rides.

Our march on Astorga had caused us to anticipate an expedition into Portugal but, being isolated, we had no way of knowing what was being planned or what was happening to the rest of our 8th Corps. Quite often, when we were apart, we had no idea what was happening to the various brigades of our division. This is typical of campaigning. It was not until 4 June that, at 8th Corps Headquarters in Salamanca, I learned for certain what was being planned. An army consisting of the 2nd, 6th and 8th Corps was to invade Portugal from the east. The prince of Essling* was the commanding general and General Eblé† was commander-in-chief of the artillery, his chief staff officer being General Ruty‡. General headquarters foresaw great difficulties in this expedition, but it was clear that the campaign was begun without any apprehension either by officers or by the troops, who seemed to have no interest even in discovering which enemy they were likely to encounter.

The army was not yet ready to begin the campaign; an expedition into Portugal in the fierce heat of the summer could not be contemplated, any more than leaving two places as important as Ciudad Rodrigo and Almeida under the enemy's control in our rear. These places did not command the road, for there was none, but they commanded the Portuguese tracks.

The siege of Ciudad Rodrigo. The 6th Corps, under Marshal Ney, was to conduct the siege of these two strongpoints, and the 8th Corps was to protect the 6th from the attacks of the English, who were known to be quite near. These attacks were not greatly feared, given the prudence of their general who, unfortunately for us, was rightly determined to remain on the defensive throughout the campaign.

On 16 June the divisional artillery left Villamayor and we went, with all of the 8th Corps, towards Ciudad Rodrigo to support the siege.

On 2 July two brigades from the division, with the artillery and headquarters, crossed to the left bank of the Agueda and took up position at Mariella on the right of the 6th Corps.

A forward reconnaissance was made on 4 July just beyond Almeida in Portugal. The English had their scouts on the left bank of the little Azava river, which has steep banks and flows into the Agueda just below Mariella.

† Marshal André Masséna had been made prince of Essling at the end of January 1810.
‡ General Jean-Baptiste, Count Eblé (1758–1812) saved our army in November 1812 by having bridges over the Berezina built and then destroyed after we had crossed over. He died of illness at Königsberg shortly afterwards.
§ General Charles-Étienne-François, Count Ruty (1774–1828). As well as serving in the revolutionary campaigns and in Egypt, he took part in campaigns from 1805 to 1807 and commanded the artillery of the Army of the North at Waterloo.

On the 10th Ciudad Rodrigo capitulated after twenty-six days of open trench warfare and sixteen of bombardment. The town surrendered at the moment of assault, when the troops were already at the foot of the breach. The engineers were under the command of Colonel Valazé, who was wounded, and the artillery, at Marshal Masséna's wish, was commanded by his senior general, Eblé.

The 6th Corps had been under great pressure during the siege. Food had been in short supply, and incessant rain had been followed by terrible heat. As well as the many wounded, there were also a great number who were sick. Consequently, a period of rest was urgently needed before an attack could be made upon Almeida, particularly as the commander-in-chief required that the same corps should undertake the new siege. This was despite General Junot's request that he should be allowed to take responsibility for it.

Ciudad Rodrigo is in Spain and Almeida is in Portugal. These two towns confront each other, in a position to observe and control the communications between the two countries; they are built on two parallel streams, tributaries of the Douro.

On the 14th, the division returned to the right bank of the Agueda and the artillery bivouacked at San Felice de Chico. General Clausel was at San Felice el Grande. In spite of its rocky nature the countryside kept us supplied with wheat and rye.

Up to this point, I have spoken only of my division, the 1st of the 8th Corps, and not of the other army corps. This is because I was not in a position to know anything of their movements; frequently, in fact, I did not know about those of the brigades of my own division. It has to be said that there was not a single officer attached to the staff of a division, or the staff of an army corps, who could have had an exact knowledge of the marches, the positions or the actions of the different corps of which it was composed, and yet, and yet! The desire to write and to be praised, has given us many, many false accounts.

I received the order to provision my companies with sufficient biscuit for fifteen days. Having been unable to obtain anything from the local authority, and as the wheat was still standing in the fields, I undertook the task of harvesting it, threshing it, grinding it and making it into biscuit myself. I had under my command men of all trades. I took sickles from the peasants, had the flails made by the artillery workers and the leather workers from the train.* I seized one of the mills on the Agueda and succeeded in producing an excellent biscuit. The peasants had thought that, by refusing to supply our requisitions, they would avoid providing them, and were very surprised to see us so easily furnish our own needs. It was certainly the only time they saw corn threshed with flails. I do not know if they profited from the lesson.

---

* The *train d'artillerie* – consisting of the drivers and horses that moved the guns – was usually a separate organisation in the Napoleonic army.

The peasants of that country threshed the wheat in the field on a threshing floor, while a flat slab encrusted with flints, on which several people stood to provide more weight, was dragged in a circle by oxen. They winnowed the wheat, first shovelling aside the straw that had been cut into small pieces, and then collecting the grain into a winnowing basket. The straw was taken to the granaries and, when mixed with barley, was fed to horses and other livestock.

If we, ourselves, had taught something, we had also learned something as well, notably about the care and maintenance of horses. Horses in Germany and Spain were better nourished than ours. They were healthier and more active. In these countries the horses were fed on finely chopped straw mixed with hay or with a few handfuls of oats or barley. I did the same in Spain and in Portugal and my horses were very healthy.

The siege and capture of Almeida. In order to reach Almeida, Marshal Ney had to push back the English advance guard occupying Fort Conception, as it barred the road between Ciudad Rodrigo and Almeida. This fort had been mined, and the English certainly hoped to blow it up when we had gone into it, but the French attack was so rapid that the English were able to blow up only a small part of it. Marshal Ney forced the English back over the Coa, a torrent on the right bank of which the town of Almeida stood; he took several hundred prisoners and laid siege to the town.

As it was not possible to enter Portugal until after the worst of the hot weather, the marshal could position his troops and organise his attacks at leisure.

As at Ciudad Rodrigo, the 8th Corps was to support the 6th. I was still encamped at Banovares on the 10th when I received the order to go at once to the front at Almeida, where, although I belonged to the 8th Corps, I was to assume the provisional command of the siege park. I arrived there on the same day. There were still only a few artillery detachments there.

The following days were spent in collecting wood, making *gabions* and *saucissons* and filling sandbags. The ground from which the attack was to be made was rocky, so it was impossible to protect the approaches by means of trenches, and artificial cover had to be constructed.

During the night of the 15th/16th August a trench was opened, 250 *toises* from the town, without too great a loss of life.

I was ordered to undertake the extension of the attacking front so that the batteries could be established; this work was checked and approved by General Ruty.

On the night of the 18th/19th work was done on the construction of eleven batteries, eight of them firing *à ricochet* to rake the front of the bastion under attack, for the demi-lunes* and the branches of the covered way threatened the assault. Two

* Breastworks placed in front of a fortification.

of the batteries were intended to form the breaching batteries, after the enemy fire had been suppressed. The front to be attacked was composed of the San Pedro bastion and the two demi-lunes.

The ground made the construction work for the attack and for the batteries very difficult. It was impossible to provide cover without hitting rock, so sandbags and bundles of branches were constantly needed for shelter. Zig-zag trenches, ending up in two parallels approaching the town, were constructed without firing one cannon shot – although several of the batteries were ready to fire – but with the loss of many men.

All the batteries were ready to fire at five in the morning of 26 August and firing began from all the positions at once; sixty-four big-calibre guns were aimed at the small target presented by the town. What an awakening for the wretched inhabitants!

The enemy replied vigorously. Their aim was less accurate than ours, and the town was soon in flames. At seven in the evening, two bombs, fired by batteries numbers 4 and 8, fell simultaneously on the old castle that contained the powder magazine and the arsenal. The gunpowder, then being loaded in the castle courtyard, caught fire, and this spread to the magazine, causing an appalling explosion. The entire castle and part of the town was blown up, the rest of the houses were shattered. Fragments of guns and gun carriages, stones and earth hurtled as far as our trenches and on to our batteries. In the fortifications on the left, gunners and their guns were engulfed in the debris. Fortunately for the inhabitants, they had sought refuge in a vast underground tunnel that ran under one of the walls to the right of the assault.

In the morning of the 27th Marshal Masséna called upon the town to surrender. Negotiators were sent from the town into our camp. Firing stopped but, as the talks dragged on, it began again at eight in the evening and this persuaded the governor to sign the surrender. English officers who were in the town opposed the capitulation that the inhabitants and the garrison favoured. The Portuguese, like the Spaniards at Ciudad Rodrigo, were angry at the inactivity of the nearby English army.

We entered the town at noon on the 28th. The garrison, which still consisted of three thousand six hundred men, was made up of militia and troops of the line. The first were sent back to their homes, and the remainder joined our army. Many of these soon deserted. We already had Portuguese in our ranks, most of them being officers who had taken up the French cause at the time of the first invasion of Portugal. They were, generally speaking, good soldiers, who remained true to us.

A hundred and twenty-two cannon were found in the town.

Had the terrible explosion not occurred, it was assumed that Almeida would have been capable of sustaining an open trench siege for twenty-five days. The bastion under attack was strongly entrenched. Nevertheless, there were quite considerable weaknesses in the fortifications, of which the greatest was the inadequate protection afforded by the demi-lunes; their lack of depth was such that, from outside, it was possible to observe part of the escarpment and the trench. The glacis were too steep and the ditches too narrow and too shallow.

Chapter Five

The Portuguese Campaign (1810–1811)

From Almeida to Busaco. Almeida was the only fortified town in Portugal between the Douro and the Tagus. Its situation was determined by that of Ciudad Rodrigo, and also, doubtless, so that it could serve as a depot for an army operating on that part of the frontier – the only place in the sector from which Portugal could be invaded. It was inadequate to fulfil the latter function.

The ground was difficult for the besieger, and few of the supplies required by the artillery could be obtained locally.

On the 30th I returned to my division which was now encamped before Escarrigo and Almofalo. The 11th Company of the 8th Foot Artillery and the 8th Company of the 6th Horse Artillery were under my command, the latter being well led by Captain Coquard.

On 4 September, I went with General Clausel on a reconnaissance that took us to within a league* of the Douro, and then on another to Pinhel. We were trying to find a way by which the artillery could be moved. I had never seen a country-side so battered and torn up as this part of Portugal. The roads were barely fit for horses.

It was truly guerrilla country, for the hills and mountains were very steep, and the banks of the Douro fell sheer into the water at the bend where the river flowed into Portugal.

On the 13th the divisional artillery moved to Aldea del Obispo, a village at the foot of Fort Conception in Spain, in order to rejoin the artillery of the army Corps. Fortunately for us, the English had abandoned this fort after having blown up some of the defences. It was said that they did not have enough heavy guns to defend the place; it is likely, too, that they were afraid they might be captured there. Although the fort could have been defended, it could not have held out against us for long and the garrison would certainly have been taken, although, had we been compelled to besiege it after our siege of Ciudad Rodrigo, we should have needed to consume some

* League, about four kilometres.

94

of our provisions and the siege of Almeida would have been delayed; thus we might, perhaps, have been prevented from invading Portugal.

The army began its march on 16 September. The 8th Corps, on the right, went towards Pinhel; the 6th, in the centre, towards Alverca and the 2nd, forming the left wing, was directed to Guarda, while the advance guard pushed as far as Celorico. The divisional artillery bivouacked before Pinhel on the banks of the Pega river, with that of the 2nd Division near by. The park was on a hill to the rear. The Pinhel river, with its steep banks like all of the streams in that mountainous country, had to be crossed, in order to reach the town of the same name. The town was approached by a steep cobbled ascent.

Pinhel was a small town built on a promontory, and would have been pleasant if the surrounding countryside had not been uncultivated and bristling with rocks. There was a fine episcopal palace there, furnished with taste and enclosing, when we arrived, an excellent library consisting largely of French books. There were some remarkable houses in the town that testified to the wealth of the inhabitants. Of course, as the town had been abandoned, everything was pillaged and laid waste. In an old ruined castle I saw two huge cannon, made out of iron hoops. The Portuguese would not do us much harm with such things.

During the night, I received the order to instruct my reserve to march off with the park. A bad idea, as this would deprive the reserve, or such of it as was with me, of the forge and its operatives, while the difficult paths we had to follow would compel some or other of them to leave their carts behind. The drawbacks were obvious, but as the command is never wrong, I was allowed, after the 18th, to recall my reserve, without attracting any reprimand.

On the 17th the 8th Corps went to Venta de Cego; the 6th to Janlues and the 2nd to Celorico. The advance guard proceeded to Fornos on the right bank of the Mondego.

We passed near to the little town of Trancoso which is surrounded by a turreted wall.

The entire countryside was rocky and mountainous; there were no roads, merely narrow, dangerous and stony pathways where the artillery avoided accidents only with enormous difficulty. Nothing but craggy climbs and sheer descents lay in our path. I had to send gunners, armed with pickaxes and mattocks, ahead of me to clear the way. One soldier went ahead carrying an iron bar equal in length to the width of our gun carriages, to indicate how wide the path must be made. As an army on the march is concerned only with its own welfare, the artillery had to wait behind to allow the infantry and the cavalry to pass ahead; this meant that the artillery always arrived late at the halting place, tired and worn out. Officers and troops could not take care of themselves until their horses had been cared for, the carts repaired and the ammunition stowed away. Meanwhile the best – or least bad – accommodation had already been taken and the food supplies carried off. On a campaign the foot-soldier is the least unhappy, as he has only to think of himself, the cavalryman must care for his horse, while the artilleryman must ensure that his guns and his caissons are in good order, as well as attending to the welfare of his animals.

In their retreat, the English had laid waste the countryside, seizing and burning, as the population fled before them; they cut the bridges and destroyed everything that might have been of use to us, furnaces and mills, food and forage. They wanted us to starve, for starvation is a terrible tool of war, one that cost them nothing, and which seemed not to the liking of the Portuguese. From this introduction we learned what lay before us in so devastated a country.

We marched towards Viseu, along the steep ridges intersected by the ravines of the Sierra Caramula, which cut deeply, on the right, into the steep and beautiful valley of the Mondego, of which we caught occasional glimpses. The artillery nearly always marched alone, abandoned by the other troops and often not knowing which path to follow. The passage of the army left no trace, other than the occasional stragglers who, themselves, often had no idea which way to go; there were no locals remaining to give us information. To guide me, I had only the incomplete maps of Lopez and Mentelle with which I had taken care to provide myself.

Marching thus alone, with my two companies, we found ourselves at midday on the 18th, after a climb of more than two hours, on one of the highest mountains on the right bank of the Taveres. From this eminence the whole country could be seen. I was horrified at the desolation that was spread before me and at the sight of the path that we had to traverse. A headlong descent into a deep valley was followed by a climb up a tortuous track that soon became lost to view. It would be impossible to cross the mountains before nightfall with our exhausted horses. Therefore, I decided to bivouac at the bottom of the valley, where we found some forage for our weary animals. If, in this gorge, we had been attacked by the guerrillas, the leader of whom was known to be the most daring in the area, it would have been impossible for us successfully to defend ourselves, for we could not have used our cannon and they could have sniped at us from behind the rocks at their leisure.

At four in the morning of the 19th, I despatched twenty gunners to prepare and widen the path and at six o'clock we set out. We climbed yet another steep mountain, marched along the peaks, then descended into a delightful valley, fertile, cultivated and dotted with temporarily abandoned villages. The valley seemed even lovelier as we had just come from a desert. This was a contrast we met with frequently in this part of Portugal, where the mountains, arid and uninhabited, were cut through with charming, shady valleys. The vegetation was luxuriant on the banks of the streams and oleanders grew everywhere.

Having crossed the mountains and the valleys, we had again lost track of the army and, while men and horses rested in the pretty valley, I went, with four mounted gunners, to find out where the army now was. All the houses were deserted, but I managed to catch an old peasant as he fled from us, and he showed us a path to Viseu, where our army corps should have arrived on the previous day. But it was fast growing dark, and at eight in the evening I ordered my group to bivouac on a plateau near a wretched, abandoned village.

On the 20th I sent the company quartermaster out to reconnoitre. While waiting for him, I let the horses rest and had the carts repaired. The quartermaster and the troops with him came back at about midday – they had pushed as far as Viseu and been welcomed like the raven [sic] returning to the Ark.

During the morning we were rejoined by the artillery of the 2nd Division which, having followed the same route as ourselves, had slept at the foot of the plateau where we had spent the night. Together we headed towards Viseu. Now we were entering a pleasant land, well cultivated and covered with vineyards and fruit trees. Although they were deserted, the villages looked less poverty-stricken than those in Spain; they were cleaner and better built. Good stone bridges crossed the rivers and even the small streams.

At Viseu we rejoined the 8th Corps.

Viseu was a very fine town built on the side of a hill in a charming and fertile countryside; the houses were attractively built and well furnished, proclaiming a comfortable way of life. Their upkeep indicated better hygiene and better taste than those in Spanish cities.

From the 20th to 24th we rested at Viseu.

At Viseu, as at Pinhel and all the villages we had seen since entering Portugal, all the inhabitants had fled. Being forced to get supplies by any means it could find, and obeying the sad law of warfare, the army resorted to pillage; and, since circumstances did not restrict looting to taking only what was necessary, the inhabitants suffered far more than would have been the case if they had stayed at home. Discipline in the army slackened because soldiers acquire the habit of looting. Unfortunately the officers, even those on the staff, presented a bad example. The effects on obedience and respect were evident.

The town had already been looted when we arrived for, on the pretext of searching for supplies, the whole place had been laid waste.

We left Viseu on the 24th by two different routes. All the 8th Corps marched off to bivouac near Sabugosa. The path taken by the 1st Division was the worst. In the course of the short journey, I was forced to have the walls of an enclosure just outside a village knocked down so that my carts could pass. Just at that moment General Junot came past and, as he rode over the ruins, his horse fell and threw its rider. 'Bad omen,' I remarked to Captain Coquard, who was near by. 'No,' he answered, 'We shall take Portugal.' However, we did not feel like laughing.

25th. The country around Casal de Maria is lovely and picturesque but not very fertile. The valley bottoms are cultivated carefully but the heights are uncultivated or covered with Scots pines.

On the 26th we camped in a broad valley near the village of Martigao, at the foot of the mountains forming the Sierra d'Alcoba. In the evening, the 6th Corps, which was ahead of us, came into contact with the Anglo-Portuguese army in a strong position at Moira, which gave the battle its French name, although the English call it Busaco.

The battle of Busaco. At the beginning of the campaign the English army had been concentrated around Viseu; following the setback that Marshal Ney had inflicted on their advance guard, we had seen no sign of any English soldiers. A rumour ran around our army that Lord Wellington* had re-embarked, abandoning the Portuguese as, after Talavera, he had abandoned the Spanish. All of us rejoiced at the prospect of repose in the towns on the coast. What gave this belief more credibility was that the enemy had permitted us, unopposed, to cross the steep Portuguese mountains, leaving only a few groups of alert and well-commanded guerrillas to hinder us. If they had killed only our artillery horses, the invasion of Portugal would have been impossible for us.

As a result we were far from anticipating what was in store for us of danger, misery and suffering.

To reach the Portuguese plains, it remained for us to cross the last mountain chain, that of the Sierra d'Alcoba. These mountains formed an unbroken range along the right bank of the Mondego valley that we were following. The river had forced its way through the mountains, and was so steeply banked that no army could travel along it; therefore we had to cross the Sierra d'Alcoba where the Anglo-Portuguese army had taken up positions on the mountain to dispute our passage.

This position had been admirably chosen; it is likely that Lord Wellington, wise and prudent, had let us cross the mountains unopposed so that he could confront us in this place at a time when we were weary and worn out by ten days of difficult marching.

The 8th Corps arrived very late at its quarters on the 26th. On the 27th, after an hour's march, we reached a position confronting the enemy on the heights where the 2nd and 6th Corps were attacking. We formed the reserve. From my position I was able to watch the action perfectly.

---

* Field Marshal Sir Arthur Wellesley, duke of Wellington, Viscount Douro (1769–1852).

Lord Wellington's army was at least as large as ours. If their soldiers were less active and less spirited than ours, yet, being on the defensive and lacking nothing, they were a force to be reckoned with. This army positioned on the plains extending along the Sierra d'Alcoba consisted of their main force, all their reserves and all their artillery. The English occupied all the defensible points, and most importantly, a hamlet on the slopes. This was almost completely sheltered from our artillery; and being high above the countryside, was able to dominate and observe our efforts, hampered as they were by ravines, to attack. From here they were able to draw reinforcements wherever they were needed.

In order to force our passage we should have to dislodge the English from their various strongpoints and, to do so, our infantry would have to contrive, without cannon, to reach the plateau, then to attack and repulse the main English forces. The English troops were rested and their supporting artillery would have time to be brought to bear on any threatened position. It would take the audacity of Masséna and the spirit of the French to undertake such a task. But when one had witnessed the taking of Ebelsberg, one no longer had misgivings.

Forming up on our left, the 2nd Corps attacked first. Helped for a time by a thick fog, it was able to reach a plateau. It pushed back the first troops it met but, attacked by several English divisions brought up to the position, and under a hail of bullets, it was thrown back from the heights and forced to retreat, having lost its senior officers.

The 6th Corps was too far from the point of the attack to provide a useful diversion. It took over a hamlet half-way there and managed also to reach the plateau, but again, greeted by a hail of bullets and charged by a large number of fresh troops, it was repelled with great loss.

My division was sent to support the 2nd Corps, and the 2nd to support the 6th, but in such an attack our artillery could not be of much help.

This unhappy assault cost us more than four thousand men, among them many generals and colonels. The English admitted the loss of eight hundred men.

If the rumours to be heard in the army were to be believed, General Reynier, whose corps was the most battle-hardened, had demonstrated great skill and courage; on the other hand, Marshal Ney might have been at less than his best. Marshal Masséna was not the man to be discouraged by such a setback. He did not consider retreat and made his dispositions to receive the English if they should go on the offensive. They were careful to do nothing of the sort. Wellington needed positions such as he enjoyed at Busaco to fight us.

We remained in our positions until the 28th.

From Busaco to Coïmbra. Following the setback of the 26th we carried out the reconnaissance of the countryside that should have been done at the outset. If that had been done first, a route would have been discovered by which the position at Busaco could have been turned. It is true that the Portuguese officers serving in our army did not know of the route and that, in that uninhabited region, there was no one left to tell us of it. The cavalry, sent out to reconnoitre, discovered it. What a quantity of spilt blood could have been saved!

When the new route was discovered on the 27th, our army made a flanking movement, with the 8th Corps on the right forming the advance guard. In order to deceive the English, who could have attacked us successfully during our flanking movement, we waited for the cover of darkness.

We were directed towards Sardao across the Sierra d'Alcoba, to the north of the position occupied by the enemy. It was already daylight when I set off with my artillery to follow the division.

Immediately, in the first village we came to, we found the streets so narrow that I was forced to find a way across the fields; then, the deep track that we followed was so constricted that I was compelled to leave it and climb up on to the heights. This was not easily done with our heavy wagons. Once more, we found the same tracks, the same climbs and the same steep slopes that we had encountered when we first entered Portugal. In some places, on the ridges, the narrow untrodden path presented so little level ground that the carts were overturned. This was an accident that I was able to prevent, by putting gunners near each of mine to balance the cart by bearing down on the wheels on the side opposite to the drop. We followed a ridge shaped like a donkey's back, with a drop on the right and a drop on the left. At last we reached the top of the Alcoba mountain chain and saw the sea and all the countryside spread before us. This rich countryside with cities and villages, trees and greenery looked to us like an earthly paradise. We had been in sight of Busaco throughout the journey.

The English must have been quick to notice our turning movement, but it was too far advanced for them to be able to contest it. It was also impracticable for them to cut across our route on the heights of the Sierra d'Alcoba. To avoid being cut off themselves, they retreated swiftly towards Coïmbra, blowing up a few caissons. The discovery of the path we were following was the equivalent of a victory for us. Our goal was achieved and the Anglo-Portuguese were retiring. If only we could catch them on the plain!

We came down from the Alcoba heights rapidly, by means of an unusually steep slope, losing all the elevation that we had spent the entire morning attaining. The mountains rising steadily from the Spanish border fall abruptly into Portugal, as the Alps rising gradually from the Swiss side fall steeply into Piedmont, and as the Vosges descend into Alsace.

This journey was one of the most difficult and exhausting for the artillery. Our horses suffered dreadfully and we lost many of them; even the strongest were affected.

We had no food to give them but green corn, a poor diet for a working horse. They ate it greedily, but it did not remain in their bodies and was purged like young grass. It was not until ten at night that the first of our artillery wagons reached Sardao, which lay at the foot of the mountain. We bivouacked beyond it. Our division was already a league further on, on the road to Coïmbra. The 2nd Division and the general headquarters spent the night at Sardao.

On the 30th we reached the main Oporto to Coïmbra road, joining it at Pedriera. This was a fine, wide road, passing through fertile, well-cultivated country. There were many deserted villages. We bivouacked on this side of Mealhada, a place directly opposite to Busaco on the other side of the mountain, and from which there was a path leading to it. It was, doubtless, along this track that the Anglo-Portuguese army had retired. An advance guard of cavalry and light infantry were pursuing them in front of us.

On 1 October, it seemed as if the English were preparing to oppose us near Fornos, but at about midday, they retreated again, leaving Coïmbra to us. We entered the town on the same day.

Coïmbra. The only aim of the apparent resistance had been to give them time to evacuate the town and destroy any supplies that we might have found there. A number of the inhabitants had fled; a host of vessels and boats could be seen on the Mondego, heading downriver towards the sea. The speed of our march had denied the English the time they needed to evacuate everyone and to destroy everything, so plenty of supplies were still to be found in the town.

This method of waging war, leaving ruin behind, may be heroic among people who are defending their independence and are prepared to sacrifice everything for their freedom. It was not to the taste of the Portuguese, who detested the English nearly as much as they loathed us. As for the English, it did not matter that they spread ruin in Portugal in order to starve us, for they were not making war in their own country. They themselves did not suffer at all; on the contrary, they alone supplied the population with what was needed and they hoped, soon, to sell them a great deal more. England never loses sight of her own interests.

A large city – it was the third largest in Portugal – Coïmbra was mercantile and rich. It occupied the side of a fairly steep hill on the right bank of the Mondego, which was spanned there by a fine stone bridge. The setting could not have been more delightful and attractive.

When we entered it, the town was almost completely deserted, the houses all shut up. A few hours later it resembled nothing more than a scene of utter ruin, the usual fate of abandoned places. With my own eyes I saw officers of the staff, axe in hand, hacking open the shop doors and placing sentries inside, so that they could loot at their leisure. What a dreadful example for the troops! How could they demand their respect? There was needless destruction of supplies that might later have been of use to the army. Such lack of foresight on the part of army commanders is inexcusable. I regret to say that General Junot, whose corps was the first to enter Coïmbra, did nothing to prevent it.

The Mondego valley and the surroundings of Coïmbra were delightful. There were beautiful, well-cared-for gardens on the outskirts, and orchards that were full of all kinds of fruit trees, particularly oranges. The whole beautiful countryside breathed peace in spite of the traces of war; there was fertility and luxuriant vegetation, with forests of tall trees on the mountain slopes. How different from Spain! Here, every plot of land between the rocks was cultivated whereas there, even naturally fertile land remained uncultivated as a result of the indolence and apathy of the inhabitants. Beyond the mountains there were few, if any, trees and bare, arid plains, while on this side all was green. There is a great deal more rain in this country than in Spain.

There seemed to be the same contrast between the natives of these two countries, who loathed each other, but were now united in hatred of us. Even in Portuguese villages the houses were better built, cleaner and better cared for. In the towns they were furnished with a taste that indicated greater affluence and concern with comfort. In Portugal we saw many libraries with a good number of French books – things practically unknown in Spain, where the women, even those of good family, were unable to read. Everything here seemed to demonstrate a higher intelligence, greater activity and education. As for their physique, the Spaniards were handsomer than the Portuguese. The Spaniard was well built, with an attractive face; the women varied from province to province but were generally beautiful, slightly masculine and lacking elegance. The Portuguese were stocky with plain faces but intelligent eyes. I saw few Portuguese women; they were small, ugly and dark.

From Coïmbra to Sobral. On 2 October, our division pushed the enemy out of Condeixa, a large town two leagues beyond Coïmbra on the Lisbon road, where we found large stores of oats, bacon and wine that the retreating English had not had time to destroy. I seized a large store of oats for my wretched, exhausted horses. Condeixa was a warehouse for English goods. We found there kettles, whips and tablets of polish that my soldiers mistook for chocolate. They had prepared a huge pot of it, and would certainly have poisoned themselves if my servant had not brought some slabs of it to me. I could not convince them of their mistake until I polished my boots with some of the so-called chocolate.

General Junot again demonstrated his lack of foresight by allowing the supplies at Condeixa to be squandered.

We remained at Condeixa on 3 and 4 October while the other army corps rested at Coïmbra. A new advance guard was formed there of cavalry and light infantry under the command of General Montbrun.

We marched towards Lisbon on the central road leaving, on the left, the route over the mountains to the Tagus and, on the right, the coast road. We reached Pombal on the 5th and, on the 8th, Leiria, a pretty little town in a valley. We noticed that during their passage, the English, if they had not had time to carry off or destroy their supplies, had set fire to the warehouses. The countryside was beautiful and fertile in the valleys but uncultivated and covered in briars on the hills. In places the road was wide and paved, although it was sandy and difficult in others. The English retreated ahead of the advance guard and were given no respite, some men being killed and some prisoners taken. All the time we hoped to catch them and, doubtless, beat them. Morale in the army was excellent.

Yet the troops noted with disgust the relative luxury enjoyed by some officers whose numerous baggage wagons choked the roads. They took every opportunity to have the satisfaction of playing some nasty tricks, when this could be done with impunity; the worst were the artillerymen, who had a harder time than the rest. On the mountainous and difficult paths they would happily allow these wagons, carrying the baggage of certain staff officers, to pass. Then, arriving at the top of the hills, they would urge their horses to a fast trot and, without disturbing themselves, would bump their heavy carts into these wagons which would topple over to the left and right. It gave the poor devils some satisfaction, which could be allowed them as long as it did not go too far. I have never been able to understand how career officers on campaign could permit themselves the enjoyment of luxuries in front of troops who lacked the necessities of life; troops who could look forward neither to promotion nor to reward and whose devotion was entirely disinterested.

We had had continual fine weather until 8 October but, on that day, the rain began and came down in torrents. It continued, and our sufferings grew. The countryside was deserted and we found no more provisions. Arriving last at our quarters, we had to set out, in an unknown neighbourhood, to look for food and forage for our horses. Returning at midnight, we had to march again at dawn. It was quite impossible to keep our draught-horses in a healthy condition.

On the 11th we reached the little town of Alemquer on the river of the same name that flows between steep banks in a narrow valley. There were handsome houses here, richly and tastefully furnished but, as with all abandoned towns, everything was in disorder, pillaged, broken and burned.

On the 12th, the division marched towards Sobral. Leaving Alemquer was very difficult for the artillery; indeed, that of the 2nd Division was forced to stay there and I was not able to rejoin the 1st Division at Sobral with my guns until the 13th. My other wagons did not arrive until the following days. Happily the country was better and we found oats for our horses.

The English were positioned on a height in front of Sobral that was only about two hundred yards from our advance posts. General Clausel ordered me, overnight, to position a battery of four guns to cover the attack that was to take place next day. This I did, concealing the guns under great barrels.

Towards noon on the 14th all was ready for an attack on the position that the enemy had crowned with a trench during the night. The grenadiers and the infantrymen of the 4th Battalion of the 19th of the Line, captured it at first. A moment later the enemy, with superior forces, took the offensive once more, and pushed us back. They then made ready to attack us in their turn. Our attack was not sustained, in spite of the presence of the commander-in-chief. We lost 120 men to no purpose in this assault. In this skirmish I saw English officers urging the soldiers on with blows of the cane.

The English abandoned this position on the 15th as well as several others in front of their lines. Sobral, where we took up our position, was a well-built town in a diverse countryside where an excellent wine was produced.

The lines of Torres Vedras. The army is halted. Up to this point we had pushed the English back before us; we had imagined that we should continue to drive them along as far as the Tagus and the sea, where we should force them to fight or to re-embark. Suddenly, as we left Sobral, we found ourselves confronted by a strong defensive line; the heights in front of us, and all those we could see in the distance, were fortified. This was the famous line of Torres Vedras, of which we had never before heard, and with which we should in time become well acquainted. This came as a terrible shock to us. We had thought ourselves to be victorious, to be near the end of a glorious campaign, and about to move into winter quarters in the Portuguese capital, whereas we were now obliged to spend the winter in a devastated and ruined countryside at the foot of these terrible lines, the strength of which no one could doubt.

As far as Abrantes, the Tagus flowed from east to west, but then took a more southerly direction forming, with the ocean into which it emptied, a fairly acute angle with Lisbon at the tip. It was to close the base of this triangle by a fortified line stretching from the Tagus to the sea, several leagues to the north of Lisbon, that the English had established an immense entrenched camp. They must have toiled at this fortification ever since their arrival in Portugal – that is to say, for more than a year – while the French remained ignorant of it. All they knew, at the very most, was that the English controlled Lisbon and some fortified places. The line stretched from Alhandra on the Tagus to the sea near Torres Vedras, extending for at least twelve leagues. Here the countryside was rough, and the line did not consist of a simple enclosure, but was made up of a series of forts and redoubts placed on hills and cliffs, each one being complete in itself and independent of the others. They were all maintained and joined by an unbroken line of earthworks. All the vagaries of the terrain had been utilised with great skill; the slopes had been made steeper and the rivers flowing down from the Sobral plain, one flowing to the Tagus and the other to the sea, had been incorporated in the defences.

This formidable line of fortifications did not satisfy Wellington, so fearful was he of our general and our army. A second line was placed behind the first, and then a third, which would have made possible the embarkation of his army had the first two been overrun.

These lines were armed by seven hundred guns, mostly heavy guns, and defended by a regular army of seventy thousand excellent troops, English, Portuguese and Spanish, not including the numerous militias composed of refugees and inhabitants. The English employed all the peasants, who were crowded into this immense entrenched camp, in various tasks and in the work of fortification that continued without cease. Supplies for all these people and for the army were brought in from the provinces beyond the Tagus, and by the English fleet – the mistress of the sea. All this information was brought to us by the Portuguese, who communicated with their compatriots in our service.

It was this triple line of formidable fortifications, thus armed and defended, that we should have to attack with, at most, forty-five thousand men and campaign artillery which possessed barely sufficient ammunition for a single battle, from our position in a ruined and hostile country at the beginning of winter. As for Lord Wellington, he had only to stay on the defensive and await events. But the difficulties that faced us and would have to be overcome, while destroying the army's illusions, did not diminish its confidence in itself or in its commander-in-chief.

Following the battle in front of Sobral, the English had abandoned this position to us on the 15th although they had repulsed us on the previous day. But as soon as we tried to pass Sobral to continue on our way, aggressive firing from a line of redoubts had warned us of the existence of the famous lines of Torres Vedras. We advanced no further. The 8th Corps halted at Sobral and bivouacked on the plains surrounding it. The 2nd Corps took up position at Villa Nova and the 6th Corps, in the rear, remained at Alemquer. The whole army gathered opposite Torres Vedras.

When we arrived, there were still some supplies to be had in the countryside. These were quickly exhausted and, in order to live, recourse was had to marauding. Each corps, each branch, organised itself in its own way. Detachments, at first sent out into the immediate neighbourhood, were forced to go further and further away. These parties, commanded by officers of various ranks, split up as they fanned out.

The result was that the men, separated from their leaders, gave themselves up to every sort of pillage and even to the practice of cruelty on the miserable peasants who had thought that their wretched poverty would protect them from such violence. This was done, not so much to force the peasants to reveal hordes of grain, or the hiding place of cattle, as to compel them to hand over money.

I organised my marauding service so perfectly that, as soon as a hoard was found, a train of wagons brought back supplies of corn, wheat and forage to the houses in Sobral that we occupied; provided, that is, none of it had been lost or stolen.

It was not enough to find the grain, it had to be milled and then bread made from it.

There were bakers in every corps, but millers were more rare. I had several among my men. I seized a windmill that had been abandoned near Sobral. So that it should not be put to any use, the English had taken away all the ironwork that had been dove-tailed beneath the upper millstone to engage the end of the central axle and cause the millstones to move. I had the missing parts forged, replaced the sails with the cloth used for mattresses, and my windmill worked. ·

The artillery was not allowed to operate it for long. Under the pretext that it was near the advanced positions and too exposed, the mill was taken from me, and, a few days later, given to the infantry. I looked around for a replacement. In a narrow valley between the outposts of the two armies I found a watermill. I put it in order. Because of its location it could only be used in daylight. Thanks to my mill and my marauding service, the troops under my command never lacked for bread, either of wheat or of corn flour, and my horses had, at least, some maize. On leaving Sobral, apart from the provisions we took with us, we left behind us a room filled with maize.

Wretchedness became so widespread that discipline suffered to the point where even the most basic military duties were neglected.

One day, accompanying General Clausel on a tour of inspection, we came upon a bivouac that had been established to protect Sobral and support the advanced positions. All the detachment's weapons had been stacked and not a single man, not even a sentinel, was on guard. The general ordered me to have the weapons removed and taken to the park. I had time to go there, obtain two wagons, load them with the guns – having first removed the priming – and then have them taken to the park before one soldier returned to the bivouac. Hunger had driven all of them, officers and men, to go out pillaging although they were only a couple of paces away from the enemy's advanced posts.

I could not believe that the English general, well knowing the situation we were in, would not dare to attack us in our unfavourable position at Sobral, which present-ed a flank to their attack. We stayed there from 13 October until 14 November.

Our proximity to the English lines exposed us, quite uselessly, to daily battles. Our commanding general decided to move the army to the rear, and concentrate it in a better position between Santarém and Tomar. As we were, at that time, unable to take the offensive, all we could do was confront the lines of Torres Vedras and this could be done equally as well from Santarém as from Sobral. It was suggested that we might cross the Tagus and attack these terrible lines from the rear, an action more easily undertaken from Santarém. As for those of us who were not on the general staff, we could not understand why we were stationed there, confronting enemy lines that we could not cross, unless we were waiting for the arrival of the Army of Andalusia to come to our aid. This army had only, we thought, to march down the left bank of the Tagus to enable us to take the offensive.

The retreat to Pernès. Our stay in that town. The 8th Corps was to begin its retreat through Alemquer, Cartaxo and Santarém. I was ordered, with an engineer officer, to reconnoitre this route, which we found more or less suitable for the artillery.

On 14 November, at eight in the evening so that our retreat was concealed from the English, the whole army began to move. Because we could be vulnerable to attack as we retired – although the enemy showed no inclination to leave his lines – the 8th Corps were told to take a path leading through marshland, a route that we had appreciated was impractical for the artillery which was routed by way of Villa Nova. We reached Azambuja at six in the morning at the same time as the 2nd Corps.

Together with the artillery of the 2nd Division we left Azambuja at midnight on the 15th reaching Santarém at eight on the morning of the 16th.

Santarém is a large town built on a hillside sloping down to the Tagus. It is in a fine position and the magnificent, fertile Tagus plain can be seen from the higher part of the town. The town itself is not beautiful and its streets are narrow. Many convents, some of them very large, surround it, but all their inhabitants had left.

Pernès is a little town built on a steep mountainside, at the foot of which the Alviella flows. Most of the inhabitants of this and the surrounding villages had remained in their homes, but marauders, and the habit of pillage into which the army had fallen, soon led them to flee. In truth, the Duc d'Abrantes* was far too weak in preventing the pillage which, while it demoralised the army and quickly deprived it of the squandered supplies, also caused us to be detested.

There were a dozen mills on the Alviella at Pernès. My first care was to seize one of them that had four mill wheels, and have it repaired. As at Sobral, the infantry were jealous and reproached us with having no less than two sorts of bread, one for the soup and one for the ration. This was true, for our supplies were abundant, I had good millers

---

* General Junot.

and good bakers and I could not see, as it did no harm to anyone, why I should not give my men, with whom I was pleased, this small indulgence. I was forced by the chief of staff – General Pierre Boyer[*] – who was called in the corps 'Peter the Cruel' – to give my mill to the infantry, who thought that, if they had one, they would have plenty of food. I could foresee the time when 'Peter the Cruel' would forbid me to grind corn.

Very little consideration was shown to the artillery on the march. We were left behind in the difficult gorges of Portugal without any help. But when, as a result of our discipline, the organisation of our marauding parties and hard work, we were able to ensure our survival, then we were envied and robbed of our gains, instead of being held up as an example to be followed.

We remained for three and a half months in this position at Pernès, with little to do except survive; we had no news from France and could not correspond with our families. It seemed as if we had been abandoned. The officers under my command ate with me and it was my servant, Souillé, who did the cooking. The only meat we had was goat and pork; but there was no shortage of bread and wine. One day our stew was stolen and our landlord, a poor cobbler, came under suspicion and, for fear of punishment, he fled and was not seen again.

Coming back from a raid, Souillé brought me a small still and I set about making brandy.

While we were at Pernès, not knowing what the future held, I built up stores of dried vegetables, salt bacon and hams, all of which during our later retreat, when marauding raids were impossible, were of great use. It was as well, too, that I had biscuits made in advance for the soldiers and that we also carried flour with us. I had caused Souillé, a clever, intelligent and well-informed lad, to dress the skins of the goats that we had eaten and these were useful in our bivouacs.

It was during our stay at Pernès that General Junot, while on reconnaissance, was struck by a bullet at the base of his nose. This did not penetrate his head but, diverted, came to rest in his cheek and a simple incision was all that was needed to extract it. This wound was later blamed for the general's insanity; his character was, in any case, a violent one, but he was good-natured.

The army's position between Santarém and Tomar was much better that the previous one, more concentrated and better placed to resist attack. This was especially true of our 8th Corps which, at Sobral, had daily been obliged to exchange fire with the English to no purpose other than the loss of some soldiers on either side. But we could not continue indefinitely like this, face to face with the English, looking daggers at each other. Unable to attack, if no help was sent to us quickly, we should soon be forced to retreat in these deplorable conditions.

---

[*] General Pierre-François Joseph, Baron Boyer (1772–1851).

Since our latest move, the commanding general had decided to send the artillery general, Foy,* to the Emperor, to advise him of the exact situation of the army in Portugal. It would have been impossible to make a better choice for such an assignment. General Foy left with a strong escort and we awaited the result of his mission with understandable impatience.

As things stood in Portugal, it seemed to us impossible that the Emperor, sole instigator of the war, would not make a final effort to secure the conquest of the peninsula. Once the English were forced to re-embark, the Spanish and the Portuguese would submit, there would probably be peace with England and an end to war in Europe. It was learned later that Napoleon, at that time, already had other preoccupations. Being unable, up to that point, to subdue Spain with an army of three hundred thousand men, wearying of that war and while it was still unfinished, he contemplated the madness of going yet further to conquer Russia. There are many, less mad than he, whose *folie de grandeur* has led them to the lunatic asylum.

Either because he wanted to position himself better, or because he really wanted to attempt to cross the Tagus and attack the English, as well as to keep his army on the alert, the prince of Essling, while awaiting the help he had asked for, instructed General Eblé, an officer admired and loved by all the artillery, to build whatever was needed for a bridge. Everything was lacking; there were no boats, no tools, no wood and no ropes. General Eblé started by having the tools – axes, saws, etc. – made out of the iron obtained from demolished houses. He had trees cut down and used his tools to saw beams, cut planks, forge anchors and grappling hooks, and to plait ropes. Finally, through his energy, activity and intelligence, he contrived to produce all that was needed for a bridge that could cross the Tagus. General Eblé's workshops were at Punhete where the Zezere flowed into the Tagus. All his efforts and all his work were in vain. Help never arrived, the attempt to cross the river was abandoned and everything that had cost so much difficulty to produce was burned.

At the end of December, the arrival of some significant help was announced; this was an army of at least thirty thousand men under General Drouet,† bringing supplies, munitions and money. Since our arrival in Portugal none of us had received any pay. In fact General Drouet reached us on 26 December, with a single division, the Conroux Division of the 9th Corps, nine thousand men at most, without any supplies, munitions or money.

And it was to be with the assistance of these nine thousand men, without a single barrel of gunpowder, that Napoleon ordered us to cross the Tagus, take the lines of Torres Vedras and fling the English into the sea.

* General Maximilien Sébastien, Count Foy (1775–1825).
† General Jean-Baptiste Drouet, count of Erlon (1765–1844), later became a marshal of France on 9 April 1843, under Louis-Philippe.

We hoped that, at the very least, in addition to the official despatches, they would have enough concern for us to send us the letters that must now be waiting at Almeida or at Salamanca. But nothing came. A new disappointment – the Imperial government showered us with them.

1 January 1811. A sad New Year's Day. All of us who were seated around the more than meagre table had danced, exactly a year ago to the day, at the prefecture of Châteauroux. It is true that we had been less than enthusiastic about going to make war in the peninsula, but were resigned to it and were far from anticipating such prolonged toil and suffering, in the course of which we should fail to have a serious encounter with an enemy we longed to fight and who, we felt certain, we could overcome in open battle.

It was better to suffer in silence. When I heard the officers around me grumbling, I reminded them of our poor soldiers, without shoes or shelter and lacking every necessity, who quietly endured their troubles, often with good humour. It was my philosophy always to remember those below me, and compare my fate with those less fortunate and never to be envious of those who were above me. Our triumphs were waning and our armies would shortly have to bear other sufferings, both mental and physical, than those of the Army of Portugal.

At last, we were told that our communications with Spain were, for the time being, restored, and that mail was being sent to France. On 10 January I wrote my first letter to my family since I had arrived in Portugal. It had been six months since we had had news from France, or from our families, and nearly as long since we had been able send news to them; six months since we had been able to reassure our relations and friends of our fate. Those who loved us could not even learn if we were still on earth. But what did this matter to Napoleon? We were not beaten. We were not victorious. We could no longer conquer new territories for him, to feed his pride and ambition. What satisfaction would it be to add to his Empire a new department on the Tagus with a capital at Lisbon? He abandoned us, as he had abandoned his army in Egypt.

At the beginning of February, General Foy returned to the army, bringing with him a small body of two thousand men. This did not provide us with the munitions of which we were running short. But the hopes of early help that came from Paris restored, to some extent, the shaken confidence of the army and stilled the growing complaints. The leaders, with the exception of Masséna, set a bad example of discontent.

Meanwhile, as we waited, the supplies grew less; our horses, weakened by hunger, died; soon, in the artillery, we should be forced to abandon our guns. All depended on the intervention of the 5th Corps which, under the leadership of Marshal Soult, should come down via Abrantes, on the left bank of the Tagus. I greatly doubted that our commanding general was much deceived about the good intentions of the duke of

Dalmatia,* who was well known in the army for willingly leaving his comrades in difficulties.

On the 17th, the English made several offensive moves. The park and part of the 8th Corps artillery was sent to Thomar. Only three guns now remained behind for each division.

The duke of Abrantes sent me out on 24th to reconnoitre the two bridges over the Alviella that lay to our rear. I concluded that preparations were being made for our retreat. These bridges, half a league apart, were made of wood and were strong enough to carry the artillery. They would be easy to destroy after the crossing and no tools except levers would be needed. Near to one of them there was a house, materials from which might be used to rebuild the bridges. If we retreated, it would have to be burned.

On the 24th the order was received to destroy twenty of the wagons that were in the artillery park of the 8th Corps; the ammunition was thrown into the Baboa. Twenty-one more wagons were destroyed on 1 March; this figure did not include the company baggage wagons. In spite of these reductions, it was only possible to harness four horses to each of the remaining wagons; this included animals that were sick and convalescent.

The retreat from Portugal. Retreat had been decided upon, and it was urgent. We could achieve nothing where we were, and should soon be dying of hunger. Some corps had no food left, except their reserve supply of biscuit.

The blame for the retreat did not rest on the shoulders of the army, or on those of its commander-in-chief, whose firmness of purpose had sustained morale and confidence despite the shameful recriminations of some staff officers. Blame should be placed, instead, upon the unspeakable state of neglect in which we had been left. As it had been Napoleon's wish to wage war in Spain and Portugal, why had he not come in person to take charge of it? Such difficulties would not have been insuperable for one of his genius, and his subordinates would, at least, have obeyed him.

We were without any regrets at leaving a country where we had suffered so much. The army's morale was not affected, nor was its confidence in its leader; in any case, we did not believe that Portugal was to be completely abandoned.

Our retreat would not be easy. The weather was dreadful; there were tempests, rain and wind. Our horses were exhausted, the country was difficult with its steep ascents and descents, the valleys were swampy and would provide no food for men or horses, and the inhabitants had been stirred up against us. We should have to carry our sick and wounded with us, while a rested, well-fed and numerous enemy was forever at

* Marshal Soult.

our heels, together with the numerous guerrilla bands now more passionately opposed to us than ever.

It was of the utmost importance to conceal our retreat from our enemies for as long as possible. The marching orders were precise, of course, and everything was carried out calmly, without difficulty or confusion.

On 4 March the park and divisional reserves of the 8th Corps, together with our sick and our baggage wagons, went to Chao de Maçans across the Tomar. We were to retreat into the valley of the Mondego. The 2nd Corps was to go there by a more direct route. The 8th Corps were to march by way of Condeixa and Coïmbra and would have to cross the mountain chain that separated the Tagus valley from the coast.

The 6th Corps, which was the nearest to the Lisbon to Coïmbra road at Pombal, was to form a rearguard, positioning themselves on the road in order to halt the English if they should attempt to cut us off.

The movement began during the night of 5 March. And, at five in the evening, I left the little town of Pernès with my much-reduced artillery.

At the same time, the infantry divisions of the 8th Corps also left their positions. We headed for Chao de Maçans and Ourem by different routes for the way chosen by the infantry would have been impassable for us. On my way, I destroyed the two bridges I had noted on 24 February and burned the neighbouring house. We passed Torres Novas, where the general headquarters had been, and, at midday on 7 March arrived at Tomar, a small town with wide, straight roads. I noticed, by the way, a very handsome textile mill that looked to me as if it belonged to a Frenchman. I was in no doubt that it would soon be burned by the English who, even in an allied country, were in the habit of destroying anything that could compete with their own industries and trade.

Having reached Pombal at midday, we had to leave again at two o'clock for Chao de Maçans. The road still led over mountains and valleys; the ground was covered, now with olive trees, now with heather. Having lost some horses, I was forced to burn yet another baggage wagon and now there were only ten carts left to me. Leaving Tomar, we climbed the Scotch-pine-clad heights and followed them for a long while, having a fine view over the whole countryside. We bivouacked before Chao de Maçans; this was just a big village. The wretched town of Ourem, perched on rocks, lay on the other side of the valley. General headquarters was at Chao de Maçans, and it was there that we rejoined the infantry divisions of the 8th Corps. The 1st Corps had protected Pombal during this march and the 2nd Corps was covering Chao de Maçans.

At seven in the morning of 8 March, the 8th Corps had set out for Pombal on the main road to Coïmbra. With my artillery, I led the column. The bad road, the difficulties of the route, following the foothills of the Estrella, which separated the Tagus valley from the coast, and towards which we were heading, combined with the weakness of my horses – fed only on a little grass – together with hail and rain, so delayed the column's march that at four in the evening we still had covered only two leagues. Out of forty-eight horses, only thirty-six remained in a state to continue, and I could foresee having to blow up four caissons. It was six in the evening before we reached Manoria, where we bivouacked in the woods. There was nothing but heather for my horses to eat. The enemy were close behind and the 2nd Division provided cover for us. We were then at the highest point of the chain of mountains.

We set out again for Pombal at four o'clock on the 9th. We had only to descend, but the ground in the valley was swampy and difficult for the artillery. When we reached the wide 'Route Royale', we found the cavalry of General Montbrun and the 6th Corps already in position there, near to Venda du Boica. We crossed this town and went to bivouac at the same place where I had camped when we arrived in Portugal. We stayed there throughout the day of the 10th.

Now, in front of Pombal, Marshal Ney with the 6th Corps, General Drouet and Montbrun's cavalry faced the Anglo-Portuguese army which, leaving its lines, was advancing up the 'Route Royale' from Lisbon. Confronted by Marshal Ney, Wellington seemed undecided whether to attack. Was he afraid that he might lose his reputation for prudence by fighting a conventional battle? We had halted, either so that we could support Marshal Ney if he should be attacked, or to give us some rest, or perhaps to allow the 2nd Corps, then on the march on the other side of the Estrella mountains, time to reach the Mondego valley. Perhaps all three of these reasons caused us to halt at midnight, but we certainly did not complain and it allowed our poor horses to have a little rest.

On the 11th the artillery continued its march at one in the morning and, with all the corps, camped that evening at Redinha.

Marshal Ney abandoned Pombal on the same day; however, when he saw the English enter it he attacked, pushed them back over the Arunca and then resumed his retreat. He camped to our rear at Venda da Cruz.

With my division, we went to Condeixa on the 12th. The 2nd Division remained at Redinha in order to give support there to the 6th Corps that was due to arrive. It would not have been unwarranted if our division had also remained with the 2nd, for Ney was attacked on that day as he retreated towards Redinha.

The Anglo-Portuguese army, constantly reinforced by the arrival of new troops had, by the 12th, increased to twenty-five thousand men.[*] With such a force, its general thought that he could attack the 6th Corps, which consisted of fewer than half that number. He attacked the front and attempted to outflank the 6th Corps on both sides. Ney halted his men before Redinha in a favourable position, kept one division

---

[*] This figure is given as 16,000 by some authorities.

in reserve and using his infantry, cavalry and artillery with the skill and boldness he always displayed in the presence of the enemy, pushed the English back on all fronts, putting 1,800 of their men out of action. If he had not feared risking too much he would have routed them completely.

Once the English were repulsed, Ney resumed his retreat to Condeixa.

The division, which had camped near Condeixa, passed through that town on 13th and, instead of turning towards Coïmbra, followed the road to Miranda de Corvo, turned to the right and reached the valley where the Loison* Division of the 6th Corps had been since the previous day. This latter division had been detached at the beginning of the retreat to cover the 2nd Corps. When it left Punhète it had burned the materials for the bridge built by General Eblé. Our 1st Division was, provisionally, to link up with the left of the 6th Corps confronting the enemy, and with the 2nd that was arriving from the Estrella mountains. This explained our change of direction, which originally had been towards Coïmbra and the lower Mondego. General Junot, with the 2nd Division and Montbrun's cavalry, continued to march on Coïmbra in order to occupy the town and rebuild the bridges.

There were two villages at the head of the valley I entered with my division; general headquarters had occupied one of them since the morning. This village had not been sufficiently guarded – negligence that was, perhaps, explained by the defeat of the English on the previous day. At about six in the evening, English cavalry had surprised and sabred several dragoons; in alarm, general headquarters was promptly evacuated. The prince of Essling[†] had retreated on to a hill at the head of the valley, where I had established a battery.

From the ridge on which I was bivouacked I had spent the whole evening watching numerous enemy skirmishers on the road to Miranda de Corvo. It was feared that the enemy might occupy, in force, this area through which we should have to pass, so the two divisions – those of Clausel and Loison – were united, and we left at midnight for Miranda de Corvo. Our march was undisturbed and we reached our destination at five in the evening of the 14th, meeting troops of the 6th Corps moving into position on our way. Our hasty move to Miranda de Corvo was motivated by news coming from the commander-in-chief that Marshal Ney, fearing to be cut off, had abandoned Condeixa.

Until this time we had not believed that we were to leave Portugal, We had marched towards Coïmbra and the lower Mondego thinking that we were to establish ourselves in that region, protected by the river, and wait there for the hoped-for help so that we could again take the offensive. What had taken place at Redinha on the 12th had demonstrated that the English were not too formidable in open combat.

* General Louis Henri, Count Loison (1771–1816).
† Marshal Masséna.

If the rumours that were circulating were well founded, it appeared that Marshal Ney's impatience to leave Portugal, together with the tendency to insubordination that he had shown throughout the campaign – and he had never concealed it – would be sufficient to foil the prince of Essling's plan. By retreating precipitately, without having been attacked, from Condeixa, which he had been ordered to defend, Marshal Ney, so brave and determined during the retreat, had delivered up the road leading from Coïmbra to the lower Mondego to the enemy, forcing the commander-in-chief to return up the valley formed by this river and its tributaries and subsequently continue his withdrawal into Spain. I report this rumour, although I do not usually pay much attention to army gossips, as it gained credibility from the fact that General Junot and the 2nd Division, together with General Montbrun, were suddenly recalled from the lower Mondego, where they were constructing a bridge over the river and where, after the 6th Corps retreated from Condeixa, they were in danger of being cut off.

Throughout 14 March, during our march towards Miranda de Corvo, the 6th Corps fell back on us, followed by the entire English army. Marshal Ney, as always, recovering his great qualities and courage in the presence of the enemy, conducted a skilful withdrawal by echelons, profiting from all the irregularities of the terrain. He killed many of the English, while himself losing few, retiring slowly, step by step until he joined up with us before Miranda de Corvo, where the English showed no sign of wanting to attack us.

We left our bivouacs at two in the morning of the 15th to go to Foz d'Arouce. Now the army was completely reunited. The Anglo-Portuguese had been halted by the skilful retreat of Marshal Ney, making it possible for our division and General Montbrun to rejoin us, and for the 2nd Division to come down from the Estrella mountains. All the army's artillery was now on this route.

When the basin of Miranda de Corvo had been crossed, we were continually among the gorges formed by mountains that were not high but were close together and covered with pines. As ever, our road lay through the mountainous part of Portugal, bad and difficult for all, but especially so for our heavy artillery vehicles, and we found the long, narrow village of Foz d'Arouce far from easy to pass through. Then we had to cross the stone bridge over the Ceira, a tributary of the Mondego, afterwards climbing a steep hillside and bivouacking on the top. The 8th Corps was on the right bank and most of the 6th Corps on the left bank and in the village.

Donkeys belonging to the 6th Corps were no longer of any use and had become an encumbrance so, on the orders of Marshal Ney, these animals were killed near the bridge, which was immediately named the 'Bridge of Asses', but this was soon altered to 'Bridge of the Defeat'. The enemy, following us, had taken up a position on the heights above Foz d'Arouce. A section of the 6th Corps was separated from the main body of the army by a deep river, crossed only by a single bridge. When they saw that this section was not sufficiently alert, the enemy suddenly attacked the village and the bridge an hour before nightfall. There was immediate panic among our troops, who rushed on to the bridge and piled up there. As darkness fell on the resulting chaos, they opened fire on one another and many soldiers were drowned attempting to cross the river. Colonel Damour, having been wounded by his own troops, was taken prisoner and a good number of his men were drowned together with the regimental eagle. Marshal Ney, calm as ever in the face of danger, soon rallied his troops and went to the help of those who had not lost their heads in panic and were confronting the enemy. He attacked the English in his turn and as usual repulsed them, forcing them to retire for a while.

The day of the 16th was spent on the right bank of the Ceira and, at ten in the evening, the artillery of the 8th Corps marched off. We climbed steadily on the left of the Mondego, crossing the streams that flowed down the mountains to the river, and passing over the steep foothills on either side of them. During the night of the 16th/17th we ascended the Sierra Murcelha and descended into the Alva valley. We crossed the bridge over this steeply banked river boldly. The English had fortified the position and blown up the main arch of the bridge as a precaution in case our route into Portugal took us by way of the left bank of the Mondego. Our sappers had soon rebuilt it. The Murcelha bridge that we crossed was level with the Alcoba on the right bank and, from the artillery park, we could clearly see the east side of the Busaco mountain.

We should have remained on the banks of the Alva but, at four in the afternoon of the 18th, we were ordered to leave at once for Galizès, where we arrived at one on the following morning. Almost immediately another order, to continue on our way, was received and we marched three leagues further; then all the artillery went on for yet another league, on the road to Celorico. At five in the evening we halted at last, having marched for twenty-five hours with exhausted horses harnessed to heavy vehicles!

This sudden departure had been the result of a movement by the English threatening our left flank, which was, as always, ill guarded by the 2nd Corps who were, as usual, off marauding.

All the countryside through which we passed was most picturesque, very fertile, more fertile even than that of Viseu. The road was good – or, at least, less bad. The villages, close to one another were, as usual, deserted. Marceira lies in a delightful hollow containing several villages on the slopes. This road into Spain that we were following along the left bank of the Mondego seemed to me to be much less difficult that the one by which we had entered Portugal. Such an experienced general as Marshal Masséna must have had his reasons for preferring the other.

Marching, sometimes by day, sometimes by night, and often both day and night, we reached Celorico, a little town on a sugar-loaf hill, on the 21st, and then, on the 24th, arrived at Guarda, where the 8th Corps was to halt.

Guarda was an old town built of stone blocks in the midst of a bare landscape bristling with rocks. As a defensive position it was good, dominating its surroundings without itself being dominated. The nature of the terrain made it difficult to approach.

We remained at Guarda until the 28th. We should have stayed there longer, but the enemy was attacking with stronger and stronger forces, and we left in a hurry. We went towards Ciudad Rodrigo, passing through Sabugal and Alfayatès.

As we went through the latter place we learned of the birth of the king of Rome,[*] and I was ordered to announce the fact with a salvo of 101 cannon shots.

The artillery crossed the border into Spain on 3 April, and slept that night at Ciudad Rodrigo. On the previous day the 2nd Corps had taken part in a very lively engagement with the English at Sabugal and had lost many men there.

When we had crossed into Portugal on 15 September 1810, the artillery of the 8th Corps possessed 142 wagons, guns, caissons, etc. and 891 horses in the train. When we returned to Spain we had only forty-nine wagons and 182 horses, so our losses consisted of ninety-three wagons, destroyed or burned, and 709 horses of the train, but the enemy had neither captured nor killed a single wagon or horse.

The 2nd and 6th Corps had also suffered losses, but theirs were not so great. Their horses had not been overworked and doomed as most of those in our corps had been. Also, they had received a strong reinforcement of mules collected in the province of Salamanca.

So this was the end of this pitiful Portuguese expedition.

I had no idea what we were to do in Spain. It was quite certain that, for the time being, our army was in no state to undertake even the smallest offensive action. Our supply situation was deplorable; we lacked everything – food, ammunition, clothing, boots, money and horses. However, the morale of the troops was not affected. Six months of deprivation in a country without any supplies, obtaining no provisions from outside and depending on marauding to live, had not lessened the army's courage, but had exhausted it and destroyed its discipline. Much had been left to the soldier's initiative and the soldier had taken advantage of it. We had left sad memories behind us with the Portuguese and they would curse the name of France for a long while. Survival had been necessary, it is true, but bad soldiers had behaved like brigands towards the unfortunate peasantry, who might well have thought themselves safe from such marauding, by reason of their poverty and misery. I have seen things

---

[*] François Charles Joseph Bonaparte, king of Rome (1811–32). The son of Napoleon Bonaparte and his second wife, Marie-Louise.

so dreadful that they can never be forgotten. If, in their turn, the Portuguese showed themselves to be savage towards our prisoners and our wounded, this can be understood, although not excused.

To think that we believed, when we crossed into Portugal, that we had only to show ourselves to cause the English to flee and to throw them back into the sea; whereas, under the skilful command of a prudent general, living in abundance, and practically without fighting, they had forced us into a retreat that could, with more aggression from our adversaries, have turned into a rout.

The failure of this campaign in Portugal has been laid at the door of the commanding general. This is quite wrong. The responsibility must lie with Napoleon, who, alone, wanted this war and forced it upon his generals without giving them the means of ensuring success.

Two French armies under the command of Junot and of Soult had already been obliged to abandon Portugal and, although it was known that the English had received reinforcements and had been strengthened, and that the Portuguese troops had been reorganised under the command of their officers, it was under these conditions that an army that should have consisted of seventy thousand men (but had only fifty thousand men when it entered Portugal), had been sent to conquer this difficult country, already in a state of insurrection against us. Our army's retreat had not been secured and we were abandoned for the whole of the winter almost without help, without supplies and without ammunition.

It had required all the military skill, the watchfulness and the determination of Marshal Masséna to sustain for so long the morale and confidence of an ill-supplied army that was grappling with such great difficulties, and then to conduct a long withdrawal before a numerically superior force without allowing himself to be diverted or shaken.

The generals under the command of Masséna were skilful and brave, but unhappy about the war, and, although none of them had experienced a defence of Genoa[*] or a victory of Zurich[†] in the course of their service, they were unwilling to serve under his orders and were too often obdurate. It was the hurried abandonment of Condeixa that forced the commanding general to leave Portugal, and Marshal Ney's opposition became so determined at the end of the campaign that the prince of Essling was forced to remove him from his command.

It has been said that Marshal Masséna had aged and that he was weary, but he was barely fifty years old and it was no more than a year since he had, by his resolve, captured the strong position of Eibersberg [sic] and had won the title of prince of Essling.

* Siege of Genoa, April–June 1800.
† In 1799, Masséna routed Field Marshal Suvarov's army.

Masséna was a looter like any old soldier. Unfortunately, looters were not rare in our armies, even those who sought to enrich themselves at the expense of our own troops. A woman, who was often the cause of embarrassment, had accompanied Masséna all through this campaign and certainly this did nothing to raise his prestige. I can only make a judgement as a soldier and, having seen the difficulties that he had to overcome, I have to say that, in the course of the campaign, he maintained his usual standard and was, like all of us, the victim of Napoleon's short-sightedness and reck-lessness. Among our generals there were few who could have left Portugal without suffering a single defeat or reverse.

Chapter Six

My Second Spanish Campaign (1811)

From our arrival in Spain until the battle of Fuentès d'Onoro. Starvation had compelled us to leave Portugal. Physically, we were in the most lamentable state; we were unhappy with this war and furious that we had been abandoned, but we were not at all discouraged. Our commanding general always seemed anxious to continue the struggle against the English, demonstrating, by his attitude and resolve, that he had not aged as much as some liked to imply, and was less weary than were some of his subordinates – if they were to be judged by the grumbles of their staff officers.

We needed rest and we needed resupply, for we were completely destitute. The situation in that part of Spain where we found ourselves gave little hope of either.

As far as we knew, we were battling with the English on two fronts: in Andalusia, where Marshal Soult was besieging Cadiz and protecting Badajoz, and on our front, where they were attacking and beginning their siege of Almeida.

There was no question of a rest for us.

We re-entered Spain on 3 April 1811 and slept, on the 4th, at Ciudad Rodrigo, leaving again on the 5th for Salamanca; on the same night General Foucher, who was in command of the 8th Corps Artillery, and was marching with us, received the order to turn back; these successive marches and counter-marches wore us out. We did not reach Salamanca until the 10th.

The countryside was marshy and thickly wooded; the guerrillas, who swarmed around us, were more numerous and bolder. To leave the column was madness. Three soldiers, who had been left behind by the wagon train, were attacked on the 8th but we heard their cries and they were rescued. One of them had suffered seven blows from a spear; fortunately he was not dangerously hurt.

It was only twelve leagues from Salamanca to the neighbourhood of Toro, where we were to camp, but it took us three days to cover the distance because our horses were so exhausted. There were about five thousand souls in the little town of Toro, and fourteen convents – seven of monks and seven of nuns. The country was pleasant, fruit trees were growing there, something that was rare in Spain. We remained in the town and its environs for quite a long time.

The Army of Portugal, after a few days' rest and having received some meagre supplies, marched towards the English, to compel them to raise the siege of Almeida. Clausel's division, the artillery of which I still commanded, remained behind to cover the rear.

The order reached me on the 16th to go with the artillery train of my division into cantonments at Castro-Menbibra, leaving my guns at Toro. The little town of Toro stood on a hill and we were only half a league away when, always on the alert, I noticed a movement; some horsemen coming down from the town appeared to be gathering behind a hillock that lay in our path and concealed them from our view. I was anxious, and feared an ambush, as I had with me only the soldiers of the train, few of whom were armed with guns. I halted the detachment and brought them into a position to fight, while trying to make them appear, from a distance, more numerous than they were. I sent out a sergeant and my gunner orderly, a highly intelligent lad, on to the hillside to reconnoitre. Instead of merely observing and coming back to me, when they saw two or three guerrillas who were scouting for the group near by, they fell upon them. My orderly was killed and the sergeant returned alone to warn me of the ambush. I waited calmly for a little while, expecting an attack. Seeing no one approaching and supposing that the guerrillas were hesitating or falling back, I moved forward with those of the men who were best armed, hoping to save my orderly if that should prove possible. The guerrillas, believing us to be stronger than we were, fled and scattered and we found nothing but the poor dead soldier with his stomach ripped open. They had cut through his belt, in which he carried some money, in order to rob him. We took his body with us and buried it at our halting place at Bénafarcès, where we found a detachment of the 4th Battalion, to whom the train belonged.

At Toro, on 20 April, I had, at last, the great happiness of receiving the first letters from my family for seven months. There were so many letters for the army that it would have taken too long to distribute all of them at once. They were handed out monthly. On 20 April I received those from the months from September to October. Those dated from the following months would be handed out later, when *messieurs*, the employees of the postal service, might have time for it. Those poor lads must not be over-tired! We did not grumble. All our good fortune arrived at once, for a few days later, when still at Toro, we were paid for one month out of the ten that we were owed, and in money that was no longer in use.

Our back pay was provided for us from taxes raised in the country and paid by the Spanish in the local money. Excellent! The army paymasters paid us in *écus*, each worth six *livres*, but these were no longer legal tender in France and would not be accepted by the post. The paymasters exchanged the *livres* for five francs ninety-two cents – well below their real worth. This went to prove that the paymasters were incorrigible scoundrels and that we were incredible fools to let ourselves be duped like that. But we were so very happy to get our hands on some money after waiting for ten months.

We missed Italy greatly when we were in Spain. Apart from bread, meat and wine this country offered us nothing. In the towns we had no acquaintances, there was no theatre, no entertainment, no promenades, and the countryside was barren, devoid of trees or gardens. It was impossible to leave our cantonments. For our necessities, clothes, boots and toilet articles we had to rely on traders who came from France and exploited us outrageously. It was sad to see how everything combined to take advantage of the needs of the unhappy soldier who risked his life daily, and endured every discomfort for the common good.

In our various cantonments around Toro, where the countryside was infested with guerrillas, I had to take great care to ensure that we were not taken by surprise, for we were isolated from the division. I placed one post in the middle of the village and, during the day, another on the top of the clock tower. By night the roads were blocked with wagons and, where there were many side roads, I had permanent barriers erected. All were aware of a rallying point, to be used if there should be an alert.

Our cantonment was finally established on the 17th at Villabendimio, a village near to Toro, where I lodged with the priest, a good man. Throughout my stay in Spain I had more to be grateful for than to complain of with these venerable clergymen.

On the 22nd the 2nd Division of the 8th Corps left the area round Toro and Salamanca and returned to Ciudad Rodrigo.

The country on this side of Toro was very similar to that between Palencia and Benavente and between Old Castile and La Mancha – bare, but producing a large yield of wheat and barley.

In my isolated position in cantonment at Villabendimio, I redoubled my safety measures; the departure of the 2nd Division increased the number of guerrillas who surged down upon us.

At the end of April, the prince of Essling concentrated the army at Ciudad Rodrigo, with the exception of our division, which remained in the rear to safeguard communications. On 3 May it left the town and marched upon the English. They were found to be entrenched before the Dos-Casas, a steeply banked river. Masséna's army consisted of thirty-six thousand men; there were more than forty thousand under Wellington's command. Their centre was at the village of Fuentès d'Onoro. He attacked them that same day, crossed the river and pushed them from the village. They retired in good order on to the surrounding hills.

The armies continued to confront each other on the 4th.

At dawn on the 5th the attack began again. Several positions were taken from the English and, at the moment that the attack became general and success seemed imminent, the marshal was told that the ammunition was nearly exhausted. The fight had to be terminated. The delighted English were quick to take the offensive.

The battle of Fuentès d'Onoro (or of Poso Bello) remained indecisive, but it should have been a conclusive victory, leading to significant consequences. If he had been beaten, Wellington would have retreated and, pursued by troops more agile and active than his own, might have been routed. We know, by the example of Corunna, what the rout of an English army entails.

This battle was, I believe, Masséna's last. If it was the cause of his unmerited disgrace – and he left Spain shortly afterwards – then Napoleon himself must bear the well-deserved blame for his neglect of the Army of Portugal. As for the shortage of ammunition, that was not the fault of our general, the far-sighted Eblé, but rather of those who, responsible for supplying it to the army, allowed it to arrive in half-empty caissons.

Marshal Masséna was reluctant to call off the attack. It was no longer possible to relieve Almeida. A few bold soldiers contrived to pass through the English lines and take instructions to the governor, General Brenier,* to blow up the fortifications and withdraw, which he did. On the 10th, at ten in the evening, the garrison of fifteen hundred men, having completely destroyed Almeida, passed the English, who failed to stop them, and rejoined the French division that had been sent to meet them, losing only two hundred men.

Marshal Masséna, having resupplied and reinforced Ciudad Rodrigo, returned, with the army to Salamanca, from where he was recalled to Paris.

The reorganisation of the Army of Portugal. The prince of Essling was replaced by Marshal Marmont.

Even if there were some who were gratified by this disgraceful incident, this was not true of most of the officers and soldiers, who gave full credit to the strength of character displayed by our commander-in-chief throughout this difficult war. They did not blame him either for our failure or for our sufferings. His departure did nothing to appease an unhappiness that verged on anger. If, by striking at him, Napoleon had wished to turn him into a scapegoat, then he was mistaken for it was he himself whom the army blamed for its troubles.

Marshal Marmont's second-in-command was General Reynier, the commander of the 2nd Corps.

The whole Army of Portugal was reorganised and many officers were sent back to France. The army corps were abolished and reorganised into five infantry divisions and one cavalry division.

---

* General Antoine-François, Count Brenier de Montmoran (1767–1831).

All the artillery of the army was brought together at Salamanca on the 28th to assume its new organisation; there were to be only five cannon for each division and six for the mounted division. At my request, I remained in command of Clausel's division, now the 2nd Division of the new army. The 8th Company of the 6th Horse Artillery, commanded by Captain Aubé, came under my orders.

The march on Ciudad Rodrigo. On 3 June, I rejoined my division at San Pedro de Rosadas, and we marched towards Ciudad Rodrigo. We passed near the market town of Tamamès, where, on 8 October 1809, General Marchand,[*] at the head of ten thousand French, attacked fifty thousand Spanish under the command of Duke del Parque, who were positioned on the heights. Repulsed and pursued to Valladolid, he again took the offensive and beat the Spanish at Alba de Tormès,[†] inflicting so great a defeat on them that they took no further part in the campaign.

We reached Ciudad Rodrigo at two in the morning on the 6th. We found the 1st Division there, as well as the cavalry division. We left at eight in the morning, with the marshal, to carry out a reconnaissance across the Azava. The English retired before us. The town was resupplied and the three divisions marched together towards Extremadura. It seemed to me that the march on Ciudad Rodrigo, by the three divisions under the command of the senior general, was a feint, made to divert the attention of the English and deceive them into thinking that we intended to attack in the north, while we were about to attack them in the south.

During this march our other divisions, under General Reynier, actually advanced towards the Tagus.

The operation in Extremadura. It was decided to join General Reynier on the Tagus to help Marshal Soult force the English to raise the blockade of Badajoz. He had already tried to do this and had clumsily allowed himself to be beaten by Wellington at Albuera.[‡] His army was not responsible for the difficulties in which he had voluntarily abandoned the Army of Portugal beneath the walls of Lisbon – where his intervention would probably have made it possible for us to force the English to re-embark. It was with great joy that we went to the aid of the brave garrison at Badajoz.

On 7 June we left Ciudad Rodrigo for Tamamès.

On the 9th we crossed the Sierra de Gata, separating the province of Salamanca from that of Extremadura, by way of the Banos Pass.

[*] General Jean-Gabriel, Count Marchand (1765–1851) Became a general in 1799 during the Revolutionary wars. He took part in the Spanish and Russian campaigns. He was at Lützen, at Bauzen and at Leipzig in 1813. He served the Bourbons following Napoleon's abdication. He was acquitted of the charge of having delivered Grenoble up to Napoleon and was made a peer of France in 1837.
[†] On 26 November 1809.
[‡] General William Carr Beresford (1768–1854) was the Allied commander at Albuera.

After following the valley of the Hombro, we climbed a long, steep ridge to reach the pass and went down into Banos, a small town that had been partly burned and lay in a narrow valley surrounded by high mountains.

We were at Oliva on the 10th and reached Plasencia on the 11th. This was a large town built on a hill in a sparsely cultivated region that was, in places, covered by green oaks. The women of this place, and most of those in Extremadura, were not so swarthy as those in the kingdom of Léon.

There was a good road between Plasencia and the Tagus, leading through a gently undulating countryside clad in woods and broom and with plenty of forage. We reached the river on the 14th and crossed it on the 15th. A flying bridge was built above a stone one, the middle arch of which had been destroyed. The cavalry and the draught horses crossed by means of a ford.

The Tagus was about 80 *toises** wide at this point. The banks were very steep and the mountains surrounding it were arid and uncultivated. The French had built a fort on the mountain overlooking the left bank of the river with a redoubt at the edge of the water. Another redoubt had been built on the other bank.

Between Madrid and Badajoz we followed a good, metalled road that crossed the barren, mountainous countryside.

On the 16th we reached Trujillo, the homeland of Pizarro[†] and of storks. This town was built on the two slopes of a hill crowned with a vast old fort; it was almost entirely deserted.

Throughout our travels, the country through which we passed was uncultivated and all the villages had been abandoned. This was not because the land was barren, but rather because the inhabitants had given up the attempt to cultivate land on which the harvest brought them no profit. In any case, everything they needed for husbandry had been taken from them – horses, carts and seed.

Medellin, where we arrived on the 18th, was a little town on the left bank of the Guadiana; here we crossed the river by means of a bridge with twenty arches. The town was on a broad plain that would have been very fertile if it had been cultivated. A third of the houses in the town had been demolished. Hernando Cortès[‡] was born here and his house was shown to us with pride. The town was dominated by a large fort built on a hill, and was unusual in that a crenellated wall, taller than the one surrounding the town, bisected it. There was a vast cistern beneath the chapel of the fort.

Marshal Victor[§] utterly defeated Cuesta[¶] on 18 March 1809 between Medellin and Don Benito.

* A *toise* = 6.3 ft.
† Francisco Pizarro (1475–1541) the Spanish conquistador.
‡ Hernando Cortès (1485–1547).
§ Marshal Claude Victor-Perrin, duke of Bellune (1764–1841).
¶ General Gregorio Garcia de la Cuesta (1740–1812), a Spanish commander.

We reached Don Benito, a well-built town of some eight thousand souls, on the 21st. The country around was very fertile, for Partido de la Serena, of which it formed part, was one of the best districts in Extremadura.

The English were not waiting for us. Our marshals had met at Merida, on the Guadiana above Badajoz, and marched towards that town on the 18th. Wellington raised the siege at once and retired to a good defensive position on the mountain, where our marshals considered that it would be useless to follow him. Our army entered Badajoz on the 20th and relieved the brave little garrison that had survived two sieges and repulsed two assaults, killing between seven hundred and eight hundred of the English.

When Badajoz had been relieved and the garrison reinforced and resupplied, the two armies separated, and we went to take up quarters near the Tagus. We left the banks of the Guadiana, which were covered with oleanders just as our river banks at home were bordered with weeping willows.

Return to the Tagus. On 13 July my division advanced to the frontier of the kingdom of Cordoba; we were followed by many guerrillas and, in spite of all my care, several of my wagon train soldiers, who had been sent out to find forage, were captured and killed and their horses were stolen. We returned on the 18th to Trujillo, and the entire army went into camp at Talavera, near Plasencia, the capital of the Navalmoral de la Mata region. The artillery equipment of the five divisions remained here and the personnel were sent into various cantonments. We stayed in these quarters until 9 September. It was in Trujillo that I saw the comet for the first time.[*] Marshal Marmont had chosen these cantonments near the Tagus so that he would be able, as required, to move either to the north of Sierra de Gata to Ciudad Rodrigo and Salamanca, or south towards Badajoz. These were the two lines of communication held by the English between Spain and Portugal.

We were not idle while we were in these quarters, for the army fortified certain routes across rivers and mountains and repaired and replaced artillery equipment.

Towards the end of August, the English made a movement in the direction of Banos. We marched towards this place and to Plasencia, where the headquarters was established. It seemed certain that this movement of the English indicated some attempt on Ciudad Rodrigo.

The second march on Ciudad Rodrigo. We left our cantonments on 9 September and marched once more to the north. As the road between Banos and Tamamès that I should have followed with my artillery proved to be very difficult, I obtained

---

[*] This would have been the great comet of 1811, first seen by Jean-Louis Pons when it was visible to the naked eye on 11 April 1811. The comet remained visible without optical aid for 260 days.

permission from General Clausel to take another direction, accompanied by an escort. My maps and my information indicated that this route would be better. I rejoined my division near Tamamès on the 22nd.

Two leagues before Ciudad Rodrigo we took up position with the 6th. The 5th was to the rear with a division of the Young Guard that had been detached from the Army of the North. Everything indicated a minor engagement.

The advance guard pushed as far as Alfayatès, and we retired to Ciudad Rodrigo, which was resupplied, then we went back to Banos by a third route that I had not travelled along before.

We returned over the Sierra de Gata and again went down into the Tagus valley; I did not know why these marches and counter-marches were ordered.

On 9 October we were at Plasencia, and on the 10th at the ford at Tietar, We reached Navalmoral on the 11th and Oropeza, a little town with an old castle in a fertile countryside, on the 12th. We arrived at Talavera on the 13th. This was a town that might be considered large in Spain and which lies on a plain covered in olive groves near the Tagus. It was near here that the indecisive battle of the same name took place, after which Wellington returned to Portugal.

Leaving Talavera, I was given, as an escort, a battalion of the *infanterie de marine*,* the commander of which claimed for himself the control of the entire convoy. He dictated when it should leave, when it should halt, and where it came to rest; this was contrary to the rules that invested the responsibility in the leader of the convoy and accorded him complete control. This commander pretended that he was unable to start his march until after I had left, and held his battalion well to the rear, in spite of endangering the whole convoy by his actions; this was particularly the case beyond the Tagus, where the Principe's band operated. I made a complaint when we reached Galvez. I was then given an infantry battalion, the commander of which behaved in the same way. It was said that infantrymen disliked being commanded by an artillery officer. I was not in the mood to tolerate this sort of thing, and complained to the marshal himself and he agreed with me.

The return to France. At Galvez on 15 October I received some news that filled me with joy. This was my appointment as commander of the 1st Squadron of the artillery train and the order to report to Strasbourg to the depot of the corps. Nothing could have made me happier than to return to France and to be garrisoned at Strasbourg. But being authorised to leave Spain was not sufficient, one had to be able to do it, and all the country was so infested with guerrillas that it was necessary to wait until one could join a mobile column.

* An army corps serving alongside the French navy on overseas operations.

So, it was not until 2 November that I was able to leave Galvez in order to go to Toledo, where I had to wait for a convoy to leave for Madrid.

Toledo was a big town in a picturesque setting. It was built in very hilly country on the right bank of the Tagus, where the river encircled it on three sides. We used the Alcazar, built by the Moorish kings, as our citadel. Only its interior was noteworthy. The courtyard was surrounded by a gallery supported by columns, each formed of a single block of granite. The cathedral was huge and majestic, but a closed choir interrupted the view of the interior, this being a defect that was common to almost all the churches in Spain.

On the plain, on the opposite bank of the Tagus, was the place where the famous Toledo blades were made. The bishop's palace, the cathedral and the town hall formed the three sides of a triangular 'square'. From the town wonderful views, extending far over the countryside, could be enjoyed, but there were practically no trees to be seen, so the vista was a little monotonous. General headquarters were at Toledo, where I found General Foy, the commander of the 1st Division, and was invited to dine with him.

On the 6th I left Toledo at last and arrived at Madrid on the 8th where I was forced to remain until the 29th, so that for twenty-one days I had the time to look around and wear out my boots.

Madrid is perfectly planned. The roads are well placed and aligned, something that is unusual in Spain. The town lies on a high plateau above the left bank of the Mançanarès, but the surrounding countryside is bare and unattractive. There are fine promenades with many fountains both inside and beyond the city walls. The best is the Prado, lying between the town and the Retiro, a sort of fort to which the royal family retreated during Holy Week. The gates of the town are handsome, simple monuments to military architecture.

The artillery museum contained nothing of interest except relief maps of different systems of fortification, notably those of Montalembert.* The museum was quite well stocked.

The royal palace was a handsome, square building overlooking the Mançanarès. The Corinthian columns of the façade were built into the wall instead of being free-standing, and the interior courtyard resembled a cloister. There was a magnificent staircase, similar to the one at Caserta Castle near Naples, and two handsome alabaster lions were to be seen there.

There was not a single genuinely interesting weapon in the armoury.

After my long, enforced stay in Madrid, I left the capital on the 29th under a powerful escort composed of the Imperial Guard that was returning to Valladolid.

---

* General Marc René Montalembert (1714–1800), pioneer of nineteenth-century fortifications. He introduced the polygonal layout.

 howtext THE FRENCH ARMY LEAVING LEIPZIG howtext
The defeated French converge in a chaos of troops, wagons, caissons and gun
carriages in their retreat towards the Lindenau causeway, the only road over the
swamps to the west of Leipzig, in order to escape the encircling Allied armies

～ MARSHAL ～
JOACHIM MURAT, PRINCE AND
KING OF NAPLES

～ MARSHAL ～
NICOLAS
JEAN-DE-DIEU SOULT

～ GENERAL ～
JEAN ANDOCH JUNOT,
DUKE OF ABRANTES

～ GENERAL ～
ANTOINE HENRI,
BARON JOMINI

෨ MARSHAL ANDRÉ MASSÉNA, PRINCE OF ESSLING ෨

✍ MARSHAL PRINCE JOSEPH ANTON PONIATOWSKI ✍

∽ ALEXANDER I, CZAR OF RUSSIA ∾

❧ Field Marshal Gebhard Lebrecht von Blücher ❧

❧ NAPOLEONIC ARTILLERY ❧

Guns were dragged into position by teams of horses (*top left*). After firing, the gun was run back from its recoil, the smoking barrel sponged (*top right*), another round rammed home and the vent primed before the next shot was aimed. Heavier guns were used for the more static siege work (*above*)

There were seven stages to be covered between Madrid and this town and it took us twelve days to complete them.

Nothing could be more tedious than this method of travelling, and one's patience was severely tried, especially that of those who, like me, were impatient to reach France and to see their families once more.

We were forced to wait again for another convoy at Valladolid, that horrible town, bleak and filthy.

At last, on 25 December, we came to Irun, the last Spanish town, where we should have slept. However, with several companions, as eager as myself, we continued on our way and, on that same Christmas Day, crossed the Bidassoa.

It would be quite impossible for me to describe the emotion we all felt. When we saw the frontier we all started to run and, the Bidassoa once crossed, I believe that, if fear of what the others would think had not held us back, we should have kissed the soil of our beloved country.

What a contrast it was! A truly happy Christmas. Everything delighted me. There was such a difference in appearances, customs, character and behaviour. We were greeted by cheerfulness and smiles and, instead of the dark and ugly clothes of the Spanish, we saw the delicate and elegant costume of the French Basques.

I went to Spain on 31 January 1810 and left it on 25 December 1811. I had been there for two years – and for what purpose? I had been on campaign throughout the entire period, marching, in camp, bivouacking, never remaining in garrison, suffering both physically and mentally and without any recreation, seldom even engaged in battle, but always under the eyes of the enemy, denied any respite and constantly alert. And all this to no purpose and with no apparent result. The Wagram campaign, when everything had been so swiftly achieved, had been quite different, for then fatigue had been cheerfully borne because the goal had been clearly seen and quickly reached.

The wars in Spain and Portugal were iniquitous wars and disastrously void of glory. While two hundred thousand men – excellent soldiers – were uselessly occupied for five years in pursuit of an illusory conquest, Napoleon raised three hundred thousand conscripts to march to conquer Russia.

Chapter Seven

The Russian Campaign (1812)

Returning to France: Strasbourg. At last, on Christmas Day, 25 December 1811, I crossed the Bidassoa. But I was then obliged to remain for three days at Bayonne so that I could receive my back pay, and also to dispose of a mule and various articles that I had needed on campaign.

Not caring to travel by stages from Bayonne to Strasbourg, I left my horses in the care of my servant who was to join me at Saint-Dié and travelled to Paris by way of Toulouse, where the depot of the regiment to which I was attached was then stationed. Public coaches took eight days to cover the distance between Toulouse and Paris. As far as Orléans the inns were bad and dirty. In Languedoc the people were oafish and crudely insolent. They had no liking for the military.

I stayed for three days in Paris. At the war ministry I was told that I was recommended for promotion to the rank of lieutenant colonel, and that the command assigned to me was only an apprenticeship for this rank. I was told, too, that this command – awarded to senior artillery officers – was a mark of confidence that there would be an end to the wastage previously suffered under the commanders of artillery trains, and that, as a matter of principle, artillery officers would be placed at the head of these train organisations in order to instil in them the sense of discipline for which our branch of the service was so justly known.

I was at Nancy on 16 January and at Saint-Dié on the 17th, so very happy to be with my family after such a long absence. I waited there very patiently for my horses, which were travelling in stages, and Souillé arrived with them after a journey of forty days.

Reaching Strasbourg on 8 February, I settled myself, with my family, and took up my new duties.

The organisation of the artillery train formations left much to be desired. A few days after my arrival a young quartermaster blew his brains out, leaving me with a large deficit that cost me a half-year's pension as an officer of the Légion d'Honneur.

I had fifteen days' rest between the campaigns of Wagram and Spain, and six weeks between those of the Peninsula and Russia. It was not much, but that was the soldier's fate in times such as we lived in, and one was obliged to bear it.

I had scarcely started on my way when my destination was changed. Orders arrived for me to proceed to Berlin to the general headquarters of the artillery.

Berlin. Old Prussia. Elbing. I travelled by way of Frankfurt, Leipzig – a large and handsome town in beautiful countryside - and Düben, where the sand dunes began, and at last reached Berlin on 15 April.

The capital of Prussia was one of the finest cities in Europe; the houses were like palaces and the public buildings were magnificent. There were fine promenades in the centre and at the gates of the town and impressive roads of nearly a league in length. But this construction could be criticised as being only an illusion and intended solely for effect. It is hard to understand how such a fine town could have been built in such an unattractive countryside. For twenty leagues around there was nothing but sand dunes and forest, the villages were poor and the peasants looked wretched.

The king of Prussia had left his capital, there were no Prussian soldiers to be seen, and the French performed all the civic administration of the town. It was easy to see that the inhabitants did not like us, but they bore their ill fortune bravely. If we were to be at war with Russia and if the Prussians were to be on our side, it would be against their will and we should be well advised to be wary of this ally.

War had not been declared and there were many who hoped that it would never take place. Why then were these preparations being made and troops concentrated on the Vistula? It was to be hoped that the Emperor would finally set a term to his ambition, and devote more time to the welfare of the French people, who were worn out by these endless wars. What could be the goal of a war against Russia? If successful, what could we acquire from them? If defeated, all these false friends, who only supported us because they were forced to do so, would turn against us. This was the opinion of all the officers around me.

I had started to make my journey by stages, accompanied by my faithful servant, Souillé, who had followed me everywhere since 1804. However, I grew tired of this slow method of travel, and left him to continue the journey with my horses, while I took advantage of horses requisitioned in the country to proceed in double stages. This was at the same time quicker, more pleasant and more economical for, as the Germans had continued the excellent habit of feeding the military personnel billeted on them, I had only to pay for the tips I handed out to servants.

Instead of joining my army corps, which was already on the Niemen, General Lariboisière,* the commander-in-chief of the artillery, instructed me to take delivery

---

* General Jean-Ambroise Baston Lariboisière, count of La Riboisière (1759–1812) . An artillery officer who had become acquainted with Napoleon in the La Fère Regiment, he served as director general of the artillery parks of the Grande Armée, and took part in all the campaigns of 1805, 1806, 1807 and 1808. Serving in Russia, he died at Königsberg as a result of the hardships he suffered during the retreat from Russia in 1812.

of the four thousand remount horses intended for the artillery and which were to be supplied by Prussia, first at Marienburg and later at Elbing; I was also to allocate these animals to the various formations of the train as they should be needed. I left Berlin after a short stay and travelled to Marienburg by way of Custrin, which was completely protected by two streams of the river Warta flowing into the Oder. The fortification of this town consisted of only a bastioned rampart with a few small demi-lunes, and its underground works were in a bad condition, so I doubt that they would have provided shelter from bombs.

The route as far as the Vistula lay through sand dunes. I crossed the river at Thorn, where it was wider than the Rhine at Mayence.

On the right bank of the river was the small town of Graudenz, built at the foot of a fort of which the French had been unable to obtain possession by the treaty of Tilsit, and which was still denied to us.

On 3 May I reached Marienburg, a small town on the river Nogat, the right branch of the Vistula. This was a dirty town, foul and filled with rubbish with which whole roads were cluttered and which the city police made no attempt to remove. The inhabitants detested the French. There was an old château there that had earlier been, so it was said, the residence of the Grand Masters of the Teutonic Order. Clearly, neither these Grand Masters nor their knights had inculcated habits of cleanliness in their subjects, nor developed any charitable impulses in them. I was billeted with an old rascal who had a wife even more wicked than he was himself.

Fortunately, I did not stay very long at Marienburg, and on 1 June the remount depot was established at Elbing.

The busy and attractive city of Elbing, with about eighteen thousand inhabitants, was built on the bank of a navigable river that emptied into the Frische Haff. This was a long, narrow lagoon separated from the Baltic by a flat tongue of land and connected with it only by a narrow channel. Several rivers, as well as a branch of the Vistula, flowed into this stretch of water. The expanse of the Frische Haff was continually diminished as a result of the silt carried down into it by these rivers, and the residents living near the water acquired land that was extremely fertile by building drainage ditches and dykes.

It was said, in the area, that it was the Teutonic knights of Marienburg who were the first to build the dykes that had enriched the inhabitants.

If I had judged the inhabitants of Elbing by my host, who was a doctor, I should have received a favourable impression, but he was an exception, for they were uncouth like true Prussians, dishonest, greedy and filled with hatred for the French. All of them, especially those in authority, did everything they could to harm our army. Our dealings with them were very unpleasant.

The kindness of my hosts made me forget the rudeness of their compatriots. In the course of my long stay a child was born to them; I was present at the baptism and saw, for the first time, a Protestant christening. Unhappily, the doctor's father died a few days later, and I also attended the funeral. I was given a place of honour at the meals that were served at each of these two contrasting family occasions. This courtesy shown by my hosts did not in any way prevent them from being good patriots.

Farine,[*] a colonel of dragoons, commanded the remount depot. I was responsible for receiving the horses for the train and was in command of depots in several different places. This obliged me to move frequently and I had the opportunity to visit all of Old Prussia and to observe the hatred with which we were regarded, and which amused me at the time. They were indeed nasty people.

I was at Elbing when, on 22 June, the army was told, by means of a grandiloquent proclamation, that war was declared.

The Emperor, of course, blamed Russia for everything that was wrong, he accused the Tsar of having broken his promises, and declared that Russia was doomed. This proved an ill-fated prophecy, for less than two years were to pass before the Tsar proclaimed, in Paris, the overthrow of Napoleon and the dismemberment of France.

The French army crossed the Niemen on 24 June.

I returned to Elbing in order to hasten the despatch to the campaign artillery of the horses I had collected. Towards the end of October, I was ordered to form two artillery train companies to provide the horses for two artillery batteries of which I was to take command. These were to join the 34th Division that was forming at Königsberg under the command of General Loison, and was composed of conscripts from the Confederation of the Rhine.

I provided these two companies with the finest horses, and few batteries could have been better equipped. Apart from the troops of the train, I had, under my command, two companies of foot artillery, each with a hundred men and, as adjutant, Captain Odeyer.

From Ebling to Vilna. I left Elbing on 31 October in order to go to Königsberg, the capital of Old Prussia. Until this time the autumn had been wonderfully fine, but during the night, the temperature dropped and, when we set out on 1 November, we were disagreeably surprised by the extreme cold.

I arrived at Königsberg on the 2nd and was so rudely greeted by a certain baron, who was to give me lodgings, as well as by his wife, who was a veritable shrew, that I was forced to seek another billet where I was made more welcome. I remained at Königsberg until 15 November, awaiting supplies that had been sent by sea from Danzig, but before they had all arrived, I was ordered to leave, with the cannon and

* General Pierre-Joseph, Viscount Farine du Creux (1770–1816).

several caissons, to follow the infantry that had already reached Kovno. I left Captain Odeyer at Königsberg, with instructions to follow me with the remainder of the supplies.

We had had only very vague news of the army, communications with its rearguard having been disrupted. The uncertainty of our destination and my own knowledge of the poverty of Poland made me determined to take advantage of my stay in Königsberg – that city of provisions – to obtain personal supplies of wine, rice, coffee, sugar, soup tablets etc. at a cost to me of more than 400 francs. It was as well that I did so for, without it, I do not know how I should have survived the retreat from Vilna to Kovno. I was able later to help several comrades who, without me, would have died of hunger, notably General Neigre.* He was a colonel at that time and came to take refuge in my bivouac at Ewia when he was utterly destitute.

The weather grew colder and snow covered the ground.

We set out again for Kovno on the left bank of the Niemen. We reached Tilsit on the 20th It was here that, a few years earlier, the two Emperors, who were now at war, had sworn eternal friendship.

After Tilsit we left Prussia and entered the Grand Duchy of Warsaw. Our road lay between almost endless pine forests. Only Jews lived in the villages. The misery and squalor afflicting these people was horrifying. Their houses were mere hovels resembling stables. In Poland there were only aristocrats and the wretched; there was no middle class, for the feudal system, with all its abuses, still reigned there. It was this regime that had destroyed the country. Pride, and the rivalries of the nobility, had been its ruin.

There were many fine views along our route as it followed the course of the Niemen. Castles could be seen in the distance, providing a contrast with the miserable appearance of the villages, yet not, apparently, indicating any great affluence either.

We arrived at Kovno on the 26th in increasing cold.

Kovno was a little town in Lithuania standing on the right bank of the Niemen at the junction of the river Vilia.

The Niemen, separating the Grand Duchy of Warsaw from Russia, was a beautiful river, about 300 paces wide, and the Vilia, near the bridges, was about 230 paces.

There was a large depot at Kovno containing the year's supply of food, drink and ammunition; the town had been fortified with earthworks.

I remained at Kovno to await the arrival of the caissons that should have reached me there, but an order from General Happensburg, one of the Emperor's aides-de-camp and the governor of the town, obliged me to leave without these supplies. This

---

* General Gabriel Neigre (1774–1847).

measure, taken no doubt as a result of the general's knowledge of the Grand Armée's retreat, was unfortunate, for if I had stayed at Kovno for a few more days, my sixteen cannon, in good condition and well supplied with ammunition, would have been available to support the retreat.

I had to leave Kovno with only the supplies that I had brought with me. No one in the town knew what was happening.

The cold became so intense, in spite of the fact that it was only 4 December, that the hills became impassable and we were forced from the road and had to take to the fields.

On the 5th we came to the little town of Zimory. As we had had to spend the night in small villages that were not upon our route, the magistrates in those places had refused to provide forage in exchange for my vouchers, so I had commandeered it. They came to complain to the commandant at Zimory; this was a German *chef de bataillon,* a stupid and arrogant individual. We quarrelled, and things became so violent that we repaired immediately to the duelling ground. A *chef de bataillon* who was passing through intervened and finally made monsieur the commandant of the town see reason.

I was quartered with the postmaster at Ewia on the 6th. In the morning, just as I was about to mount my horse, my host took me aside to tell me that matters were going very badly and that the Emperor had passed through Ewia in a sledge that same night on his way to Paris.* We had no news of the army and I could hardly believe what this Lithuanian had told me. Nevertheless, I was very disturbed and did not know what to think. The position must have been very bad for the Emperor to abandon the struggle and leave the army secretly, almost alone, and without any preparation having been made for his journey. A dark shadow fell across my soul at this news, coming as it did, there in the midst of a snow-covered countryside, with half-burned villages all around and in the bitter cold.

I came to Kykouty, a miserable, burned village, on the 7th. There at last I met some army personnel. The bad news they gave me still failed, however, to convey any idea of the extent of the disaster that had befallen us.

Two leagues from Vilna on the 9th, the road fell steeply through forests. This was Mount Ponary.

Encountering the ruins of the Grand Armée. The difficulty in descending this steep and icy slope with my horses and cannon in a temperature of twenty-two degrees forced me to decide to halt my convoy on the summit, and examine the route myself

* General Armand Augustin Louis de Caulaincourt, duke of Vicenza (1773–1827) was an equerry to Napoleon during the Russian campaign and returned with him to Paris from Smorgoni. He succeeded Duroc as grand marshal of the palace in 1813.

before undertaking it. It was as I, accompanied only by a single officer, went down the hillside on foot that I came across the first signs of the ruin of our army. I could not at first believe that this was, indeed, the Grand Armée. But very soon I could no longer doubt.

It was, indeed, the miserable wreckage of the magnificent army of four hundred thousand men that, six months earlier, had crossed the Niemen, and that had, in every engagement, consistently defeated the Russians. The appearance of this disorderly mob was truly pitiful. It is impossible to imagine a more tragic picture, and I was unable to comprehend what I saw or to express the anger and despair that I felt.

It was a rabble, a mass of haggard men, slovenly, and in rags, who stumbled forward lurching into each other, seeming to see nothing, hear nothing and understand nothing. All ranks were muddled together, officers and troops, cavalry and infantry, French, Italians and Germans, without their weapons, clad in tattered finery, cloaks, sacks, the skins of newly killed animals, and with footwear made from old clothes and hats.

Here before us was the result of this senseless war; here was a revelation of what the mad ambition of a single man had done to these soldiers: soldiers who had marched as victors into almost all the capitals of Europe and, having defended France from foreigners, had then been dragged into wars of conquest. I cursed ambition; I feared what the consequences of such a disaster would be on us all, and I thought of all my brave comrades who had gone to Russia, many of whom would never return.

The road down into Vilna was choked by this crowd and by vehicles unable to move forward. And this was nothing but the beginning of the confusion of the next two days, for it was at the foot of this cursed hill that the army abandoned the last of its cannon and was about to lose everything that had survived the passage of the Beresina.

Finding it quite impossible to move my convoy down into Vilna, I finally positioned my artillery at the top of the Ponary hill, and went forward as far as the town in search of orders, should that be possible.

It was with great difficulty that I found Marshal Ney, whom I had known in Portugal, and General Loison, of the division to which I was attached, who was with him. They delayed giving me my orders until the following day, and it was not until the afternoon of the 9th that I was instructed to remain in my position on the summit of Ponary hill. I had no doubt that Marshal Ney wished me to march with him as part of the rearguard. This appeared to be likely as the army was without any cannon and I had two complete batteries with good horses.

I hurried to leave Vilna but, when I reached the foot of the hill, I found that it was impossible to clear a path through the crowd. Men, horses, carts were piling up in the road, crammed together, crushing and overturning each other. Ignorance, fear and stupidity kept this mass of humanity on the one road, rather than seeking another way across the countryside.

Realising that I could not force my way through, and impatient to rejoin my artillery park, I set off in spite of the darkness through the forest on my left, and after climbing the side of a gorge, I reached the top without too much difficulty.

Officers of the artillery train who had stayed at Vilna had assured me that there was another road to Kovno, going round Ponary hill. The chaos was such that it had not been pointed out or clearly marked.

I reached my bivouac where I awaited the morrow anxiously.

Throughout the day and night of the 9th my soldiers busied themselves in climbing on to carts and lending help. It was given to those who paid them best.

At Vilna I had seen the remains of the army plunging like a torrent into the town. From daybreak on the 10th the same scene was repeated before my eyes at the top of Ponary hill. Not a single organised formation appeared, but just a mass of men from all countries thinking of nothing but flight. And no orders reached me.

I was waiting, all ready to move, when, at about eight or nine o'clock, I was summoned by the king of Naples,* who was in his carriage. He had been surprised as he passed by to see sixteen cannon in good condition by the roadside, and sent for the commander. I explained the situation to him and the fact that I had received no orders. Murat leant towards me and said, very softly, 'Commander, we are f....d; jump on your horse and clear off!'

Behold the leader to whom the Emperor, as he deserted the army, had confided the task of reorganising the ruins and restoring its morale. I obeyed the instructions of this commanding general and ordered the gun teams to be harnessed. I mounted my horse and we returned along the congested road towards Kovno.

The retreat to Kovno. Twenty of my men, all of them Dutch, had died of the cold while we waited on the top of Ponary hill and others were in danger of a similar fate. The cold was so intense that I could not remain long in the saddle; attempting to repair the traces of a harness, the tips of my fingers froze and the skin stuck to the iron buckles. I was wearing, as well as a jacket and undershirt of wool, my uniform greatcoat, a tunic of sheepskin with the fleece inside, and over everything my regulation cloak. Despite all this clothing the cold went right through me.

My losses of soldiers of the train had forced me to entrust the driving of the guns and wagons to the gunners. So matters were already in disarray when I set off again on the 10th. We were marching all day and sometimes part of the night, without any regular shelter.

* Marshal Murat, who had been appointed to command the survivors of the Grande Armée when Napoleon had left for Paris on 5 December 1812.

The gunners, employed as temporary drivers, did not enjoy this work which was in any case difficult, and they neglected their horses and abandoned or overturned the gun carriages, often on purpose. I received no support from the disheartened officers, and so was unable to save a single one of these gun carriages; and the gunners disappeared into the crowd.

But the main reason for the losses I suffered was a fatal measure taken by Marshal Bessières* to protect the army treasury wagons.

These wagons had been abandoned by the roadside. The marshal halted my convoy and, in spite of my protests – for harried as we were by the Russians we had more need of guns than of money – he ordered me to load my wagons with the barrels of money. That which I had foreseen took place. The lure was tempting; accordingly the carts loaded with money soon vanished. The confusion was so great, and it was so easy to avoid scrutiny, that there was no way in which anyone could be held responsible for these losses.

At the last stopping place before Kovno, when I went to the artillery park at about three in the morning to give instructions for the harnessing to start, I saw an officer of the train – Belchamps – who was loading two barrels of money into one of his company's carts. His sense of duty had become so confused that he had the impudence to suggest that I should do the same. I was furious and heaped reproaches on him; he disappeared that same day.

I reached Kovno on the 12th quite early but we were in a wretched state, having lost guns, caissons, gun carriages and most of my men – officers as well as troops. The crowd at the entrance of the town was so great that I could not force my way through, as I should have done. Hoping that things would be easier on the next day, I parked outside. But, day and night, the horde continued to flood into Kovno, always in the same state of chaos.

On the 12th one of the treasury carts was abandoned at the gate of Kovno. My gunners quickly learned what was in it and, despite my threats, I could not stop the looting. However, in accordance with my orders and with a view to keeping my gunners at their posts, a captain, whose name I regret I have forgotten, took several sacks of money from them, and I entrusted it to his care, so that he could issue it to the troops and the officers as part of the pay that was due to them. An account of this would be sent to an army paymaster. One hour later this captain had vanished and I never saw him again. This looting was another reason for the troops who took part in it to abscond.

At about two in the afternoon, the Cossacks, who had been following the rear of the army, took up their position in a convent in front of Kovno and began to bombard

* Marshal Jean Baptiste Bessières (1768–1813).

us. Chaos resulted. My soldiers of the train abandoned their horses or led them away. Nevertheless, I managed to rally some of them in spite of the hail of bullets directed upon us by the enemy, and I was able, at last, to go into the town with the guns that remained to me. In compliance with direct orders from Marshal Ney I abandoned some caissons, first blowing them up, for I did not want them to be of use to the Russians.

The defence of Kovno. When I entered Kovno I placed my three guns as a battery on a small hill to the rear of, and dominating, the fortifications.

My guns, and a battalion from Lippe (Westphalia), were added to the town's usual defences.

The commander of this battalion was killed by the first enemy shots and his troops were scattered. Only those few gunners who were not serving the cannon were available to sustain the fusillade. It was at this moment that Marshal Ney and General Gérard,* who were in our midst, seized guns and began shooting, contributing to the defence.

My first cannon shot dismounted one of the enemy guns that had been mounted on a sledge, and the second ploughed through a column of Cossacks that was attempting to cut off our retreat by crossing the Niemen on the ice. This was enough to dampen the ardour of the enemy who, with a little more courage, could have wiped us out.

However, what made our situation more precarious and could have had disastrous results, if the enemy had been more enterprising, was the fact that all firing from the town's guns had stopped at the beginning of the attack. These guns had been spiked, just when they were most needed, either because of a misheard order, or through loss of presence of mind on the part of an artillery officer. I cannot describe the anger and indignation that Marshal Ney directed towards the unhappy officer who had committed such an act. If he had not been prevented he would have run his sword through his body.

At Kovno I was able to observe, once again, how panic was spread, turning men into the likeness of fear-driven animals.

The alleyway through the fortifications was narrow and steep and the ground was icy. Soldiers who fell were trampled under the feet of men and horses, and the wretched wounded were abandoned pitilessly. The fortifications came to an end at the banks of the Niemen, which was now frozen solid. As a result there was an unobstructed pathway, without any obstacle between the two banks, and by this means the blocked way through the fortifications could have been avoided. Although this path was barely a hundred paces from the gate, and although I went along it several times

---

* General Maurice-Étienne, Count Gérard (1773–1852).

to show the way, I failed to persuade even those on foot to use it, and the crowd, blinded by fear, insisted on rushing into the town by a difficult and dangerous route.

We bombarded the Russians until nightfall, and this, fortunately, made them more circumspect. I believe that these were the last cannon-shots that the French army fired in Russia.

We evacuated Kovno at eight in the evening after burning down the warehouses and the bridges. Lacking horses, I was able to take only four 6-pound cannon and a caisson with me. These were the only guns to return over the Niemen.

There were many stores of food and drink in Kovno. No one thought to make a distribution of these things to the starving troops, so there was looting and many tragedies resulted. Houses were burned down and drunken soldiers, warming themselves at these fires, fell stupefied, never to rise again. The route that we followed on the evening of the 13th was strewn with the bodies of the wretches overcome by the cold. At Kovno there had been a massive supply of weapons intended for the armament of the Lithuanian conscripts; all was destroyed.

The duke of Fézensac,* aide-de-camp of the prince of Neufchâtel and peer of France, gives an account of the occurrences at Kovno in his memoirs, an extract of which appeared in the *Revue des Deux Mondes* of 1 April 1843. This account is generally accurate, but some of the details are not. The duke should not have spoken of this defence, except as by hearsay, for he certainly was not present whereas I was one of those involved.

The duke of Fézensac reports:

An earthworks, constructed hastily before the Vilna gate, seemed to Marshal Ney to provide an adequate defence to hold the enemy all day. During the morning the rearguard arrived in the town. Two cannons, supported by some troops provided by the Bavarian infantry, were stationed on the ramparts and these few men prepared to confront the attack. The first cannon shots dismounted one of the guns, and the infantry fled; the gunners were preparing to do the same when Marshal Ney appeared on the ramparts, seized a gun and fired on the enemy. The troops returned to their posts, the battle continued and went on until nightfall when he ordered the retreat.

In the state in which the army found itself, it would indeed have been very difficult to build an earthworks in a hurry, but in twenty degrees of frost it would have been completely impossible, for the ground was frozen solid. As an important centre of supplies Kovno had, throughout the campaign, been fortified with a continuous circle of

* Raymond-Emery-Philippe-Joseph de Montesquiou, count of Fézensac (1784–1867).

earthworks to counter an attack. I had inspected this fortification when I arrived in Russia, as I invariably visited the defences of any place I passed through, and I wrote a clear description of them in my diary.

It was on a hillock, behind the fortifications and near the Vilna gate that I placed my battery, which consisted, not of two, but of three guns. The ramparts should have been protected by the town artillery but those guns had unfortunately been spiked.

An entire battalion of the Lippe was assigned for the defence, not just a few troops of Bavarian infantry. The Bavarians were better soldiers than the Hessians. None of my guns was dismounted; on the contrary, it was one of my cannon that dismounted the only Russian gun that we found in front of us.

The Hessians fled to the last man, and not one had returned. This bad example had not deterred our gunners; they had not left their posts and had no need of encouragement by the bravery of Marshal Ney.

Finally, if the duke of Fézensac had been present, he would hardly have failed to mention General Gérard, who had fired shot for shot with Marshal Ney, as I have always maintained.

I met my adjutant, Captain Odeyer, at Kovno with the wagons that had been intended to complete my batteries. As soon as I arrived, I ordered him to send them to the heights above the left bank, on to the route to Gumbinnen. But, because the climb had become too slippery, only a few of them could be taken there, and the rest remained at Kovno where they were blown up at the time the town was evacuated. I found Captain Odeyer again at Königsberg; he had abandoned his position on the heights in time to avoid being cut off by the Cossacks who had finally crossed the Niemen on the ice. It was this movement by the enemy that had forced us, at first, when we left Kovno, to follow the road to Tilsit.

From Kovno to Königsberg. The rearguard, formed from the remains of the 3rd Corps, and under the orders of General Marchand, left Kovno at eight in the evening of the 13th; they marched along the Tilsit road, and my artillery led the column. I marched with the first gun, and continued on my way, instead of stopping at Tapiecizky where the column halted without my knowledge. I reached a village near Mikity on the following morning, and waited there for several hours before being joined by the second cannon. The others, warned in time, followed the column that had taken a direction to the left, between Tapiecizky and Mikity; but the road was too difficult. I learned later that my three wagons which had followed this route were overturned and had been abandoned.

At about nine o'clock on the morning of the 14th I hurried to set off with my two guns, in the hope of rallying the remains of the 4th Corps that, it was said, had taken the road I was following to Tilsit. However, as I only met a few isolated individuals, and having only the solidly frozen Niemen as protection on my flank, I was also afraid that these stragglers would attract parties of Cossacks, so I took a road to the left, leading to Neustadt, which one of the inhabitants had pointed out to me

I had no escort except about twenty gunners and a single officer, a young Dutch lieutenant who, throughout the campaign, had never left me. The horses were very weary and in poor condition. We halted when we were obliged to do so and we always found shelter as there were many villages on the way.

Throughout this journey, completely alone on the vast, snow-covered plain where we could be seen from far off by enemy detachments, I had to exercise the greatest care; all the more so as the attitude of the inhabitants left me in no doubt as to their hostility to us. I was certain that we should have been attacked if they had known that we were not being followed by other troops. On our arrival in a village where we were to shelter, I sent for the burgomaster and told him that everything with which we were supplied would be paid for in cash by me but, also, that at the slightest threat from them, I would have the village burned down. As a result, I had my guns trained on the main road, near to the last house that I occupied with my men. We kept watch in turn so that surprise was impossible.

The cold continued as bitter as ever, to the point that it was impossible to remain on horseback; but on dismounting to walk, one felt so numb that one could neither move forward nor remount. On foot, crushed with exhaustion and the need for sleep, I found it difficult to overcome the urge to lie down at the roadside, which would certainly have been fatal. Mirage-like impressions continually confused me, and yet I was not hungry. While at Kovno I had sent my servant away with Captain Odeyer, having first supplied myself with provisions, and there were stores of food in the villages where we found ourselves; we were even able to sleep under a roof. But, on the march, I had great difficulty in preventing my men from stretching out and sleeping by the roadside; sometimes I failed and those who slept in the snow never woke again.

I had assumed that the 3rd Corps, being unable to follow the road from Kovno to Königsberg via Gumbinnen, had headed towards Neustadt. I went this way and was happy to arrive at that town on the 16th; there I found the gunners and horses of my battery that had followed the main part of the column. The guns and the carts had been overturned and abandoned.

The country after leaving Neustadt was thickly populated, but the people became more and more hostile to us. The barons, while welcoming our generals to their châteaux, excited their vassals against us and encouraged them to make us pay the highest possible price for everything.

We went to Tapiau on the 19th and to Königsberg on the 20th.

We had a short rest at Königsberg, and took advantage of it to restore some small degree of order to the men and equipment remaining to us. There was a division there that had not taken part in the fatal campaign and we were able to attach ourselves to it. Typhus broke out when we arrived. The artillery suffered especially cruel losses – General Lariboisière, who, a few years earlier, had been responsible for the construction of the raft on the Niemen at Tilsit where the two Emperors met, and General Eblé, known throughout the army as 'Brave' Eblé, who was as good, as efficient and as faithful as he was brave. I had known him in Portugal before the lines of Torres Vedras, and I had the sorrow to be present at his death throes. I also lost a young quartermaster who had been with me for a long while and to whom I was very attached.

The town hospital was crammed with our sick and wounded; the hostility and arrogance of the townsfolk grew as our misfortunes increased. They no longer tried to hide their joy and, had they known the extent of the disasters that had befallen us, it cannot be doubted but that they would have risen up against us. Fortunately, they could not believe that this rabble of undisciplined soldiers, clad in rags, was the Grand Armée, and thought that we were to be followed by other troops.

Some did arrive, in groups, mostly consisting of officers without soldiers. The disorder was so great from the beginning that everyone halted as they wished. One day I saw an officer of the gendarmes of the Imperial Guard leave Königsberg on a sledge, sitting on a barrel that I recognised as being part of the army treasury.

To defy us the inhabitants sang rude songs about us: the refrain of one of them was explained to us: 'Five French to pay for one Prussian, it's not too much', and of another, 'Frederick has only to slap his thigh with his glove for the French to flee'. It was as well that we did not then understand them, for despite our dreadful situation we had not been reduced to letting ourselves be insulted.

Being virtually the only able-bodied senior artillery officer, I was given command of a battery that had been put together with difficulty from Prussian equipment. A few days before the evacuation of Königsberg, Marshal Berthier* reviewed the division. My battery was still not ready and the marshal reprimanded me. I answered that I could only parade what had been delivered to me. But General Charbonnel, who was in charge of the organisation, had either been unable, or had neglected, to complete it for the review, and held me responsible me for the failure, so that I received the blame despite my protests. It is thus that the blame for the carelessness and errors of leaders falls on the heads of their innocent subordinates.

Time was short and a swift reorganisation had to be made, after a fashion, from whatever materials there were at hand: not in order to dispute the Niemen line with the Russians, for the river was completely frozen, and we were quite unable to do so, but to put up some resistance against the enemy corps who had crossed on the ice. Our commander-in-chief, Murat, had lost his head, and everything showed the effects

* Marshal Louis-Alexandre Berthier, prince of Neuchatel and Wagram (1753–1815).

of this loss of energetic leadership. What was needed at such a moment was the organising genius of the Emperor, his coolness and authority.

Soon consideration had to be given to leaving Königsberg in order to withdraw behind the Vistula. A Prussian corps which formed the main force of Marshal Macdonald's army had just defected to the Russians; they were advancing together on Königsberg from Tilsit.

In this evacuation of the capital of old Prussia could be seen again the lack of intelligent leadership.

The massive supplies intended for the siege of Riga were still in Königsberg. As they could not be moved, it would be necessary to destroy them so that they were denied to the enemy. And, in truth, one wonders what the officers in charge of this duty were thinking of. For, to get rid of the projectiles, the ice covering the Pregel was broken and the cannon-balls were rolled into the river, watched by the inhabitants gathered on the bank and laughing at this absurd method of cheating our enemies of them.

What was even more terrible for us than the loss of these supplies (we had already lost many more in Russia) was the forced desertion of our unhappy sick and wounded who were filling the hospitals of Königsberg. The townspeople could not be relied upon to provide care but at least, although the Prussians were harsh, they were not cruel and it was certain that our comrades in arms would not be abandoned to the same fate as that of the wounded of Verona and Coïmbra, massacred in 1797 by the Italians and, in 1811, by the Portuguese. We left surgeons and nurses behind with them, as well as money for their needs.

After the artillery remaining at Königsberg had been destroyed as far as possible, and the contents of the warehouses, instead of being distributed to the troops, had been delivered up to the greed of the Jews and the townspeople, the army evacuated the town during the night of 4/5 January 1813. At three o'clock in the morning of the 5th I reached Brandenburg with my division, the 34th, under the command of General Marchand.

Chapter Eight

The Campaign in Germany (January–August 1813)

From Königsberg to Posen. The Emperor had left the army hurriedly before the final disasters overtook it, and had returned to France to raise a new army. To raise, equip and train an army presented difficulties and required time, especially in view of the successive demands that had been made upon our country. Should we be ready in time to withstand the Russians and survive the defections that were impending?

The residue of our army, having fled from Russia and now being scattered throughout a hostile population, were in no position to offer much resistance to the Russians. However, although the Russians had not suffered as we had, yet the campaign of 1812 had, fortunately, placed them under a severe strain. This was the reason for their indecision in their pursuit of us across the Niemen, although the Prussians – who were still officially our allies – urged them to persist. Some groups of Cossacks did, in fact, cross the river, but they were more of a threat to the people they pillaged than they were to us.

On 10 January 1813, we reached Elbing, where my old host, the good Doctor Quiednau, welcomed me warmly and where we found the general headquarters of our new commanding general, the king of Naples.*

Here I parted company with the division, as it was going on to Danzig. Some of our other troops were sent to Thorn, also on the Vistula, to reinforce the garrison there; Prince Eugène occupied the town.

With the general headquarters, we withdrew to Posen on the Warta, a river that flowed between the Vistula and the Oder before it joined the latter at Custrin. I marched with the artillery of the Imperial Guard and the Royal Neapolitan Guard, under the command of General Desvaux,† for I had no fixed destination and did not know to which corps my battery belonged. We numbered ten thousand men, at most, and we formed the centre of the Grande Armée.

---

* Marshal Murat.
† General Jean-Jacques, Baron Desvaux de Saint-Maurice (1775–1815) He was to be killed at Waterloo.

We reached Tuckel on the 15th; this was a little town built on a hill with only a single line of defence around it. Two thousand Prussians were quartered there and they sought an excuse from the governor to refuse to give us lodgings. Marshal Mortier* was notified of this refusal in the most offensive manner.

On the following day, while we were at the small town of Zempelburg, the two thousand Prussians who had left Tuckel for Friedland passed through singing songs that insulted us. If we had been permitted, what a punishment these jokers would have had! But we had to control ourselves; a clash at this time could have had the most serious consequences by giving the Prussians an excuse to break our alliance.

On the 17th, while we were at Bunowo, the Old Guard, in whose company we were marching, were quartered at Commin. They suddenly came under attack from Cossacks who fired cannon shots on the village at five in the morning. They seized their weapons and rushed out and, by their presence alone, put the Cossacks to flight. A Prussian battalion, lodged in the same village, did not leave their billets, with the exception of a few who came out to fraternise with the Cossacks. Despite our disasters and our terrible situation, the Imperial Guard continued to inspire terror in our enemies, the sight of them was sufficient to put the enemy to flight. I think that a row of bearskins on the parapet would have been enough to defend a town.

Until this time, the Cossack troops that had crossed the Niemen had not been too formidable, but their continual harassment wore us out.

After passing through several little towns, all full of Jews, we reached Posen on the 22nd and on the 27th I was at last told where I should go. I went, with my battery, to the 2nd Division of the Observation Corps, commanded by General Girard.†

Posen was a big town and spread over a large area, for its outlying districts stretched as far as the surrounding villages. The numerous newly built roads of modern appearance gave it quite a pleasant air. It had many attractions but I did not have the time to enjoy them. Our small army corps, gathered in and around Posen and composed of all nationalities, had too many problems to allow any of us the leisure to enjoy the resources and pleasures of a large town. We had no idea what might happen to us if we should retreat further, nor what was the situation and strength of our army. We patiently awaited events.

It was said that the Emperor had informed the Senate of the state of the army. Whatever he had been able to tell them must have been less than the truth. Did he

---

* Marshal Adolphe Édouard Casimir Joseph Mortier, duke of Treviso (1768–1835). He had assumed command of the remnants of the Old Guard in January 1813.

† General Jean-Baptiste, Baron Girard (1775–1815) took part in most of Napoleon's campaigns in the course of his distinguished career. He was mortally wounded on 16 June 1815 during the battle of Ligny while taking the village of Saint-Armand.

himself know the true position? It would have been necessary to have been with the army in these final days in order to give a real account. France would have to bear great sacrifices if we were to be rescued from our present situation. Not to do so would mean the loss of the few who had escaped, and there were already too many families in mourning to risk adding to their number. We hoped that in France, our fate would be of great concern and that, while we had so much to undergo, both mentally and physically, the pleasures of the winter season would be mitigated.

It was unlikely that the Russians would allow us to remain in this country for long. The extraordinary levies that were being raised in France were far from complete and the Prussians seemed to be on the point of turning against us.

The 2nd Division, to which I was attached, was to be composed chiefly of recruits for whose arrival we were still waiting.

While we were at Posen with the general headquarters, our commander, the king of Naples, despondent and quite unable to bring order to anything, abruptly left us to return to his estates. He delegated the command to Prince Eugène, whom he summoned from Thorn.

As a prince and a member of the Imperial family, Eugène's authority was free from the jealousies that, unfortunately, divided our marshals, but among whom there were those who possessed the experience, energy and organising ability that he lacked. However, he was loved and respected by the army, and it was certain that he would carry out his difficult and thankless task with complete devotion.

Of the remains of the Grand Armée, twenty-five thousand men were at Danzig and twenty thousand at Thorn and various towns on the Vistula. There were barely twelve thousand of us with the general headquarters at Posen. Our situation was dangerous, for the Niemen and the Vistula, both still frozen, no longer protected us from the Russians, whose scouts had long since crossed the latter river.

Early in February, the Russian army decided at last to cross the Vistula. Emperor Alexander was well aware of the Prussian attitude towards us, and knew that they only awaited his advance to declare war on us. We had been amazed that he had delayed so long before advancing.

As it was quite impossible for us to oppose the Russians from the position we were in, it was essential to retreat again beyond the Oder, the third line of defence.

The retreat over the Oder. On 2 February I left Wilda, a village near a Posen suburb where we were in barracks, in order to take up a position at Obernick, a small town on the Warta that was already occupied by twelve hundred Westphalians.

After daily alarms, and having been joined by the 4th Regiment of the Vistula Legion that had been forced to abandon Rogasen, we left Obernick on the 12th and travelled down the Warta.

A Cossack position fled at the sight of us at Zirko on the 14th and, three days later on the 17th at Landsberg, the Russian General Czernichef hastened to yield the place to us. He marched towards the Oder, crossed the river and surprised an Italian regiment on the march and overwhelmed it. A short time later he encountered General Grenier coming from Berlin and himself suffered a rude setback.

At Landsberg I received a new proof of the unreasonable demands our allies made on their compatriots, burdens for which we were always blamed.

Under my command I had a weak detachment of Westphalian artillery, commanded by a *chef de bataillon.* He was billeted with me and a few other French officers at the château. This commander threatened, and came near to hitting, our host's servants in order to obtain wine. This he succeeded in getting, while we, the French, contented ourselves with beer.

On the 19th we pushed forward to the Oder in the hope of meeting a Cossack troop that was about to cross the river. The thaw had started and we were hopeful that we might drive them into the Oder. But they had already crossed by the time we arrived and, as the ice had now broken up, we could not follow them.

The Cossacks kept us in a continual state of alarm. We were not afraid of them, but they were always there, harassing us, forcing us always to be alert, but we could never catch them.

As we travelled along the Oder we were able to judge the feelings of the inhabitants towards us. Our advance guard, consisting of Poles, were believed by the peasants to be Russians. As the Poles approached the villages the peasants came to meet them, bringing all manner of refreshments, while bestowing the crudest insults on the French. We ate their food and laughed at them. It was our only revenge.

On the 20th we reached Custrin, where we left the Westphalians to reinforce the garrison there, and crossed the Oder to make for Berlin. General Girard left us on the 21st and was provisionally replaced by General Bronikowsky.*

A road dating from the sixteenth century encircled nearly all the small towns we passed through. We slept at Alt-Landsberg on the 24th, leaving again at eleven in the evening to reach Berlin on the 25th.

I positioned my battery where I was directed. As all the battery's equipment was Prussian, crowds gathered around us and I saw that the time was coming when an effort would be made to seize it, but the determined aspect of my troops inspired respect and the crowd finally dispersed.

We now came under the command of General Poinsot.†

---

* General Nicolas Bronikowsky, count of Oppeln (1772–1813), was badly wounded at the defence of Wittenberg on 18 April 1813 and wounded again at Leipzig, where he was taken prisoner on the following day.

† General Pierre Poinsot, baron de Chansac (1776–1833).

Having camped, together with general headquarters, at the Potsdam gate, where the Prussians forbade us to enter, we went to take up our positions at the bridges over the Havel.

Some troops had joined us in the course of our retreat from Posen to Berlin. General Grenier was garrisoning Berlin and, together with his corps, we began to form an army of forty thousand men, one that would be capable of resisting an attack.

The retreat to the Elbe. The Russian advance on the Elbe made Prince Eugène decide to abandon Berlin, withdraw to the river and reform in the rear of the troops that were already in position there and those that were arriving from France. The Elbe, rising in the mountains of Bohemia and flowing into the North Sea, was our fourth line of defence, the last one before the Rhine.

The army completed its retreat on 5 March, and our division slept at the little Saxon town of Brück.

If it had not been for the arrogance of the Prussians, who seemed to believe that we had retreated because we were afraid of them, I should have been glad to leave the miserable country of Brandenburg with its uncouth inhabitants. I understood the patriotism that inspired their hatred of us. We had been at war with them far less often than with the Austrians, but we had treated them more harshly and our Emperor had spared them no humiliation. It was the coarseness of the people and their presumption that offended us. They spoke only of their great Frederick. Jena and Auerstadt, the flight of their army and the crushing of Prussia after a campaign of only six weeks, seemed entirely to have escaped their memory. They remembered only Rosbach[*] [*sic*].

In Germany, the Prussians were called 'the Gascons of the North'. This was unfair to the Gascons, who, although they were boastful swaggerers, had a lively spirit and good qualities such as never flourished on the banks of the Spree.

Now we found ourselves in Saxony and, from the moment of our arrival, the inhabitants treated us kindly and were quick to keep us informed of the movements of the Russians. I was astonished to find so much sympathy from a people on whom alliance with us had already imposed such a heavy burden.

Even the landscape changed: as we marched towards the Elbe the country improved, becoming more populous and more prosperous. The breed of horses was more handsome.

We reached the little town of Wagen on the 10th. Here the division was placed under the orders of General Gérard, and Marshal Davout commanded our corps.

On the 12th we came to Meissen, where the famous porcelain factory is located. This town stands on the left bank of the Elbe, the two streams of which were united here by a superb covered bridge built on stone piers; we burned this during the night.

---

[*] The battle of Rossbach (5 November 1757), in which the Prussians, under Frederick the Great, defeated a numerically superior French army under Prince Soubise.

Our route followed the lovely valley of the Elbe as far as Dresden, where we arrived on the 13th and remained until the 19th.

Dresden is a large town in a fine position on both banks of the Elbe; that part of it standing on the right bank, named Neustadt, is modern, the other is the old town. A quite remarkable long stone bridge united the two towns and was considered by the inhabitants to be the eighth wonder of the world. They displayed anger and annoyance when Marshal Davout had two arches of the bridge blown up when we evacuated the city.

While we were in Dresden we learned that Prussia had declared war. We were neither surprised nor worried, for it had been anticipated. The king of Prussia had long ago retired to Breslau in Silesia while we occupied his capital. When we abandoned Berlin at the approach of the Russians, he hesitated no longer and began to raise conscripts and volunteers in Prussia who were certainly not intending to help us against the Russians.

This declaration of war was, doubtless, the reason for Marshal Davout's decision to abandon Dresden and draw nearer to Prince Eugène by descending the Elbe towards Magdeburg. The Russians, with whom the Prussians were hoping to link up, were advancing with their principal forces on Dresden.

The unhappy king of Saxony, not wishing to find himself in the middle of belligerent armies, had left his capital, abandoned his estates and retired, escorted by his cavalry, to Ratisbon in Bavaria with his family and his treasure.

We evacuated Dresden on the night of the 19th and slept at Meissen. Our route from there to Torgau still led us down the Elbe valley.

A considerable amount of work was done on the fortifications of Torgau, and, when this was completed, it would be a first-class position. There was a covered bridge over the Elbe in the town, and the bridgehead had defensive earthworks. The approaches from the river also had two separate lunettes. The main fortress was a system of bastions. A fort was built on the left, and this needed to be joined to another on the top of a nearby hill, where Frederick had fought the battle of Torgau.* There were two more lunettes on the left bank that protected the gap between the bridgehead and the first two lunettes.

I had observed that there were short 12-pounder guns included in the armament of the place; these cannon were more dangerous than useful to those who served them, because a volley that failed to pass through it would soon damage the embrasure.

I accompanied General Bronikowsky to Torgau and, during our visit to the governor of the place, the Saxon General Thielman,† I formed the opinion that he had been

* November 1760.
† General Johann Adolf, Freiherr von Thielman (1765–1824) had fought with distinction at Borodino, but later defected on 12 May 1813.

greatly disturbed by the destruction of the bridge at Dresden; his conversation made me feel that we should not depend too much upon him. When we left, I mentioned this to General Bronikowsky. In fact, only a short while afterwards, General Thielman, having tried in vain to persuade his troops to defect, had gone over to the enemy, and he was not one of the least passionate against us. It was this general who organised bands of partisans, ceaselessly harried our rear formations, cut our communications and raised the Saxons against us. In this he was like the illustrious Bernadotte,* more anxious to encourage defection from us than to try his strength with us.

We were at Kemberg and Worlitz on the 24th and 25th. The latter a poor little town, in which stood the residence of the Prince Anhalt-Dessau, a handsome castle in a magnificent English-style park. This park was huge, for most of the country lay within its boundaries.

The countryside was so filled with game that we hunted there without dogs and, to find hares, we employed the little peasants who found the work both pleasant and profitable. All the country was beautiful, prosperous and well populated.

We passed through Dessau, a pretty little town where the inhabitants showed a special liking for the French. The women there, so it was said, were very *galante*.

We were in Magdeburg on the 29th, where my command of the divisional artillery ended when I was appointed, on 11 March, to be inspector general of the artillery train under the orders of General Neigre, the commander-in-chief of the army's main artillery park.

Standing on a wide plain, Magdeburg was a large town on the left bank of the Elbe, with a bridgehead on the right bank and good fortifications. Its many outer works were, nevertheless, separated from each other and inadequate, likely to provide only a weak defence. The town, of which General Haxo† was the governor, was well placed to defend the lower Elbe and had, therefore, been made the main centre for supplies of the food and equipment intended to provision the troops now entering upon the campaign.

I remained at Magdeburg as inspector general of the train until 1 July.

The offensive renewed. Prince Eugène commanded the army that was concentrated at Magdeburg and in the upper reaches of the Elbe as far as Saale, and which was already strong enough, at the beginning of April, to hold the enemy in check.

---

* Marshal Jean Baptiste Jules Bernadotte (1763–1844) was at this time crown prince of Sweden. He identified closely with Sweden, to the detriment of Napoleon's interests, and became king of that country in February 1818.

† General François-Nicolas, Baron Haxo (1774–1838) rallied to Napoleon's cause during the Hundred Days and commanded the engineers of the Imperial Guard at Waterloo, but continued thereafter to serve Louis XVIII and was made a peer of France in 1832.

It was made up of the 5th and 11th Corps, some divisions of the 1st and 2nd, and a small part of the Imperial Guard, more than sixty thousand men in all, resolute and far from disheartened by our long retreat.

As the enemy had advanced on Magdeburg on the right bank, we crossed the river on the 5th and, after a fight very much in our favour we demonstrated that we must again be taken into account.

On the 6th the army recrossed to the left bank and took up a position on the Saale, with its left flank on the river and its right on the Harz mountains, and remained here until the arrival of the Army of Main, commanded by the Emperor. We awaited his arrival impatiently so that we could go on the offensive once more.

The enemy's army, which was said to be more than one hundred thousand strong, had crossed the Elbe at Meissen and at Dresden and had advanced through Saxony towards Leipzig instead of marching to attack us before we joined the Army of Main, or attempting to prevent our doing so.

At the end of April, the Emperor came from the Thuringian mountains and advanced down the Saale; Prince Eugène marched upriver to meet him.

On the 29th Marshal Ney, who was ahead of the Emperor, crossed the Saale and made contact with the enemy's advance guard. The infantry of the Main army consisted of young recruits who had never come under fire, but there were excellent soldiers among them and they were very well led. The whole army anxiously awaited the outcome of this first encounter. The enemy cavalry, reputed to be very numerous and well mounted, was especially feared.

Marshal Ney's infantry formed into squares, and calmly withstood several successive charges from this cavalry; charges that are so terrifying for novice soldiers, and are dreadful even when anticipated. Then, forming into columns and taking the offensive, our soldiers attacked the enemy with spirit and determination and put them to flight. We heard of this outcome with something approaching rapture, seeing it as a good omen for the future.

On the same day our two armies joined each other and together crossed the Saale to march on Leipzig.

The army met the enemy on 1 May on the plains of Lützen, already famous for the victory and the death of Gustavus-Adolphus.* On the same day, in the first engagement, Marshal Bessières was killed, taking a ball full in the chest.

The battle of Lützen took place on 2 May.

Our victory was stubbornly contested. The Prussians, especially, demonstrated a resolve that could only be explained by their ardent patriotism. In spite of their hasty retreat at the end of the day, their pride made it impossible for them to admit defeat, and word of their victory was spread throughout Germany.

---

* Gustavus-Adolphus of Sweden (1594–1632) was killed at the battle of Lützen, 16 November 1632.

Their so-called victory did not prevent them from hastily recrossing the Elbe with their Russian allies. Unfortunately, our lack of cavalry prevented us from pursuing them vigorously enough to change their retreat into a rout.

The French entered Dresden to the terror of the inhabitants who had acclaimed the two sovereigns – Emperor Alexander and the king of Prussia. Napoleon attempted to calm them and forgave them. He recalled his ally, the king of Saxony, to his capital. The Grand Armée followed its enemies across the Elbe. But they had had enough time to rally and receive help, entrenching themselves near Bautzen in Lusace* behind a double line of defence.

The Emperor confronted them, captured Bautzen on the 20th as well as their first defensive line, taking the second line on the 21st and completely routing them.

He pursued them, and threw them back over the Oder on the 22nd. During this engagement a rearguard action took place near Reichenbach in which a ball, ricocheting from a tree, killed the engineer general Keigener† and, at the same time, the grand marshal of the palace, Duroc.‡

The armistice. An armistice was agreed between the two armies on 4 June. It was to last for two months and the news of it was received joyously in the army. This ceasefire was regarded as the prelude to the peace for which everyone longed.

Nowadays, it is imagined that all of us, all the soldiers, yearned for war and that we dreamed only of warfare and battles. This was not true; on the contrary, we all wished for peace. To think that a soldier longs for war is to be ignorant of his life when on campaign. Nothing could be more true than the old saying: 'The glory of the leaders is built from the blood and suffering of the troops.'

Sometimes there are those who are happy at the beginning of a campaign, but very soon, weariness, privation and all kinds of wretchedness rise to crush the desire for war. The excitement of battle briefly obliterates thoughts of danger and fear but, even after a victory, there is the sight of the battlefield: the dead thrown pell-mell into a hastily dug ditch and covered with scant spades-full of earth, the wounded abandoned without help to a fate that one might oneself perhaps share on the morrow. These sights, and the cries to be heard from the field ambulances, speedily cool the most ardent spirits and, unless the war is one of national defence, one soon grows weary.

To miseries like these must be added that of separation from one's own country and family, and the anxiety resulting from the absence of news from home.

---

* A area of eastern Germany adjacent to the Lusace mountains.
† This was actually General François-Joseph Kirgener, baron of Planta (1766–1813), who was killed by a ball that went through his body at waist height.
‡ General Geraud Christophe Michel Duroc, duke of Frioul (1777–1813).

At Dresden, on 15 July, I received a packet of letters, and among them was a deeply affectionate one, dated 15 February, from my father, another dated in the month of April from one of my brothers telling me of my father's illness, and finally, a letter from my wife breaking the news of his death. These letters also informed me that my interests had been jeopardised by an abuse of a power of attorney. However, grief and worries such as these could not be allowed to distract from service as demanding as that of an inspector general of the artillery train of the Grand Armée.

On 30 June, during the armistice, I was appointed major (lieutenant colonel) [sic]. I did not receive this news until the end of July. At the same time I learned, from the minister of war that I had been proposed for admission into the Imperial Guard. Artillery General Sorbier, however, had insisted that I remain as head of the artillery train; and, despite my promotion, I was to continue to perform the same duties. This was gratifying. I would have preferred to go into the Guard, where the service would perhaps have been more dangerous, but would certainly have been less difficult and, above all, have involved less responsibility.

Although part of the artillery, the train was a special formation with its own organisation, uniform and weaponry. This weaponry was inadequate to provide the means of resisting a serious attack. The formation was required to transport the cannon on campaign and on to the battlefield where it also remained, with its horses, within reach of the guns, so that their position could be changed when required. Thus it became the target of balls and bullets but was not able to return fire.

During my retreat from Vilna to Kovno when, lacking soldiers of the train who had died of the cold, I was forced to have the guns moved by gunners untrained for the work, I was able fully to appreciate the defects of this unsatisfactory system, which was later abolished. When the artillery was reorganised in 1828, the train was merged with the artillery, and nowadays the gunners drive the guns, as well as their munitions and all their equipment.

Officers of the train were also distinctive, and only the higher commands were given to senior artillery officers. As inspector general I was responsible for the direction of the service under the command of an artillery general.

I was ordered, on 30 June, to proceed to Dresden to take up a post at the Imperial headquarters. I left the main park at Magdeburg and reached Dresden on 2 July.

Here, as at Magdeburg, everyone desired peace; but did the Emperor really want it?

One would have thought so. How, otherwise could he have agreed to an armistice when, having been victorious in two major battles, he had forced the enemy back across the Oder and now found himself at the gates of Breslau, the capital of Silesia, the richest province in Prussia?

Nevertheless, as the negotiations dragged on and the Emperor, so eager when he wanted something, was busy only with preparations for a new campaign, one began to have doubts.

Defensive works covered the left bank of the Elbe from Bohemia to the sea. The ramparts of Dresden were restored complete with palisaded earthworks, and the fortifications of Torgau were finished. Everything moved forward together. Big hospitals were established at Dresden, Torgau and Magdeburg, and huge warehouses were filled with supplies of every sort; biscuits were being baked day and night.

The Emperor watched and supervised everything. When he was not in his study he was on horseback, exploring the neighbourhood and inspecting the troops as they performed manoeuvres before him.

Whole corps arrived to join us at this time; they were made up of young soldiers full of enthusiasm and goodwill. These corps took up positions on the Elbe, in the area of Silesia that we occupied.

There could be only one goal for these preparations and deployment of forces; it was to impress the enemy and so obtain the best possible terms for the peace or, if war became essential, to deal such a blow that the struggle would be ended at once.

Yet we knew the Emperor well enough to know that, once he found himself at the head of such a large army, it would indeed be difficult to extract the least concession from him.

Busy as I was with the multiple duties of my position, I could not be entirely deaf to the widespread recriminations and complaints that I heard all around me on the subject of the inflexibility of Napoleon's character. And those who grumbled the most were not those who suffered the most. They were not the soldiers, nor were they the junior officers, but the generals and the staff officers. But these critics did not venture the least comment; still less did the Senate, for the latter voted, without restriction or conditions, for the levies and the subsidies, and did not ever dare to inform Napoleon of the country's exhaustion and of the discontent arising from these endless wars.

All the gossip pointed towards war. It was said that Austria wished to impose conditions upon us that would be unacceptable to the honour of France. The Imperial staff, to which I belonged, left Dresden in order to move forward. Murat rejoined the army. Despite his inglorious role during the retreat and his desertion of the army at so critical a moment, the army learned of his return with joy for, on the battlefield, he was a matchless cavalry general. Always in the forefront of a charge, in brilliant uniform with the plume of ostrich feathers on his helmet, he formed a rallying point for his troops; the very sight of him was sufficient to put the enemy cavalry to flight.

Yet if we gained Murat, we lost General Jomini,* a fine officer. Offended, it was said, by the action the major general had taken against him, he took advantage of the armistice to go over to the enemy. The fact that he was a native of Switzerland could not excuse his conduct, for his whole career had been in our ranks.

As a member of the staff of the artillery and, as such, also a member of the Imperial headquarters, I was able, like all those around him to have an understanding of the operations although I was not privy to the Emperor's plans. This was something that I had not previously been able to do in charge of my batteries, when I had seen only what passed before my eyes. Even though I did not take the same part in the struggle, I found that the emotions felt on the battlefield became even more vivid, when freed from the distraction of action. As we left Dresden on 12 August, I wrote in my journal: 'We are confident. We hope all will be well, in spite of the knavery of the Austrians.' I copy this phrase from my journal because it expresses the anger we felt. Anger is no bad thing when one is setting out for a fight.

Throughout the negotiations, the Emperor had consistently spread the rumour that despite his sincere wish for peace, he could not accept the humiliating conditions that Austria, together with the Russians and Prussians, wanted to impose on us. The conditions were not made known. If the gossip was to be believed, the Emperor Francis would have betrayed the trust that led to his acceptance as a mediator, would have brought about an armistice that halted our pursuit of the enemy after Bautzen, given our opponents the time to repair their losses and to reorganise and increase their forces, negotiated with Bernadotte and separated our few remaining allies from us. Having done all this, he would have joined our enemies, sacrificing the interests of his daughter and the glory of his son-in-law to his own ambition.

Long afterwards, it was said that the propositions that Austria had undertaken to have accepted by the coalition, and to uphold on our behalf if they refused them, were on the contrary much more generous. While the independence of Germany was stipulated, Westphalia, Holland and Italy were to remain ours. It was also said that the Emperor, determined to retain the Hanseatic cities and the pompous title of Protector of the Confederation of the Rhine, had kept these proposals secret so that his refusal of them did not increase the displeasure of the generals and dishearten the army.

If the Emperor had indeed rejected such proposals, he was most blameworthy, in view of the exhaustion of France, and he made us pay dearly for his pride. It was not for us, who had for so long fought for our own independence, now to fight to impose our yoke upon others.

---

* General Antoine Henri, Baron Jomini (1779–1869). A native of Switzerland, he became a member of Ney's staff in 1805. In 1813 General Berthier placed him under arrest for some minor infraction, and this seems to have led to his joining the coalition, where Tsar Alexander made him his aide-de-camp as a lieutenant general in the Russian army.

What was the truth? Historians may one day find out. All that I can say is that, a few days later, it was learned that although hostilities were not due to resume until the 17th, the Russian and Prussian armies had made contact with the Austrian army on 10 August. As this conjunction came into operation from 10 August, it was clear that agreement had been reached before the end of the armistice, while Austria was still in the position of mediator. But what could be expected of a government that, in 1799, had caused the assassination of our negotiators at Rastadt* in order to steal their papers?

---

* The Congress of Rastadt, which was convened after the signing of the treaty of Campo Formio in 1797.

Chapter Nine

The End of the German Campaign (August–October 1813)

Hostilities start again. The armistice ended at midnight on 10 August. We repudiated it on the 11th and Austria declared war on us. This was what we had expected.

Hostilities should have begun again six days later, on the 17th.

We were stationed along the line of the Elbe from the Bohemian mountains to the sea, with Dresden as the base of our operations.

Two armies were drawn up before the Elbe. The first, under the command of the duke of Tarente,* was confronting the enemy Army of Silesia commanded by our most determined adversary, General Blücher.† The duke of Reggio‡ was in command of the second army positioned beyond Wittenberg. This army was to march upon Berlin, which was being defended by Bernadotte and the northern army.

The Emperor was at Dresden with the Guard and the reserve; ready to go wherever his presence was most needed.

The enemy's main army was in Bohemia under the command of the Austrian general, Schwarzenberg.§ The three allied sovereigns were with this army. The defector, Jomini, accompanied Emperor Alexander.

While we had taken advantage of the two months' armistice, the enemy had not wasted his time either. Less drained of men and horses than France now was, the enemy was also supported by England with arms and money and, as it was fighting on its home ground and in the midst of a population inspired by patriotism, found the assembly of an army greatly superior to our own, especially in regard to the cavalry, relatively easy. The Germans flattered themselves that we should be crushed beneath their numbers. We had raised three hundred thousand men, of whom forty thousand were mounted. The coalition possessed five hundred thousand men, including one hundred thousand cavalry.

The Russians and Prussians should not have entered Bohemia and joined up with the Austrians, to form their main army, until after the armistice. Therefore, the

---

* Marshal Macdonald.
† Field Marshal Gebhard Leberecht von Blücher (1742–1819).
‡ Marshal Oudinot.
§ Field Marshal Karl Philip, Prince Schwarzenberg (1771–1820).

166

assumption could be made that this army would not be able to move against us for several days, and the Emperor planned to take advantage of this period to dispose of Blücher and his Army of Silesia by throwing it back over the Oder. So it was in this area that he opened the campaign.

At six on the evening of 13 August we left Dresden with the Imperial headquarters.

On the 14th we were at Bautzen and, on the 18th at Görlitz, a fairly large town in Silesia.

On the 19th the Emperor pushed forward a reconnaissance into Bohemia, with the 8th Corps that was then at Zittau, guarding the passes out of the mountains. The advance guard passed Gabel on the Prague road. The Prussians and Russians had already joined the Austrians, so indicating that Austria had betrayed its obligations as a mediator before the ending of the Prague conference, and had already decided to join the coalition that had been formed against us.

Blücher had not waited for the expiration of the armistice to begin hostilities. Four days earlier, on 14 August, he had occupied Breslau and, on the following day, invaded a neutral country in order to attack our advanced posts. Surprised, the French drew back over the Bober, from where they repulsed the enemy.

The Emperor returned to Görlitz on the 20th and we left with him once more for Lauban, where we slept. On the way, we encountered retreating troops, and the Emperor made them turn back again; on the 21st we came to Löwenberg, a little Silesian town in a valley on the Bober, where we found several army corps in position.

The enemy had soon been made aware of the Emperor's arrival and, in anticipation of an attack, had destroyed the bridge over the Bober. He was on the heights opposite to us, and the bridge was quickly rebuilt under the enemy's fire. A battle was expected to take place on the following day, but Blücher, not thinking himself ready as yet to pit his strength against the Emperor, retreated. He was pursued as far as Goldberg, which was quickly captured and where many were killed.

We did not go as far as Goldberg, as the Emperor knew that the enemy had recrossed the Kalzbach; we returned to Löwenberg.

The Emperor left the pursuit of the enemy to the 3rd, 5th and 11th Corps under the command of Marshal Macdonald.

The main coalition army started to move earlier than had been expected. Either General Schwarzenberg wanted to rescue Blücher from Napoleon's pursuit, or he wished to take advantage of his absence to attack our centre of operations at Dresden for, from 20 August, he emerged from the Bohemian mountains along the left bank of the Elbe and advanced towards Dresden with his entire force.

The Emperor was informed of this, and we had to return, by forced marches, to the Elbe, a distance of forty leagues.

We were at Görlitz on the 23rd and at Bautzen on the 24th. The congestion there was so great that I was unable to find lodgings for the night.

We did not go towards Dresden, but rather to Pirna, upstream from Dresden. We left the road to that town on our right and turned to the left towards Stolpen, which we reached very late. The infantry had covered forty leagues in four days. Napoleon's intention was made evident by this march.

Knowing that the enemy was leaving the Bohemian mountains and advancing towards Dresden, the Emperor wanted to cross the Elbe at Pirna, by means of the bridges he had had built there, take up a position that would separate the enemy from the mountains that were his only line of retreat, and then attack him so that he was trapped between the French army and Dresden. To achieve this it was necessary that Dresden should be prepared to stand firm.

Reveillé sounded very early at Stolpen on the 25th, although we had not slept until late. The order for the march had been altered; we were now to head for Dresden instead of Pirna. News had arrived during the night that had changed Napoleon's plans; Dresden was under threat.

We reached Dresden at about ten o'clock on the 26th. Just in time! Before we entered Neustadt on the right bank, we saw the entire army of the coalition drawn up on the heights above the opposite side.

There had been intermittent firing on the outskirts since the morning. The enemy certainly did not know that the Emperor had arrived, for they believed him still to be in Silesia, and it was incomprehensible that, since the previous day, they had hesitated to attack a town defended by twenty thousand men.

The battle of Dresden. Napoleon immediately placed himself at the end of the main bridge and from there, with his usual clarity and precision, indicated to each regiment, as it arrived, the position that it was to occupy.

All assembled at the appointed places and, while awaiting the attack, the weary soldiers lay down in the streets and, with their heads on knapsacks, slept. I longed for rest, but I had other things to do that were more important than sleep. The guns had to be taken to their assigned positions and ammunition supplied to them.

At last, the enemy came to a decision. Between three and four o'clock, three cannon shots, fired from the heights, announced his attack.

It was a magnificent spectacle to see the solid mass of tightly packed columns, each preceded by fifty guns, coming down to attack the town from the hills that formed a vast amphitheatre around old Dresden. The redoubts responded to their fire.

The assault was fierce. The Russians and Prussians attacked on our left, the Austrians contrived to take redoubts numbered 3 and 4, but these were soon retaken by continually arriving troops.

I was near one of these redoubts with General Berty when he ordered artillery captain Souhait, my fellow-countryman, to lead one of the attacking columns that were the first to enter the redoubt and capture it. The action earned Souhait a medal.

This captain was the son of Souhait of Saint-Dié, a member of the National Convention, one of the few regicides to return to France after the 1830 revolution.

Six hundred Austrians were taken prisoner at these redoubts. I saw some of them jumping with joy at having been captured and being prevented from the need to continue the fight. Austrians were good soldiers, but the country was disunited. The races of which it was composed were so separated by birth, tongue, customs and, often, by self-interest, that many did not feel the ardent patriotism which inspired the Germans.

The battle was furious. The enemy reached the barricades at several points and the townspeople were concerned for us. Our soldiers, boldly led by their officers, repulsed the enemy everywhere, and the artillery of the town with that of the redoubts inflicted enormous losses. At last, night fell and the enemy withdrew to the hills from which he had come down to attack us.

On the following day, 27 August, we, in turn, took the offensive. The enemy, discouraged by his setback, remained on the defensive and, knowing his adversary well, expected to be attacked. Our task was not an easy one. The enemy, as well as being greatly superior in numbers, occupied strong positions on the hills, with his two flanks, the left and the right, resting on the Elbe. We should have to drive him from the hills and throw him back into the Bohemian mountains from which he had come; General Vandamme* was to block this, the enemy's only line of retreat.

The weather was terrible, rain had fallen all night long; we were soaked to the bone and a thick fog covered the countryside at times. The fog favoured us, as attackers, in that it concealed our movements from the enemy.

The Emperor had assembled his main forces on the wings and at about six in the morning, to deceive the enemy, started the action with a heavy cannonade in the centre.

He himself supervised the barrage and, to augment the assault, brought the artillery of the Guard forward. One of these batteries fired upon a group of generals and superior officers which was sometimes visible on the hills, and one of the cannon balls cut off the legs of General Moreau,† who was among them. This was a sad

---

* General Dominique-Joseph-René Vandamme, count of Unsebourg (1770–1830). A loyal and courageous servant of Napoleon, Vandamme played a useful part in most of the campaigns; his character was known to be erratic and this may have had a bearing on his failure to achieve a marshal's baton.

† General Moreau had been exiled from France, following involvement in a Royalist intrigue. He had returned from the United States in 1813 and was acting as a military adviser to the Tsar of Russia when he was mortally wounded at Dresden He died a few days later.

ending for so glorious a French officer who, after serving his country well, had allowed himself to be led astray by jealousy and personal hatred to the point of bearing arms against his old comrades, but they, nevertheless, continued to feel great sympathy for him.

An outstanding general, Moreau could not be compared, for military genius, with Napoleon. To demonstrate this, it is only necessary to contrast the campaign of the Army of the Rhine with that of the Army of Italy. Apart from military matters, he had an unstable character and this had made him liable to be misled by the bad advice given to him by Bernadotte.

In his turn he had led astray his old aide-de-camp, Rapatel, who was himself killed by a French ball at La Fère-Champenoise. One shot for the general and one shot for the aide-de-camp; that was the reward for their dishonourable behaviour.

When, a few days later, the army learned of Moreau's death, there was as much satisfaction as regret, in spite of the good memories that he had left behind. He was not forgiven for having joined our enemies and having helped them with his advice. If Moreau had not died at Dresden he would have continued to fight against us; he would have entered Paris at the side of Alexander, become one of the chief dignitaries under the Bourbons and his name would have faded like that of the traitor Marmont. His death seems to have pardoned his behaviour and today only his earlier services appear to be remembered.

The march on Dresden by the Army of Bohemia, carried out while the Emperor was in Silesia, was extremely skilful, and credit for this was given to Moreau and Jomini. If the enemy had not hesitated so long before attacking the town, there would not have been time for the Emperor to arrive, and they would have been able to seize it, and put us in a very disagreeable situation.

Bad weather and bad roads had prevented several corps from moving from Pirna on the enemy's right wing, and the fighting there achieved nothing. There was bombardment in the centre. Fortunately, on our right, Murat, taking advantage of the terrain and the conditions, charged the Austrian infantry and, as they were not able to fire in the rain, crushed them and took many of them prisoner while capturing twenty cannon and five flags.

The enemy, his left now being unprotected, was forced to retreat.

Firing ceased here and there at about four in the afternoon and we went back into Dresden, victorious, but as wet as ducks, and this included Napoleon himself. I had not a single dry thread on my body.

On the following day, the 2nd, the 6th and the 16th Corps pursued the enemy and took a huge number of prisoners. In the course of the battle and of the pursuit, a total of thirty thousand were captured; most of them were Austrians. They were utterly dispirited, being in rags and starving.

For three days, during the attack, they had been without bread. Their retreat had increased their wretchedness still more. The streets of the town were full of them, and no one knew where to house them, but the good townspeople of Dresden gave them something to eat. They cared for our wounded too, and took them into their houses. We were very friendly towards the people of Dresden and they wished us well. The sufferings that our prolonged occupation of the town inflicted on them later caused their attitude to alter. Nevertheless, in spite of this, they gave us nothing of which to complain.

We believed that our victory at Dresden was decisive and that the coalition was afraid of us, so the most optimistic rumours circulated: that Macdonald had entered Breslau, that Blücher had retired across the Oder, that the French had taken Berlin and sacked the town.

On the contrary, Dresden was our last great victory.

If, in the course of this battle, it had been possible to turn the enemy army's right flank, as Napoleon had hoped, and which had been prevented by the bad weather and bad roads, the enemy's line of retreat into Bohemia would have been cut, leading to disaster for him. But fortune now began to abandon our arms.

Setbacks for Macdonald, Oudinot and Vandamme. Marshals Macdonald and Oudinot had not been successful. They had suffered the severe reverses that were to bring to a halt all the advantages that had seemed to be promised by our victory on the 27th.

On the day after the battle, the Emperor went to Pirna with General Vandamme to organise the pursuit of the enemy into Bohemia, but an indisposition forced him to return to Dresden; at the same time news arrived of a serious setback that had been suffered on the road to Berlin by the duke of Reggio.

In an encounter with the Army of the North, the Saxons had capitulated and lost all their artillery. Oudinot was forced to retreat to the Elbe.

The Emperor was about to go to the assistance of Oudinot, when he learned that Macdonald, whom he had left victorious in Silesia, was retreating before Blücher. The marshal, continuing the offensive, had pushed his adversary back almost as far as Jauer but, following an unsuccessful attack on that city on the 26th, had been obliged to retreat. Perpetual rain had caused the numerous streams flowing down from Bohemia to burst their banks. Bridges had been carried away and the roads rendered impassable; the enemy, taking skilful advantage of these circumstances, had inflicted huge losses on Macdonald's army; fifteen thousand men and 103 cannon were lost, and the army retreated beyond the Bober, closely followed by Blücher.

In addition to this misfortune, it was learned that the 1st Corps, that of General Vandamme, in the course of an over-enthusiastic pursuit, had allowed itself to be surrounded and partially destroyed; its artillery and baggage were lost. It was not known if the generals, Vandamme and Haxo, had been killed or taken prisoner.

On Napoleon's orders, General Vandamme had set off in pursuit of the Russians on the 29th. He had followed them across the foothills of the Bohemian mountains and down on to the Toplitz plain, where he had killed many of them and taken prisoners.

Reaching the narrow gorge at Toplitz, through which the retreating coalition had to pass, the Russians turned to defend it and, seeing Vandamme isolated, rallied some of their troops to take the offensive and attack him. Vandamme withdrew to the strong position at Kulm, and presented a bold front while waiting for help.

Instead of the French, it was a thirty thousand-strong Prussian corps that appeared behind him on the hills that he had recently crossed. The Prussians, observing that the French were in a critical situation, immediately attacked them in the rear, while the Russians began an assault on their front. Vandamme, wishing to force his way through, overwhelmed their first line, but was halted by the second. Wounded, as was also General Haxo, who was with him; both were taken prisoner. Out of the entire corps, only fifteen thousand men were able to escape from this disaster by concealing themselves in the woods and on the mountain.

Should the responsibility for this affair, which had a great effect on the army, fall on the shoulders of General Vandamme, whose audacious character had led him to come down from the mountains to chase the Russians, instead of remaining in the hills that would have hindered the retreating Prussians? Or rather, was it in conformity with the Emperor's orders, that this general pushed his pursuit as far as Toplitz? There are those who throw all the blame for the disaster on the half-hearted pursuit by Marshal Gouvion Saint-Cyr,[*] a fine soldier but a detestable character, one who was always ready to put his colleagues in difficulties.

These conjectures were discussed at staff headquarters. But the unfortunate Vandamme was a prisoner and unable to defend himself, so it was on him that the blame finally rested. Bold, and impatient for his marshal's baton, he had rashly thrown himself into the Toplitz valley, without protecting his rear.

It is easy to criticise with hindsight.

Here, I am nothing but the echo of the rumours that flew around; I cannot allow myself to judge.

This disaster, Oudinot's setback and Macdonald's retreat, changed everything and, while costing us the advantage gained by the victory at Dresden, increased the already enormous difficulties that we had to overcome and restored their confidence to our previously disheartened adversaries. It would require the Emperor's genius to struggle against such problems.

---

* Marshal Laurent Gouvion, Count, later Marquis de Saint-Cyr (1764–1830).

The army's determination and its confidence in its leader were not shaken, but it was possible immediately to notice that the coldness of our German allies increased and turned to malice. Of all the troops of this nation who had been scattered from the armies of Oudinot and Macdonald, very few rallied again to their corps. They dispersed, returned to their homes, or went over to the enemy.

The Emperor was forced to concentrate his troops more and bring closer to himself his lieutenants, who now no longer enjoyed the confidence of their men.

From Dresden to Leipzig. The recent events, while revitalising the coalition and restoring its enthusiasm and determination, had also clearly indicated the path they should pursue. They would avoid a confrontation with Napoleon, who always defeated them, and attack his subordinates, wear us out, decimate our ranks (we could not, like them, make good our losses) and seize a favourable moment to surround and crush us beneath their numbers. It was this strategy that they now followed and which took them, seven months later, to Paris.

The Emperor wasted no time in hesitation. Having replaced Oudinot with Marshal Ney in command of the army confronting Bernadotte, he acted swiftly.

Blücher was pressing Macdonald hard.

On 3 September we went, with general headquarters, to sleep at Harta, a village on the way to Bautzen. In order not to alert Blücher, the Emperor left Dresden secretly at nightfall. He stayed at Harta on the 4th and slept at Hochkirsch, while we remained that day at Bautzen. In the evening, as soon as the cavalry, with Murat at its head, arrived, it fell upon the Prussians and put them to the sword.

Next day preparations were made to make a vigorous attack upon Blücher, when it was realised that he had gone. He had understood, from the violence of the attack on the previous day, that Napoleon was responsible for it. He took avoiding action and beat a hasty retreat.

Blücher's rearguard was attacked at Görlitz, and the town was taken, but it was impossible to continue the pursuit, for the bridges over the Neisse had been cut.

It now seemed that everything was to happen as it had fifteen days earlier. Blücher evaded us again but, when Napoleon prepared to pursue him, he had to turn back, for the main Army of Bohemia, now regrouped, was emerging again from the mountains and marching towards Dresden.

This coalition tactic was both simple and logical. As soon as the allied sovereigns learned, from the departure of the Imperial Guard, that Napoleon was marching against Blücher, they left the mountains and made ready to attack Dresden in his absence.

So we were forced to retrace our steps in a series of forced marches.

On the 5th we slept at Bautzen. The Emperor returned to Dresden on the 6th, which we did not reach until the 7th, by which time he had already left to join Marshal Gouvion Saint-Cyr at Pirna.

The Russians and Prussians, leaving Bohemia by the main Peterswald road, had attacked the two plains of Pirna and Gieshübel which were occupied by the 14th Corps, and which commanded the two banks of the Elbe.

The Emperor again took the offensive on the 8th and 9th with the regrouped 1st Corps and the 14th Corps, and pushed the enemy from his positions at Dohna and Liebstadt.

I remained at Dresden with the Old Guard from the 7th to the 10th.

On the 10th we left Dresden in order to go to Liebstadt by an old Saxon route into Bohemia. This seemed to imply that Napoleon wanted to pursue the enemy into Bohemia.

On the 11th, Napoleon, together with Gouvion Saint-Cyr, undertook a reconnaissance as far as the heights before Peterswald, the first village in Bohemia. This was one of the highest points in this mountainous countryside. Kulm, scene of the disaster of the unhappy Vandamme corps, could be seen from the pass.

The enemy withdrew into Bohemia along the main Peterswald road, followed by the 1st Corps. The retreat began as soon as the enemy became aware of Napoleon's arrival. The Emperor wanted to cut off the retreat by taking the old Liebstadt road but, in spite of all our efforts to carry this out, it soon became clear that it was impossible for the artillery. The Emperor gave up this plan and returned to Pirna.

Pirna was a pretty little town in a fine situation on the Elbe, which here flows between steep rocks. An old fort under military occupation that commanded the right bank dominated the town. It was here that the corps under Marshal Gouvion Saint-Cyr took up its position. General headquarters returned to Dresden with the Emperor on the 12th.

All the news was bad; Marshal Ney, in action with a superior force, had been forced by Bernadotte to retire to Torgau, and this infuriated us. All of us in the army longed for this turncoat to be taught a sharp lesson.

Our situation grew worse, despite the fact that the Emperor himself was always victorious and that fear of him was enough to cause the boldest of his enemies, General Blücher, to retreat. Events were stronger than he. The time when a victory would have been enough to end the war had passed. Our enemies were inspired by a passionate patriotism and Napoleon did not have enough influence on his force to inspire a similar sentiment. We were fighting for conquests; they were fighting for their freedom. In them burned the same spirit that had filled us when we fought against invasion at the start of the Revolution.

Our defensive line on the Elbe, which was too long for our strength, was threatened. On our left, Ney had been driven back to the Elbe; in the centre, Macdonald had been forced to return towards Dresden. On our left was the main coalition army, reinforced and strengthened, with its position protected by the mountains, waiting only for the right moment to attack our rear.

The Saxon general, Thielman, whose attitude I had remarked upon when I visited Torgau, commanded the largest of the many groups of partisans that attacked our convoys and cut our communications.

Our army, composed largely of young soldiers who were wearied by marching and by privation and bad weather, was much reduced in number by losses and by the scattering of the troops of the German contingents. The morale of the remainder was very poor. On the other hand, the armies of the coalition had been revitalised, and were continually augmented by new levies and by voluntary enrolment, as well as by reinforcements arriving from Russia. It is no exaggeration to say that the enemy forces were double the size of ours.

After the end of September the regular distribution of rations came to an end. It is true that, as ever, the distribution was made to the Guard, but troops of the line were reduced to pillage in order to live. The four-month-long occupation by a large army had already ruined and devastated the countryside for miles around, so the soldiers were now digging half-ripe potatoes from the fields, and suffering the consequent illnesses.

It was my duty as inspector of the artillery train to ensure the provision of clothing and equipment for that corps. The quartermaster general, Count Daru,* told me of the warehouse from which I could draw supplies. I searched in vain for this warehouse. Either it did not exist or, at least, existed only on paper. In the face of the determined assertions of monsieur the count I could foresee the time when I should find myself accused of having caused the disappearance of the warehouse, complete with contents. It was the same story with the stores of food supplies that did not exist either, despite the contentions of the quartermaster.

The Emperor, who was planning everything, could not scrutinise every detail and was often deceived by those he trusted. Count Daru was completely honest and well informed but, in his high rank and being sovereign in his sphere, he did not look closely enough at details and allowed himself, in his turn, to be deceived by his subordinates.

In the difficult circumstances in which we were placed, the Emperor was indefatigable. He demanded the almost impossible from the troops. He preached by example and did not spare himself. His self-confidence seemed as great as ever. He showed the same coolness and calm as he scrutinised everything, concerning himself with every detail of the endless and complicated troop movements. Officers and soldiers were reassured by his composure, in spite of the virulence of the criticism that was coming even from headquarters. They wanted him to withdraw across the Saale, even across the Rhine. Then negotiation with the enemy would be easier. This would have meant giving up Germany, something that would have been eagerly accepted by the coalition,

* Pierre Bruno, Count Daru (1767–1829).

while also sparing the lives of so many brave men and saving our garrisons on the Vistula and the Oder.

The Emperor did not see it like this; he believed that he was certain to overcome his enemies, whom he had always defeated. He sought only for the opportunity of a great battle that he thought would end the war and enable him to retain his conquests.

When the main army of Bohemia directed a new attack on our positions at Pirna, Napoleon left Dresden on 15 September and, at Peterswald on the 16th, he repelled and pushed them back. The lancers of the Guard, in a brilliant charge, took prisoner the son of General Blücher.

The Emperor returned to Dresden on the 21st believing it to be unwise, with his smaller force, to pursue the enemy into Bohemia.

At the head of Macdonald's troops, he carried out a reconnaissance along the right bank of the Elbe in the course of the following days in order to satisfy himself about the position and the movements of the Army of Silesia.

After this reconnaissance, the various army corps made several movements. The 2nd Corps went to Freyberg; the 5th moved near to Meissen; the 6th to the right bank of the Elbe in front of Meissen; the 3rd in the same area but on the left bank, and the 11th, still under Macdonald went, on 2nd October, to occupy the Neustadt defences at Dresden. In the course of the month, the 12th Corps was absorbed into the 4th and the 7th.

At the end of September and in the early days of October, the coalition's plans became clearer. Having been considerably reinforced and believing, not without reason, that we were exhausted, they decided at last to move.

Soon after the reconnaissance, made by the Emperor himself, on 22 and 23 September, Blücher, deceiving the duke of Tarente, who was in front of him, by an attack with a single corps, slipped away and quickly went down the Elbe valley, where in co-operation with Bernadotte, he attempted to cross the river downstream of Torgau. Ney had observed the preparations for the crossing and informed the Emperor.

At the same time, the whole Army of Bohemia, accompanied as ever by the three allied sovereigns, emerged from the mountains in force on to the central plains of Saxony and marched on Leipzig. This was clearly a concerted movement with the Armies of Silesia and of the North. It made apparent the intention of our enemy to combine his forces and unite in our rear.

Napoleon, who greatly desired a battle, could not contemplate embarking on one with the resources we had, and thereby engaging an enemy of double our numerical strength in artillery and, above all, in cavalry. The enemy must therefore be attacked before his armies had combined.

The Emperor's plans were quickly made.

He swiftly organised an army to be commanded by Murat, which was to confront the Army of Bohemia and delay its march on Leipzig.

A second army, made up of Ney's corps near Torgau, was to oppose of the Armies of Silesia and the North.

The Emperor, with his Guard and the reserves, positioned himself between the other two armies and was prepared to hurry to wherever his presence was most needed. His intention was to attack the enemy armies separately and defeat them in turn.

The Army of Silesia succeeded in crossing the Elbe, with heavy losses, on 3 October. Bernadotte had made the crossing lower down and without much difficulty on 27 September.

It was to this area that the Emperor went with his general headquarters.

I left Dresden with the main park on 6 October. Before leaving, the two bridges, each formed of twenty merchant boats, that provided the link between the two banks, were removed. We headed for Meissen. The 1st and 14th Corps, about thirty thousand men under the command of Marshal Gouvion Saint-Cyr, remained at Dresden. The countryside between Dresden and Meissen was very fertile and heavily populated; the view from the Gompsen and Benerick plateaux was magnificent. It was between these two villages that, on 27 August, Murat had made ten thousand Austrians prisoner. Before going down into Meissen one had a lovely view of the windings of the Elbe among the hills with, on one side, vineyards and on the other woods. From the bridge at Meissen, the view was even more picturesque, but not so panoramic as from the Dresden bridge.

On the 7th, while we were at Meissen, the king of Saxony and his family left Dresden and went for the night to Meissen. The Emperor passed through the town and continued on as far as Seerhausen.

We were at Dahlen, a nasty little town, on the 8th. The 11th Corps took up its position and the Emperor slept at Wurzen. On the 9th we were at Eilenburg on the Mulde; a large part of the army was assembled before this town.

It was obvious that we were marching in order to reach Blücher as quickly as possible, in the hope of defeating him and throwing him back over the Elbe, and afterwards to deal with Bernadotte in the same way.

On the 10th we made for Düben. Ney's corps, which was ahead of us, met and harassed a Prussian corps of Blücher's army, took some prisoners and captured some of the baggage. Ney chased them out of Düben, which we occupied immediately.

We stayed in this insignificant town, with the Emperor, the king of Saxony and his court, from the 10th until the 13th.

What was to become of the unfortunate monarch in this struggle? He had linked his quiet and agreeable life to the turbulent fortunes of Napoleon and he was faithful to an alliance that his people and, above all, his army wanted him to sever. His court was an encumbrance to us on our marches, but we greatly respected the king, his family and his suite.

Our troops were in need of some rest. The weather was terrible and the rain fell endlessly. Everywhere, the earth was turned to mud and the roads were full of ruts and holes, making marching difficult. Our young recruits, full of enthusiasm for the fight and full of goodwill, could not withstand such strain. In Napoleon's hands, the soldiers were nothing but pawns to be manoeuvred on the chessboard of Europe. But these pawns, provided by an exhausted France, were no longer the pawns of Austerlitz, made out of boxwood and ebony; these were pawns of soft wood, unable to bear the sharp and sudden movements imposed on them by his powerful hand.

Several corps of our army fought engagements with the enemy while we were at Düben, in which, as ever, we had the upper hand. Blücher retreated swiftly before us, beyond the Mulde, with the intention, doubtless, of joining Bernadotte.

Two of our army corps, marching down both banks of the Elbe, captured the bridges and defensive works that Blücher and Bernadotte had established as they passed through. The Emperor's plan then was not, as had been supposed, to drive these two generals back across the Elbe, before dealing with the main Bohemian army. Rumour had it that, on the contrary, he wanted to use the river, on which we held all the fortifications, to protect himself, then to march on Berlin, drawing in all the garrisons of the positions on the Oder and Vistula. This bold plan, the concept of a brilliant leader, required all the determination and energy that both the army and its commander possessed; but it was not to the taste, we were told, of the senior officers, who were weary and wanted only to return to France as soon as possible.

The Emperor was not in the habit of consulting his generals, but in the present circumstances, so much resolution would be needed to execute this plan that he was compelled to take their views into account. Nevertheless, he did not abandon the project, it was said, until the news reached him of the defection of Bavaria, whose army, joining the Austrian troops, could have marched on the Rhine without encountering any serious obstacles.

Now it was the turn of Bavaria to turn against us. We were angry, but not very surprised, for that country always allied itself to the strongest side. Prussia, Austria and the other German countries that we had defeated, despoiled and humiliated had seized the opportunity to turn on us, as was perfectly understandable; but Bavaria, like Württemberg and Baden, had always benefited from their alliance with us. We had enriched them from the spoils of the rest of Germany. Bavarians cared little for German patriotism, and this did not stir in them until they believed that we were beaten.

Forward reconnaissances in every direction informed the Emperor that Blücher's army, protected by the Mulde and the Saale, was marching on Leipzig to meet the main Bohemian army. Bernadotte, with his usual caution, was following him at a distance, always avoiding having to encounter his old comrades-in-arms. The

Prussians had to push him forward into battle with Oudinot and Ney, so that only they would enjoy the glory of the victories at Grossbeeren and Deinwitz.

The direction of our march now changed completely; in order to reach Leipzig ahead of Blücher we should have to lose no time.

The various corps concentrated at Düben, on 13 October, took the direct route to Leipzig. Should we arrive in time to prevent the junction of the Armies of Silesia and the North with the main army of Bohemia, so that we could fight them separately?

There was only the bridge at Düben by which we could cross the Mulde. All the troops hurried there at the same time, and so became crowded together; this caused serious congestion and impeded our march. The rain continued to fall, the roads were ploughed up and we marched along in mud while, all along the road, we left a throng of exhausted young soldiers behind us.

At last, on the evening of the 14th we reached Leipzig, together with the Emperor. Imperial headquarters camped at Reidnitz, a village near the town on the Wurzen road.

The main Bohemian army was already within sight of Leipzig. Murat had hindered their progress as far as possible, and was on that same day still vigorously repelling the first corps that had tried to seize the hills in front of the town.

It was vital to engage the enemy in battle, without waiting until all our army corps should have arrived for, from one moment to the next, the Armies of Silesia and the North might appear to join the main enemy army and crush us under their weight.

On the next morning, the 15th, the Emperor, with his usual decisiveness, prepared for battle.

Marmont's corps was located to the north of Leipzig to confront the Armies of Silesia and the North, while awaiting the arrival of the corps commanded by Marshal Ney. In the evening the main body of the army took up the positions assigned to the various corps.

Chapter Ten

The End of the German Campaign (October–November 1813)

The battle of Wachau. On 16 October, to the south of Leipzig, we were holding a line at right angles to the Pleisse, a marshy little river that lay on our right; also on our right, but further away, was the Elster. Our outposts were at the villages of Liebertwolkwitz and Wachau, situated beyond a line of hills upon which the Mensdorff farm overlooked the countryside; this was where Napoleon remained for the greater part of the battle. General Bertrand's corps had been sent to the east of Leipzig in the direction of the Rhine to protect our communications in that area.

Our army consisted of about one hundred thousand men, including Murat's army and Augereau's corps, which had just arrived. This corps contained three regiments of conscripts from France, who had only received their eagles on the previous evening. What a terrible introduction to warfare awaited them!

There were certainly at least one hundred and fifteen thousand men in the ranks of the coalition.

Although the young soldiers, most of them on our side, were not accustomed to fatigue, they were just as brave as their elders in the presence of the enemy; also, to compensate for our numerical inferiority, we had the genius of our leader, in whom we still had the same confidence.

At seven in the morning, as the mist began to lift, the enemy took the offensive. He advanced resolutely, preceded by heavy artillery fire. Our perfectly positioned artillery rained shot down upon him, but without checking his march. I have seldom heard such a deafening noise. We had a battery of three hundred field guns.

The Emperor was at the Mensdorff farm; from this dominating point we were able to see everything that was happening. The enemy's attack took a clear shape. The Austrians and the Russians were marching on Liebertwolkwitz, and the Russians on Wachau. The Prussians were coming down the right bank of the Pleisse and, between this river and the Elster, the Austrians moved towards Leipzig.

The village of Liebertwolkwitz, held by General Lauriston's corps, and the village of Wachau, held by the corps of Marshal Victor, were attacked with a determination that I had never before seen in our adversaries. Wachau was taken and retaken several times; it was soon nothing but a heap of ruins, but we still held it.

Neither was the enemy able to take Liebertwolkwitz from us. But the attacks were so violent that the Emperor, together with his staff, was forced briefly to draw back. Bullets were raining down upon us and there were many casualties.

Even as this fierce battle was taking place in our centre and on the right, an enemy corps, coming down the Pleisse, attacked the village of Markkleeberg on our right, which was held by Prince Poniatowski,* and captured it, but failed to push the Poles further back.

Until this time, we had remained on the defensive. There had been fighting all along the line since three o'clock. The enemy, everywhere repulsed with great losses, appeared to be exhausted. The Emperor took the offensive. Marshal Macdonald, on our extreme left, moved forward to outflank the enemy's right. In the centre, columns went down to Liebertwolkwitz and Wachau and, with the defenders of these villages, flung themselves upon the enemy. This advance was supported, in the centre, by the artillery of the Guard, commanded by General Drouot.† His guns caused dreadful carnage to a corps of superb Russian grenadiers. Whole ranks of them fell, but they remained steady. Threatened at one time by a determined charge of the Russian cavalry, General Drouot, with the coolness that never left him, pulled back the wings of his batteries and, sheltered behind the guns from sword and lance, continued to pour his fire upon the enemy.

Suddenly, cannon fire was to be heard from the north and from the west; now there was a battle on three fronts, a bad sign. In the north, Blücher's army and, perhaps, also that of Bernadotte, were arriving to take up position in the line. The attack on our right indicated the enemy's determination to cut our communications by nightfall.

On our front, the enemy eventually gave ground at nearly all points. But it was five o'clock and evening fell. The terrain, divided by woods and marshes and sprinkled with villages and farms, presented our attack with many problems. The enemy was able to take advantage of this and they fought with a resolution that showed no sign of discouragement.

At last, night put an end to the carnage and prevented us from achieving the defeat of our enemies.

We were victorious in the sense that, being attacked by superior forces, we had repulsed them and had even made them draw back; but it was not enough. Napoleon's aim of routing the Army of Bohemia before the arrival of Blücher had not been achieved. We had, in fact, failed.

* Marshal Joseph Anton, Prince Poniatowski (1763–1813).
† General Drouot faced high treason charges in 1816, but was acquitted.

The Emperor set up his bivouac near the Mensdorff farm.

While we were fighting the main coalition army south of Leipzig, the incessant sound of gunfire to the north and the west made us aware that the struggle in those places was no less fierce. General Margaron,* with twelve thousand men, was responsible for the defence of our line of retreat in the west. Here he had been opposed by twenty-five thousand of the enemy and had driven them back. To the north, Marshal Marmont, with twenty thousand men, had defended the outskirts of Leipzig against the whole Army of Silesia and had been forced to pull back to a more favourable position on the other side of the Partha.

On 17 October we remained in the positions we had occupied on the previous evening.

It was a wretched day; the sky hung low and grey and the weather was cold and wet. The battlefield was a terrible sight. Smoke still rose from villages, farms and ruins. We managed to collect the miserable wounded who had spent this long, dark October night on the wet earth. The dead were buried.

Both armies were wearied by the events of the previous day and only a few gunshots were heard from the outposts.

Our own thoughts were at one with the weather and the scene that met our eyes. Illusions were shattered as everyone began to understand the situation. We saw before us a numerous, courageous enemy determined, at any cost, to regain his independence. We had to start again, and in the worst of circumstances, for our adversaries were all the more passionate because they, for the first time, were advancing in battle order to bring an end to Napoleon's triumphs.

We had lost more than twenty-five thousand soldiers on the previous day, a loss made the more absolute by the fact that the only reinforcements we could expect were the fifteen thousand men under General Reynier, of whom two-thirds were disaffected Saxons.

We were assured that the enemy had lost about forty thousand men, who were, today, to be replaced with sixty thousand troops of the Army of the North, and fifty thousand arriving from the east.

Yesterday we had fought two against three; tomorrow we should fight one against two.

I had no time to think these gloomy thoughts for my work engrossed me completely. After yesterday's terrible battle, it was essential to prepare for that of the morrow.

Because of the enemy's enormous numerical superiority – a superiority due, it was said, to a plan that had been well conceived and determinedly executed – we could

* General Pierre, Baron Margaron (1765–1824).

no longer hold the positions from which the enemy had failed to dislodge us. We should have to shorten our line in order to defend it more effectively. During the night orders were given to implement this.

The battle of Leipzig. On the morning of the 18th we occupied new positions much nearer to Leipzig. Our line rested on a suburb along the road to Halle, passed through the villages of Reudnitz, Anger, Stötteritz and Probstheida, and curved back towards Lesnig. It formed an angle of which Probstheida was the most prominent part. It was from this salient that a part of our battlefield was controlled on the 16th.

On our left, behind the Partha, were Marmont and Ney, confronted by Blücher and the whole Army of Silesia. The Emperor took up his position, with his general staff, of which I was a member, near a windmill on a hillock a short distance behind Probstheida. This position, destined to become the centre of the battle, was defended by Murat's cavalry, by the corps of Victor, Lauriston and Augereau and by the artillery situated on the slopes in front. Poniatowski, who had been promoted to marshal on the previous day, was on our right with his Poles and two divisions of French, to protect the marshland of the Pleisse. Marshal Macdonald was at Stötteritz on our left, with Reynier and the Saxons a little forward of Reudnitz in the gap between him and Ney.

The enemy advanced to the attack at daybreak. Our withdrawal must have increased their confidence for it made the battle of the previous day appear to have been a victory for them.

We saw them pour out of Dölitz, from Wachau, from the university woods in close, deep ranks. They marched with resolve. Our soldiers were resolute, too. The struggle would be fierce. We waited for them steadfastly. Our artillery, still strong in numbers, occupied good positions on the slope. Our skirmishers withdrew slowly, inflicting as much punishment on the enemy as they could.

Enemy columns advanced on Probstheida, which seemed to form the objective of their main attack. The Prussians marched in front, and pushed into the village despite the cannon balls and the hail of bullets. Marshal Victor, supported by the Guard, chased them out, overwhelming them with firepower. The Russians came to their help and together, with a force much superior in numbers to ours, descended on the village and took it for the second time. Our infantry, now quite fanatical, charged again with their bayonets and, after a man-to-man fight, succeeded once more in pushing back the Prussians and Russians, who now retired, not to return.

During this fierce fight, Napoleon had stayed near to the windmill, in the midst of the shrapnel that rained all about us. A grenadier corps of the Guard, our last reserve held ready to support the infantry, was especially exposed, but the troops remained steady under the bombardment.

The Imperial Guard was not beloved by the army because of its arrogance. Treated better than anyone else, the subject of great consideration and heaped with favours, it was much envied; but it was composed of excellent soldiers, it never retreated and, during the campaigns of Germany and France, made amends for many of the short-comings of which it was accused.

Faced with our resistance in the centre, the enemy seemed to abandon the idea of a new attack, contenting himself with bombarding us. We replied, killing more of him than he succeeded in killing of us. This did not seem to worry him, for he knew that we could not make good our losses. It was essential for him to weaken us.

On the Pleisse, to our right, the greater part of the Austrian army, without any more success, had attacked Marshal Poniatowski, to whom support had been sent.

We knew hardly anything of events on our left in the north, when, during the after-noon, news was sent to the Emperor to tell him of the treason of the Saxons. He left at a gallop and we followed him with the artillery and cavalry of the Guard.

Two of the three divisions of the army corps under General Reynier had been composed of Saxons. This corps, positioned before Reudnitz, was the link between Macdonald's corps and the army of Ney, of which it formed part. While Blücher and Macdonald's attack in the centre occupied Reynier, Bernadotte, who had crossed the Partha, advanced towards Reynier. Bernadotte thought at first that the Saxons were dashing forward to attack him, impelled, he supposed, by zeal. It was indeed zeal, but it was zeal for treason that drew them towards the French general, the prince of Ponte-Corvo,* who was bearing arms against his own country. Their motives were similar; they did not give the lie to the proverb that says that like attracts like.

The Saxons suddenly turned and rained shot and bullets upon the 3rd Division of Reynier's corps, as well as on Durutte's French division, who were in the process of coming to their support; this latter division was one with which they had campaigned for a long while. The Württembergers were among the Saxons. A total of twelve thou-sand men and forty-two cannon went over to the enemy in the middle of the battle and fought against us, leaving a gap in the centre of our army. Reudnitz was left almost unprotected, and this was a village only a quarter of a league from Leipzig. If Bernadotte had shown more determination, profited from the gap and attacked Reudnitz, our army would have been cut in half and the battle would have been lost. Bernadotte did attack Reudnitz and his advance guard even entered it, but he was hes-itant; the resistance offered by Durutte's division, although it had been decimated, and that shown by the various troops sent to the spot by Marshal Ney, halted the Swedes and gave Napoleon time to hurry there. Skilful charges by the cavalry of the Guard,

* Marshal Bernadotte, later king of Sweden.

the twenty field guns that we brought up, as well as support by Guard battalions, quickly re-established our defensive line.

The behaviour of the Saxon troops on this occasion was odious. It is impossible sufficiently to revile it. It produced an enormous feeling of anger in the army and, if what we heard is true, even the Russian officers did not conceal from the Saxon officers who were joining them the scorn their actions provoked.

Bernadotte, whose intrigues had caused this treason, was not obliged to behave in this way. He had been in touch with the Saxon staff for a long while, depending more for his military success on treachery and defections than on his own courage; for, since he had achieved greatness, his caution had become extreme and his ambition knew no bounds. He had become part of the coalition only in order to obtain Norway, taking it from our ally, Denmark, and is it not true that he had the ambition, when Napoleon fell, to replace him on the throne of France?

The prince of Ponte-Corvo, who had now become the crown prince of Sweden, certainly should not have sacrificed his future subjects to the ambition of Napoleon but, also, he should not have forgotten that he was French, and owed his high position to French soldiers. He should not have borne arms against his own country. Nothing had forced him to abandon neutrality.

All through this miserable German campaign our allies had abandoned us, one after another, but each of these defections had been preceded by a declaration of war. When General Yorck* had abandoned Marshal Macdonald while the Prussians were still our allies, his corps, larger in numbers than those of the marshal's remaining troops, could have taken him prisoner with his solders or destroyed them all. They did nothing, and allowed the marshal enough time to withdraw before attacking him. It was in the midst of battle, and by surprise, that the Saxons had attacked the French troops at whose side they had for a long while fought, and even as these troops were hurrying to their support.

When our defensive line was re-established before Reudnitz, we returned with the Emperor to the windmill. The coalition attacks ended and they contented themselves with bombarding us. We replied vigorously, and at nightfall the noise was terrible, even more dreadful than two days earlier. I had never heard such a pandemonium. As for the cannonballs, one had become so used to them that one paid no attention to them.

During the day, General Drouot was even more exemplary than on the 16th at Wachau. He manoeuvred the artillery of the Guard and placed the guns with the same energy, the same good judgement and coolness as if he had been on a firing-range rather than in the middle of the most horrifying battle. He was certainly one of the

* Field Marshal Johann David Ludwig Yorck, count of Wartenburg (1759–1830).

most skilful artillery generals in the army, just as he was a model of all the virtues in his public and private life.

This battle of Leipzig, described as the Battle of the Giants and subsequently held to be the most bloody in history, was still a victory for us for, with one hundred and thirty thousand men, we had repelled the attacks of three hundred thousand enemy troops and had not, ourselves, been repulsed at any point, in spite of the betrayal by the Saxons. Nevertheless, we had lost the campaign for, being now in the midst of a Germany in revolt, we should have had to achieve a decisive victory in order to save ourselves. Driven back to Leipzig and surrounded by enemies who were not dispirited, and whose numbers increased continually while our strength fell, we were forced to retreat. Napoleon resigned himself to this for, in addition, our ammunition was running short.

General Sorbier came in the evening to inform the Emperor that no more than sixteen thousand cartridges remained. The main artillery park that had followed the army since Düben was now unprotected and, threatened with capture, had moved for safety to Torgau. Our nearest supplies were at Erfurt.

Orders to retreat were given at once; I was to go with the artillery beyond the town to Lindenau, to cover the withdrawal by defending Leipzig.

Before returning to the town, I was ordered to burn the two hundred empty caissons that were near the Wurzen gate. While I was doing this, the various corps entered the town and marched through the cluttered streets. I ordered the caissons to be pushed closely together and emptied of the powder that remained in them to avoid an explosion. The last corps, commanded by Macdonald, passed by at this time and the marshal told me to make haste, for he was bringing up the rear. I quickly caused the caissons to be set on fire and went into the town with the marshal.

Imperial headquarters had already evacuated the town, and I had great difficulty in passing through it. The streets were crowded with soldiers, cannon, wagons and carts.

Even more difficulties were encountered in leaving Leipzig. An ancient wall, the surrounding moats of which had been filled in, encircled Old Leipzig. There was a fairly wide road around it, separating it from the suburbs, with gates that closed it off from the countryside.

The army had entered Leipzig from various directions and had crossed the town by way of several roads. But, as they left, they had only one way open to them, a long highway at least half a league in length, intersected by a series of bridges, first over the Pleisse and then over the Elster and a multitude of little rivers. This route lay across a marshy meadow.

From the morning of the 19th, the coalition, doubtless surprised by our retreat, began attacking us from every direction at once.

The troops who were defending the gates gave them a warm reception in order to give the main body of the army time to withdraw. The gates were not forced anywhere, but the defenders could not co-ordinate their activities. Cannon fire sounded all around and each group fought in isolation, not knowing when they would have to withdraw to avoid being themselves cut off. So they drew back at random and, as they left the town, added to the confusion on the long road out. There, everyone piled up; everyone was swept along by the crowd; happy were those who were not knocked down. I thank Heaven that only a packhorse with my baggage was left behind there.

The bridge over the Elster was about to be blown up, I crossed it and rejoined Imperial headquarters. The Emperor had already crossed the bridge, and I continued to Weissenfels on the same day.

The retreat had been anticipated for two days and the engineers of the Guard had been sent to Weissenfels to throw bridges over the Saale. Why had they not been built over the other streams? It would have been very easy. In the course of this unfortunate German campaign I had observed Napoleon's farsightedness, so I am unable to explain this failure to predict what would happen. The blame for this negligence must fall on him and, especially on Berthier, his chief of staff, whose failure to take the initiative on this occasion was inexcusable. Such lack of foresight was soon to have dreadful consequences for us.

The retreat from Leipzig to the Rhine. The bridge over the Elster had been mined, and responsibility for blowing it up had been left to some soldiers and an engineer corporal. It would not have been beyond the skill of a cooler-headed, experienced, superior officer better to judge a more opportune moment to explode the mine.

The corporal, alarmed at the sight of Prussian skirmishers emerging from one of the suburbs, thought the danger more immediate than it was and blew up the bridge while there were several army corps on the other side.[*]

One can imagine the despair of these brave soldiers, gathered on the bank of a deep river with the entire coalition army at their heels. They had no alternatives other than to throw themselves into the water and attempt to swim across the Elster, to be massacred in an attempt to defend themselves, or to surrender. Many were drowned, a large number were slain in a useless resistance, and others were forced to lay down their arms. Many generals were taken prisoner, Reynier and Lauriston among them.

Marshal Poniatowski threw himself into the water but, weakened by his wounds, he was carried away by the current and drowned.[†] Marshal Macdonald, whose advice to me to hurry may have saved my life, did the same thing with a happier outcome.

---

[*] This incident has been ascribed to a misunderstanding of his orders by the corporal in charge of the four sappers ordered by Napoleon to blow the bridge 'as soon as the enemy appeared'. This the corporal did when Blücher's advanced skirmishers came into view.

[†] Marshal Poniatowski's horse, which he had ridden into the river, found the opposite bank too steep to scramble up, fell back on its rider and both were carried away by the rapid current.

By this time, I was already beyond Lindenau, and so far away that I did not even hear the explosion. The news quickly spread and nothing was heard around me but the most violent recriminations directed against Napoleon and, above all, against the prince of Neuchatel.*

On the other side of the Elster we left more than twenty thousand men, killed, wounded and taken prisoner, and the entire artillery of the corps that had failed to cross the river. Our losses in the battles of the 16th, 18th and 19th October were estimated to be fifty thousand men; the coalition losses, it was afterwards said, were forty-eight thousand. These figures did not surprise me, after what I had witnessed.

The Emperor slept at Markranstädt on the 19th and, on the 20th, we bivouacked with him beyond the Saale on the heights opposite Weissenfels. The arriving troops were gathered together and some order was restored to the corps. The Emperor was in charge of the retreat. Of all branches of the army, the artillery was in the least disarray. Most of the cannons had been preserved, apart from those left on the far side of the Elster.

Weissenfels was on the right bank of the Saale. The road to Erfurt, which we were following, went along this bank as far as Naumburg, where it crossed the river and continued towards Eckartsberg.

In order to place the Saale between ourselves and the enemy as quickly as possible, we crossed it at Weissenfels instead of at Naumburg and set off for Freiberg.

We were now in the middle of the battlefields of Rossbach, Jena and Auerstädt. Freybourg was in a steep-sided valley through which ran the Unstrutt. It was difficult to cross this river because of the precipitous banks. Three bridges had been thrown across it but, even so, congestion could not be avoided. The enemy was pressing upon us; cannon fire could be heard on the left and the Prussians were attacking the rear. The troops, who had still not crossed the river, repulsed them. Our rearguard, under Marshal Oudinot, did not arrive until the evening to defend the road to Freiberg, which he did until the following day.

As soon as I arrived, Marshal Berthier instructed me to take up a position at the central bridge and direct the passage of the artillery over the bridge. To carry out his orders he gave me four gendarmes of the horse guards. These praetorians, no doubt scorning to obey the instructions of a senior officer of the line, despite the fact that I was a member of the staff, soon abandoned me, and I was left alone at the entry to the bridge all the evening and throughout the night until five o'clock in the morning, when the bridges had to be destroyed.

It was not easy to cross these bridges, because of the congestion and the disorder that increased daily. They had not been stoutly built and I feared every moment to see them collapse, a calamity that would have left us isolated on the left bank of the Unstrutt, a steeply banked river that could not be forded.

* Marshal Berthier.

Marshal Oudinot, with two divisions of the Young Guard, protected our retreat, holding the enemy off at a distance while the bridges were crossed.

All the army had passed over the river by dawn on the 22nd and the bridges were destroyed. Some wagons were abandoned on the opposite bank; this was mostly the fault of the drivers who, able to cross only when there was room between the artillery convoys, abandoned their vehicles and scampered across as soon as they were told to halt.

When the bridges had been crossed and destroyed, I rejoined the Imperial headquarters at Buttelstädt, and we slept at Ottendorf. The Emperor passed the night at Eckartsberg.

We were at Erfurt on the 23rd, where the army halted to be resupplied. The advance guard of the main enemy army under Schwarzenberg was at Weimar.

At Gotha, on the 24th, I was ordered to join the advance guard to carry out an inventory of the artillery. Since Leipzig we had not known how many cannon and how much equipment remained to us.

On my lonely journey towards Eisenach, halting at various bivouacs, I was robbed one night as I slept. I lost my sabre, my pistols and my case.

It was impossible for the army to remain at Erfurt for long. Coalition forces were advancing on all sides and threatening to encircle us. Also, the Bavarians, now as fervent against us as were the Prussians, were menacing our line of retreat. The Emperor left the town on the 25th after having emptied the arsenal and the storehouses.

On the 27th I was rejoined at Neunfeld by the Imperial headquarters. I was then despatched to continue my inventory of the artillery of the rearguard, and to hurry forward any equipment that might hinder the movements of the rearguard.

I marched with the rearguard on the 28th, 29th and the 30th.

We were before Gelnhausen on the 30th when Napoleon, with fewer than twenty thousand men, passed through a corps of fifty-five thousand Austro-Bavarians under their former general, de Wrede,* who made an attempt to halt his progress.

General Wrede, a mediocre and arrogant Bavarian officer, had been heaped with favours by the Emperor, who had made him a count, awarded him the ribbon of the Légion d'Honneur and a grant of rents worth thirty thousand francs. But the Emperor had not wished to make him a marshal, and had been deserted by him when de Wrede could expect no more favours.

Our enemies had followed us closely as far as Erfurt, and Cossack bands which had captured our stragglers and looters had harassed us continually. After Erfurt, the pursuit relaxed a little. Was it possible that, by pressing us less, they hoped to give the Austro-Bavarians time to get into position to cut off our retreat?

---

* Field Marshal Carl Philipp, prince of Wrede (1767–1838).

Before the town of Hanau, our advance guard encountered the Austro-Bavarian army, which General de Wrede had positioned badly with its back to the Kintzig. Napoleon did not delay his attack until all his troops had arrived. As the Guard's artillery came up, General Drouot placed it in batteries, without even waiting for support. At one point, charged by the Bavarian cavalry, Drouot did not withdraw, but met the charge, sword in hand; his gunners, armed with muskets, were entrenched behind their guns. Troops came up in turn and the rout of the Bavarians was soon complete.

The army was now able to continue its retreat towards Frankfurt. We could hear the cannon from our bivouac with the rearguard and were uneasy, being only too aware of our numerical inferiority.

The defeat of the Bavarians had been such that, on the following day, our journey past Hanau was undisturbed. Nevertheless, on 1 November, General de Wrede, who had retired beyond the Kintzig, observing how few of our troops had been left to protect our retreat, attacked us again. He was unlucky for a second time, for he was defeated yet again and was seriously wounded. It was just what he deserved. Entering France once more, we marched over the bodies of the Bavarians, and this was not just in the figurative sense, for our guns rolled over their corpses.

On the 31st, I rejoined the Imperial headquarters and marched with them into Frankfurt. The Bavarians were occupying the suburbs on the left bank of the Main, over which the bridge was cut.

At Mayence on 1 November. Progress of the army had again been hindered, before reaching the Rhine, by the need to cross a stream by a simple trestle bridge. The disorderly congestion of wagons crowding on to the bridge was so great, that I was nearly thrown, with my horse, into the water. I saw a young mounted *garde d'honneur* hurled from the bridge but, happily for him, he fell into the mud at the edge of the river, out of which he was able to scramble.

Once more, I had the opportunity to notice the heedlessness of the service and, on campaign, the lack of care shown by certain individuals, officers as well as men, for the lives of their comrades. The passage of the wagons had forced up the pins holding the beams to the girders that supported the roadway of the bridge. The infantry, crossing the crowded bridge, were forced to march along the extreme ends of the beams, very close to the wagons. Some unfortunates were knocked into the river and their haversacks, inverting over their heads, dragged them down to the bottom. Of all those I saw falling, not one was saved. Disgusted by this sight, I went in search of an engineer officer. Among the guards of the bridge I could find only one sapper sergeant. My efforts to persuade this brute to have the pins driven in were in vain. He refused even to listen to me; I was not in his branch of the service. Yet, we had already lost so many that care should have been taken of the lives of those who remained.

At last we crossed the Rhine. It was not a moment too soon. If the retreat had lasted any longer we should not have brought back even as many as fifty thousand men under arms. This was not because our enemies, in their pursuit of us, had succeeded in killing many, for everywhere, when they pressed hard upon us, we had repelled them. Rather, it was because, after leaving Leipzig, the number of deserters constantly increased. With – or without – the least pretext, the weary, discouraged soldiers threw down their arms and gave themselves up to pillage. This example was contagious, and the army dragged along behind it a train of deserters, marauders and ruffians. The Cossacks captured groups of them; it was hardly a glorious trophy for them!

I had crossed the Rhine on 3 March 1812, on my way to a war of conquest. Now, on 1 November 1813, I returned across it, knowing that three hundred thousand Germans and Russians were at our heels. What terrible events had taken place in twenty months! I had left France great and glorious, I will not say 'happy' for wars do not bring happiness to the people. Now we brought invasion in our train.

We had always defeated our enemies, no matter how numerous, but the campaigns of Russia and of Germany were nevertheless disastrous. Even though our Emperor had always shown himself to be a great leader, and we had always been good soldiers, it was none the less he alone who was responsible, due to his insatiable ambition and arrogance, for the misery he drew down upon our country in spite of all our pains.

If his arrogance had not been blind, would he, in the hope of regaining his conquests, have left more than one hundred and fifty thousand men on the Vistula, the Oder and the Elbe, and more than one hundred thousand in Spain? These were two hundred and fifty thousand excellent solders who, if they had been added to those who were now re-entering France, would never have permitted our enemies to cross the Rhine, even supposing they had been allowed to get so far.

I reached Mayence worn-out, exhausted and weary of this war of brigandage and pillage, separated from my horses and my baggage, possessing nothing and having worn the same shirt on my back for fifteen days, my boots in holes and my clothing in rags. I believed that my servant had been, like so many others, captured by the Cossacks. I was lucky enough to find him in Mayence in good health and with both my baggage and my horses. He was a clever, sensible lad and had always marched with the main body of the advance guard.

Yet what was the wretchedness of one individual compared to that of an army that brought misery and typhus with it? Within a few days all the hospitals and public buildings of Mayence were filled with our sick and wounded. Typhus spread from the army throughout the population and claimed many victims. This sight did nothing to raise the morale of weary soldiers who were already undisciplined and habituated to marauding; many of them deserted. The good, steady troops remained; ready to make further sacrifices in the defence of their native land.

A few corps continued to occupy positions at Ocheim for several more days but were soon compelled to withdraw to Cassel at the Mayence bridgehead.

All our troubles overwhelmed us at once.

Chapter Eleven

The Campaign in France (1814)

The enemy invades France. What was to become of us?

Despite our dreadful condition, we in the army could not believe that the enemy, so often defeated, would attempt to cross the Rhine. If he were to make the attempt, we had no doubt but that France would rise against him, as in 1792. It is true that having been so long absent from our country, we did not know exactly what the popular mood was.

The talk was all of peace; everyone longed for it, from the marshal of the Empire down to the smallest drummer-boy. I did not believe in it. Our enemies, swollen with the pride of their success, would make demands that Napoleon, as long as he had a soldier under his command, would not accept.

All that one could reasonably hope for was that the enemy would allow us enough time to reorganise and raise new levies. The Emperor would know how to make good use of the time. But if the coalition were to act with the co-ordination and determination we had seen them show since their march on Leipzig, I could not imagine what would happen.

In such a critical situation, there was no time for complaints and recriminations. For us, the soldiers, we had only to obey and do the best we could, come what may.

I remained only three days at Mayence, with general headquarters.

On 3 November I was ordered to Mommenheim to command the artillery train's cantonment and to reorganise the companies. This work took up all my time from five in the morning until nine in the evening.

On the 17th we were sent to the district of Rockenhausen, at the foot of Mount Tonnerre where it formed the end of the Vosges chain like the dot on a letter 'i'.

On the 26th came the order to rejoin the general headquarters, which was already on its way to Metz. We caught up with it at Kaiserlautern.

We reached Metz on 2 December. In this military town the mood of the population was the same as that of the army; all were in favour of defence.

Matters became complicated. We learned that, as soon as Bernadotte's troops appeared, Holland had risen against us. Our domination had ruined this country, and Belgium would soon behave in the same way.

While I was at Metz I had, with difficulty, obtained permission for a few days' leave to visit my family. I was at Nancy on the 26th and arrived at Saint-Dié on the 31st. It was there that I learned of the invasion of Alsace.

On the 21st the main army of the coalition had violated the neutrality of Switzerland and crossed the Rhine by way of the bridge at Basel; they had then spread out over the Franche-Comté and Alsace. The arrival of the enemy army was preceded by a proclamation in which the foreign monarchs declared that they were not making war on France but on Napoleon. Their intention was clear; they wished to isolate our army by preventing the people from rising up. Their actions soon belied their words.

Invasion was greatly feared. Stories of Cossack cruelty had terrified the population. However, the Cossacks barely ventured into our mountains. The Prussians and, above all, our recent allies the Bavarians, were much more to be feared. They were more demanding even if they were less likely to pillage.

No preparations had been made for the defence of the Vosges. The National Guard was not armed. In the city halls pikes – absurd weapons – were issued to men of goodwill. Marshal Victor, who was in charge of the defence of this region, had too few men to guard the passes.

It was with feelings such as these that I said goodbye to my family.

In Nancy, an open town, there was no question of any resistance; the authorities seemed to have lost their heads. It was said that some Royalist families made no secret of their hope that the invaders would soon arrive. By the welcome given to our implacable enemy, General Blücher, they have since demonstrated their unpatriotic sentiments – quite inexcusable on the grounds of political passion. Since then, and even while we were still fighting against the invaders, the people of the town organised a guard of honour for the Duc d'Artois,* who had arrived in the wake of the foreigners, and the bourgeoisie, fashionably, took part in it. A certain publisher, who I prefer not to name, had even displayed such zeal in the Bourbon cause that, following the Restoration, he was awarded the cross of the Légion d'Honneur. This did not, however, prevent him, after the 1830 revolution, from parading the decoration while letting it be believed that he had won it at Wagram.

I returned to Metz on 6 January 1814.

The general headquarters left Metz on the 13th, proceeding to Châlons, which we reached on 17th.

I found that my promotion to the rank of colonel, dated the 8th, was waiting for me there.

---

* Charles, Duc d'Artois, a brother of Louis XVI and later King Charles X.

A step-by-step struggle against the coalition. On the 25th the Emperor arrived at Châlons and everything changed. The fascination exercised by this man was still extraordinary. We all knew everything about him, his obstinacy, his pride, his political failures, to which were due the disasters of the past two years – although everyone was told that they were due to the harshness of the Russian climate, treason and desertion. We had no illusions about our situation, and yet, with the arrival of Napoleon, confidence and even hope revived in the army. His presence alone filled the command with a vigour, a resolution and an energy that we had ceased to experience. One felt the presence of a leader – a good leader.

From the moment of his arrival at Châlons, the Emperor worked; he worked all night despatching his orders and, on the next morning, set out for Vitry. On the 27th a Prussian corps, left behind by Blücher to guard the town, was chased out of Saint-Dizier.

General Blücher had crossed the Rhine between Coblenz and Mayence and was heading towards the valley of the Aube to join the main army under General Schwarzenberg. Napoleon followed him, encountered him at Brienne, chased him out of that town, captured the castle from him and threw him back towards the main enemy army.

On 1 February, the whole of the united coalition army, numbering more than one hundred and fifty thousand men, moved to attack the Emperor at La Rothière. He fought them, with just thirty-two thousand men until nightfall and then fell back on Troyes in good order.

I was not with the Emperor on this occasion as, on the day after he left Châlons, I was sent to Rambouillet to reorganise and arrange the remounts for the artillery train. Since Magdeburg, and in spite of my double promotion, I had still to perform the same duties. The artillery train was short of men, and men who came from the military supply train, a completely different corps, were given to me.

I was summoned to Paris on 26 February to help organise batteries that were to be sent to the army to replace losses.

When I arrived in Paris the population was still the enjoying the effect of the brilliant victories at Champaubert,* Montmirail,† Vauchamps,‡ Château-Thierry§ and Montereau.¶ Some twenty-two thousand prisoners had been marched in front of their eyes. This was a magnificent trophy for an army of fifty-five thousand men to offer the Parisians. It was more highly valued than the official bulletins that were no longer believed.

---

* 10 February 1814.
† 11 February 1814.
‡ 14 February 1814.
§ 12 February 1814.
¶ 18 February 1814.

These were, alas, our last successes. Fortune was about to abandon us. In war there are so many unforeseen hazards that may intervene. A simple occurrence, unimportant in other circumstances, can suddenly change everything.

Napoleon with his small army had to confront the two enemy armies, each of them stronger than his own. This made it impossible for him to take advantage of his victories and, by pursuing his enemies, convert their defeat into a rout. So it was that, after having several times defeated Blücher's corps between the Aube and the Marne, he had had to hurry to the Seine at Montereau, there to fight the main army under Schwarzenberg, and had forced it to retreat well beyond Troyes. There he took up his position to observe.

Blücher, a general more audacious than skilful, often beaten but never discouraged, re-formed and with, as ever, the same objective, Paris, advanced down the valley of the Marne, opposed only by the two corps of Marshals Mortier and Marmont who, combined, commanded no more than fifteen thousand men.

But the two marshals stopped him short behind the Ourcq, and allowed Napoleon to come to their aid. Caught between two armies, Blücher was about to pay dearly for his daring. His position seemed to be desperate and, when he learned of Napoleon's approach, he decamped as quickly as he could, seeking safety beyond the river Aisne.

The only bridge over the Aisne was at Soissons, a town that was in our hands, and which Napoleon had ensured was in a condition to resist a serious attack for several days.

Even as Blücher was hurrying, abandoning stragglers in his wake, to this point, and hoping, no doubt, to capture it, a Russian corps, coming from the north to reinforce his army, was marching along the right bank of the Aisne towards Soissons, where it arrived on 3 March. Impatient to take the town, it called on the governor to surrender, threatening that if this were not done the garrison would be put to the sword. General Moreau,* who was in command, allowed himself to be intimidated

---

* General Jean-Claude, Baron Moreau (1755–1828) was seriously wounded during the crossing of the Berezina, and he incurred the wrath of Napoleon when he surrendered Soissons to the enemy on 3 March 1814. General Moreau was arrested as a result of this and imprisoned. He was brought before a court of inquiry and, later, appeared before a Council of War. There is a letter from the Emperor dated 5 March 1814 addressed to the duc de Feltre:

The enemy was in great difficulty, and we were hoping to gather the fruits of several days of hard work, when the stupidity or treason of the commander of Soissons surrendered the town to them; at noon on the 3rd he marched out with the honours of war, bringing four heavy guns. Have the wretch arrested, together with the members of the defence council. Have them brought before a military court composed of generals and, for God's sake, make sure that they are shot within twenty-four hours in the Place de la Grève. It is time to make examples of them. Let the reason for the sentence be made clear, have it printed and displayed and distributed everywhere . . .

Supplement to the correspondence of Napoleon I. Paris. E. Dentu, 1887. p. 204.

and, without attempting to resist and without even blowing up the bridge (which he had been ordered to destroy) concerned himself only with the terms of his capitulation. All his demands were met, he was even granted the honours of war, for the enemy wanted only the bridge, the loss of which was fatal for us.

On 4 March Blücher reached Soissons, crossed the Aisne and was united with the fifty thousand men who had come to join him. On the 5th Napoleon watched his prey escape. Although he had only fifty thousand men while Blücher now commanded one hundred thousand, he did not abandon the idea of attacking him. It had been a long time since we had had more men than our enemies. So, to carry out his plan, the Emperor went up the left bank of the Aisne, crossed it opposite Laon and, on the 7th attacked Blücher on the Craonne heights, from which he drove him. He rested his troops on the 8th, 9th and 10th and then attempted, vainly, to drive Blücher from Laon. After losses, in the course of these three days, of about twelve thousand men – leaving him with barely forty thousand – he conceived the bold stratagem of throwing himself upon the enemy's rear, calling in the garrisons from Belgium, from Lorraine and from Alsace in order to double his strength and to carry out the attack from the rear. Putting this plan into effect at once, he assaulted Reims, drove the Russians from it and continued to the Haute-Marne.

For this plan to succeed, it would have been necessary for Paris to be capable of putting up a resistance lasting several days, or for the enemy, halting his march on our capital city, to turn to defend his lines of communication.

The situation in Paris. Paris, however, was not in a position to defend itself, and the enemy knew it. In addition, Royalist plots had given the enemy hope that, if they could capture the city, a revolution would take place. Why then should he halt his march and give up his steadfast aim? In order to protect his communications? But we were not in a position to do more than interfere with them, and he, by marching on Paris, would cut all of ours, for our men and supplies were coming from that direction. This operation by Napoleon was so extremely rash that, as it had been conceived by such a genius, I ask myself if it was not perhaps the desperate act of a soldier playing double or quits.

The consequences of this action were immediately apparent. Marshals Marmont and Mortier, with their fifteen thousand men, having been cut off, could only extricate themselves from the coalition attacks by prodigies of courage and the loss of at least three thousand men; our main convoy, surprised at Ferté-Champenoise on its march from Sézanne to Coulommiers, was captured. This convoy had been escorted by the National Guard, the members of which did not even have uniforms; some of these brave men preferred to be massacred rather than surrender, and the rest of them only laid down their arms at the request of Tsar Alexander, a witness of their gallantry.

When it was learned in Paris that the Emperor had moved away, that the coalition was approaching and that only the small corps under Mortier and Marmont remained to protect the town, there was considerable dismay.

It was not that the mood of the population was bad. All opposition to Imperial rule had vanished at the enemy's approach and only Royalists, operating in the shadows, were spreading alarming rumours. The unfamiliar name of Bourbon was uttered only in whispers. The majority of the population thought only of the approaching enemy and the means by which he might be resisted.

To confront an enemy army of two hundred thousand men, a leader, as well as the means of defence would be needed; but everything was lacking.

The Emperor had controlled every aspect of the activities of the army on campaign and all his directions were carried out promptly. In the organisation of batteries on the move everything involving the train, men, horses and equipment, was my responsibility. Colonel Caron was responsible for the men of the artillery and Colonel Scheil, as the director of the park located in the Champ de Mars, controlled the equipment, cannon, ammunition and powder. Each day we went to report to the minister of war at General Evian's office. There, we received our orders for the organisation of new batteries and I despatched these at once to the army. All this was carried out in an orderly fashion and without difficulty.

The defence of Paris had been totally neglected, nothing had been done in this respect and the administration lacked both initiative and determination.

The Empress Regent possessed none of the skills of her grandmother, Marie-Thérèse. Old Cambacérès, who had been put at her side to act as an adviser, had become a hermit since his teeth fell out and he concerned himself only with atoning for his sins. Joseph should have been in charge, but this was the indolent brother, who had passed his time in censuring Napoleon and had not even been able to retain the Spanish crown; finally there was the minister of war, the duc de Feltre, a good and meticulous official, but entirely lacking in initiative.

The defence of Paris. Surrender. In fact, to provide the defence, there were only the depots, and the very small National Guard consisting of twelve thousand men, of whom only three thousand had guns; the others were armed with pikes that were useless except when on stage as part of the costume of actors portraying Greeks or Romans. Marshal Moncey* commanded the National Guard, and to this force were added the remains of the corps of Marshals Mortier and Marmont when they retreated towards Paris, having disputed the ground, step-by-step, with the enemy hordes.

* Moncey, Marshal Bon Adrien Jannot, duke of Conegliano (1754–1842).

The people of Paris were shouting aloud their demand to be given arms. Above all, this clamour came from the workers in the suburbs, stout fellows, most of whom were ex-soldiers. There were none to give them. Why were hunting guns not requisitioned? Because no one had the owners' permission and no one dared to take such an initiative.

As for defensive measures, a fence of barrels, without either shelter or trenches, had been placed before each barrier. The hills to the north of Paris, the only direction from which the enemy could come, had not even been fortified; only platforms for batteries had been placed there. Even on 28 March, when it was known that the enemy was already at Creil, there were still no guns in place.

It was not until the morning of the 29th that it was, at last, decided to have eighty-four guns of various calibres – mostly field pieces – taken up to these hills, at a time when the Vincennes arsenal was crammed full with heavy guns. The enemy was so close that some of the batteries opened fire that same evening.

That day, the 29th, in Saint-Germain, I encountered the procession of the Empress and the king of Rome, leaving Paris with the ministers and the members of the Regency Council. It appeared so sad, even lugubrious, that it looked like a funeral. Even the heads of the guards were low for, as they departed, the enemy arrived, and they had never before been obliged to turn their backs on danger.

The effect of this departure was deplorable. The crowd, as it watched this long procession pass, was dismayed and its mood was hostile. I listened to the mutterings; Parisians had been told to defend themselves but were given nothing with which to do it; everyone that the Emperor held dear fled at the approach of danger; twelve hundred soldiers of the guard were employed as an escort when there were no troops left to defend Paris. This desertion, which everyone soon knew about, discouraged and paralysed the most willing, and it was believed that all was lost. While the Empress and her son remained in Paris and were not afraid to show themselves to the people, their presence had rekindled wavering courage and augmented the will to resist. Now, all at once, there was a change and this emboldened the Royalists, who no longer concealed themselves.

In our almost desperate situation in Paris, with so few troops available, a popular uprising was what should have been organised; barricades should have been thrown up in all the streets leading to the gates, each house should have been defended, with-drawal carried out only step-by-step and the troops held ready to hurry to each menaced position. We should have done what we had seen done to the Spaniards at Saragossa and, by delaying the enemy, have given the Emperor time to arrive. Instead of this nothing was done, and when on the evening of the 29th the remains of Mortier's and Marmont's corps arrived, they took up position in front of the hills to give battle to an army of nearly two hundred thousand men. The National Guard, at least those of them who had arms, under the command of Marshal Moncey, formed the second line at the Clichy* gate. The artillery, other than that forming part of the armies of Mortier and Marmont, was served by various artillerymen, veterans and pupils from the schools, together with some citizens – ex-gunners – who came to volunteer themselves.

The ordinary services of the capital were in such a state of chaos that the soldiers of the armies of Mortier and Marmont would have died of hunger when they arrived if the Parisians had not taken food to them.

Early in the morning of the 30th the enemy attacked. The noise of the barrage proclaimed the fury of the struggle. I can say nothing of the periphery of the battle. My duties confined me to the Champ de Mars, where I was responsible for the despatch of ammunition; I could only judge what was happening by the approach or retreat of the noise of the barrage. The anxiety one feels in a situation like mine is perhaps worse than if one is actively engaged in a fight, when one has no time for thought.

Suddenly, at about four o'clock, firing ceased. A suspension of hostilities was announced. Marshals Marmont and Mortier, pushed from the hills and driven back to the gates, had requested it. Negotiations for the army's surrender were begun.

The army was to abandon Paris, taking its arms and baggage with it. It seemed that the sovereigns of the coalition wanted it to lay down its arms, become prisoners of war and then to retreat beyond the Loire or into Brittany. At least, by abandoning Paris we should be able to rejoin the main army. I was ordered to leave the capital at six in the evening.

What has not been said and written about the surrender of Paris? As if it were not enough to preserve national pride that twenty-eight thousand men – of which only eighteen thousand were regular troops – had, for ten hours, resisted the continual attacks of one hundred and eighty thousand men while inflicting serious losses on them, it was still found necessary to try to explain the surrender by claiming that there had been treason.

According to what I saw and heard, with regard to the courage of those in authority, the defenders of Paris did their duty and did it well, and the three marshals, Moncey, Mortier and Marmont, behaved with great bravery, doing all that it was humanly possible to do.

If there was treason and weakness, it only occurred afterwards, thanks to the evil influence of certain individuals, who placed their own personal interest before patriotism and fidelity; at the head of these latter must be put the sinister prince of

---

* During the night of 29/30 March, Marshal Moncey with pupils from the Polytechnic School and members of the National Guard organised the defence of the Clichy gate. He was made a peer of France during the Hundred Days. Following the second restoration he was imprisoned for refusing to preside over Ney's court martial, but was later restored to his former honours in 1816.

Bénévent,* who, like his worthy acolyte Fouché,† had betrayed, for money, all the governments in which he had served.

Some writers have put forward the theory that the defenders of Paris had been issued with cartridges and charges for shells that were filled with bran and sand. But this is ridiculous. It would have to be assumed, first, that these cartridges had been manufactured solely for the defence of Paris, and were not part of the normal army supplies, for this would have occasioned complaints from the army, something that never happened. Finally, the cartridges, like the charges for the shells, were not made individually but in workshops, where each item passed in succession through the hands of several workers, working in the same room. It would, then, have been necessary for all the workers in a workshop, their supervisors and the officers to be part of the same plot.

There may well have been some confusion over the supplies to certain batteries. The responsibility for this must revert to those who, charged with the defence of the place, instead of employing the heavy guns that were at Vincennes, had at the last moment armed the batteries with field guns, howitzers and cannon of different calibres. The supplies that were leaving the Champ de Mars for the Trône gate, the outlying points at Chaumont, La Villette, Pantin and Montmartre, etc. were taken right across Paris, a city they did not know well, by soldiers of the train who, perhaps, were not given reliable directions; this may have resulted in ammunition for 12-pound guns arriving to serve 8-pounders or howitzers. But who was to blame for this? In any event, it was not treason.

As soon as news of the surrender was known, Colonel Scheil, the director of the park, who was also responsible for the supplies of gunpowder, ordered his assistant, Lieutenant Colonel Maillard, to render useless, by any means available, all the powder remaining in the storehouse. In my hearing he enjoined him to leave Paris at nightfall with the last convoy. Colonel Scheil and I were ourselves to leave with the last of them at about ten in the evening.

I do not know what Lieutenant Colonel Maillard actually did. As for the powder, I have every reason to believe that it was spoiled as ordered; but this officer did not leave Paris and, doubtless, foreseeing various opportunities from which he might profit, stayed in the city.

In fact, after the army had left, he claimed that he had received an order from the Emperor to blow up the powder at Grenelle, and cited the municipal authorities as witnesses to his refusal to carry out an order that would have destroyed part of the capital. A large annuity was about to be voted to him by the municipal council as a

* Charles-Maurice Talleyrand, prince of Bénévent (1754–1838).
† Joseph Fouché, duke of Otranto (1759–1820).

reward for this refusal, when an artillery general – who I believe to have been General Ruty – revealed the scheme. Nevertheless, Maillard received a Russian decoration for it.

The Emperor was too far away from Paris to have been able to issue any instruction to blow up the powder at Grenelle. If the order did not come from the Emperor, who, among those ineffective individuals at Paris, would have dared be responsible for such an order?

In any event, the order – if it were ever given – would have been passed to Colonel Scheil, who was in Paris with me until ten o'clock, and not to a subordinate. If the order had arrived later, Maillard, who should have left much earlier, could not have received it, and by remaining in Paris was no better than a deserter.

Finally, such an order would have been made in writing and, as Maillard could never produce it, he ended by claiming that an officer whose name he did not know had given it to him verbally.

The only orders he did in fact receive were to spoil the powder and to leave Paris at nightfall with the last convoy. These orders were given to him in my presence.

When I rejoined the service in 1818 as colonel director of artillery at Bayonne, I had under my command as assistant director at Bordeaux, the lieutenant colonel Maillard, now decked out with a noble name. He was very embarrassed and uncomfortable at our first interview; from 1818 until 1822, in the course of our numerous meetings, he always avoided any discussion of what had happened on 30 March in Paris. Had there been anything that could have excused his conduct, he would certainly have mentioned it, knowing, as he did, how severely the artillery had judged him.

I give details of this matter because several versions of it have been circulated.

Some historians have taken the view that the order, supposed to have been issued by the Emperor, was an instruction to blow up some parts of Paris that were not of use to him and that this was proof of Napoleon's cruelty. This theory made a hero of Maillard, as the saviour of some areas of Paris. One thing that is certain is that, even if this schemer did indeed receive a Russian decoration, he was not able to obtain his annuity payments.

Retreat to the Loire. On 30 March, the same day as the surrender, I left Paris at ten in the evening, with all the equipment I could collect, and I slept beyond Villejuif, near where the Emperor arrived that night.

The enemy entered Paris on the 31st when I was at Fontainebleau.

On 1 April and the following days, the army arrived and concentrated at Fontainebleau. One corps was stationed at Essonne and formed the advance guard on the Paris side. Command of the army was given to Marshal Marmont, who had evacuated the capital after having defended it bravely. Generals Souham,[*] Bourdesoulle,[†] Compans[‡] and Meynadier[§] were under his command.

It was this corps that, three days later, deceived by its generals, abandoned its positions, marched towards Versailles, leaving the army unprotected and compelling the Emperor to accept unconditional abdication.

If I had remained at Fontainebleau, I should have witnessed the dramatic events that were taking place there. But, on 3 April, I had to leave for Orléans to take a convoy that consisted of eighty wagons, field guns and caissons and carts filled with powder, all drawn by sick horses that needed replacement. I was authorised to requisition relief horses from the communities that I passed through on my way. The mayors and the people eagerly offered this help. My escort consisted of only thirty gunners armed with rifles.

I slept the same night, 3 April, at Malesherbes.

On 4 April, I was about to sleep overnight at Chilleurs but, while we were halted at Pithiviers to replace the relief horses and rest the others, I saw a courier in the Emperor's livery passing by in the direction of Orléans. Shortly afterwards, he came back and, approaching me, told me that he had just been attacked by a party of Cossacks and that his postillion had been captured or killed. I ordered our horses to be harnessed without delay, and went on to Loury without halting, arriving there well before nightfall.

Near Pithiviers, the road ran through a forest. I hurried to reach it, sure that, if the Cossacks were following me, they would not dare to venture into the forest. To give them the impression that I had a strong escort and was on the alert, I placed my thirty gunners in line at the end of the convoy, thus closing the gap. By pushing on beyond Chilleurs, I had left several large villages behind me and, knowing enough of the habits of the Cossacks, felt certain that they would be tempted to stop there. In fact, I learned that, shortly after my departure from Pithiviers, they had halted there to pillage the place.

After four hours' rest at Loury, I set out again for Orléans, where I arrived on the 5th at six in the morning with all my people and all my equipment, but worn out with

---

* General Joseph, Count Souham (1760–1837) enlisted in the royal army and became a general in 1793 in the service of the Revolution. He was associated with Moreau, and was arrested and imprisoned when the latter was disgraced in 1804. After his release in 1807 he took an active part in campaigns in Italy and Spain and was seriously wounded at Leipzig. He was again disgraced in 1814, when Napoleon blamed him for the surrender of Essonne. He served under the Bourbons after 1815.

† General Étienne Tardif de Pommeroux, count of Bordesoulle (1771–1837).

‡ General Jean-Dominique, Count Compans (1769–1845) was wounded at Austerlitz and at Borodino. He refused a command during the Hundred Days and became a member of the chamber of peers under the second Restoration. He voted for the death sentence upon Marshal Ney.

§ General Louis-Henri-René, Count Meynardier (1778–1847). Having taken part in the battle of Paris, he changed sides at Essonne, receiving the title of count under the Restoration.

weariness and anxiety, having been constantly in the saddle and having had only a few hours' sleep. Warned of my arrival and of the dangers posed by the enemy groups that were hurrying towards my convoy, a regiment of infantry had been sent to meet me from Orléans; I encountered this when I was almost at the gates of the town.

I was so weary by the evening that, while dining with the general, I fell face down in my plate at the start of the meal and slept. I woke towards the end of the dinner, greatly embarrassed, but a few kindly words from the general and the sympathetic looks of the rest of the company reassured me. My neighbours had wanted to wake me up, but the general had prevented them so that I was allowed to slumber on.

It was at Orléans that I learned of the changes that had taken place in the government.

On the 9th I left Orléans to go to the artillery train depots that were quartered near Tours. I slept at Mer, passing near Beaugency. Prince Jérôme was at the hotel in Beaugency where I halted; he summoned me to see him and we had a half-hour's conversation about current events. I watched the Empress pass through Mer on her way to Orléans.

I reached Tours on the 11th and, on the 15th, was directed, with all the depots, to the Sarthe department, and a little later, to Mayenne, where we remained until peace was concluded.

The evacuation of the park to Metz was begun on 8 June. Leaving Laval on the 13th I reached Paris on the 16th, where I received the order to take up the command of the 4th Horse Artillery at Valence. My appointment was dated from the 8th.

I bought a carriage in Paris that cost me 1,500 francs and, with my horses harnessed to this, I went to Lorraine, leaving the capital on 23 June. I reached Nancy on the 29th. On 6 July I left with my family for Saint-Dié where we remained from the 8th to the 15th. Afterwards, I went alone to Valence, where I was garrisoned and arrived there on the 22nd.

Chapter Twelve

The First Restoration: The Hundred Days (1814–1815)

Garrison duty at Valence. Of my eight months in garrison at Valence – from July 1814 until March 1815 – I have only two incidents to recount: the successive visits of two princes. On 31 August, the duc d'Orléans* passed through Valence on his way from Marseilles and, on 25 September, Monsieur the comte d'Artois reached us in the course of a tour of inspection. On the following day, he reviewed the troops, and on this occasion distributed crosses of Saint-Louis. With many of my comrades I was included among the recipients of this award. He returned to Valence again on 16 October and left for Grenoble on the 17th.

Leave was granted to me on the same day, and I set out for Saint-Dié, arriving there on the 23rd. I spent a month in Lorraine, visiting my relations and friends. I left Nancy on 20 December to return to garrison duties and, with my family, reached Valence on 2 February 1815.

This was the first time for many years that we had been at peace. How much more we should have rejoiced at it if it had not been so dearly bought!

It is not for me to write history but, nevertheless, I mean to put down here an opinion of the circumstances, military and civil, in the midst of which I was living. An opinion that was, I am certain, shared by the great majority of those who were not blinded by passion or self-interest.

The catastrophe of 1814 had caused us profound distress, but we had suffered more for the sake of our country than on behalf of the Emperor. All these endless wars, attributable only to his ambition and ending in the exhaustion of France had, for a long while, made the Emperor unpopular. Everyone had had enough of despotism, and especially of a despotism that was no longer accompanied by victories. His fall was looked upon as a retribution. The Bourbons were no longer well known in the country and, when they returned to the throne and it was announced that they were to head a constitutional regime, a majority happily accepted them. If they had shown more skill it would have been simple for them to have placed their government on a solid base.

* Louis-Phillipe, duc d'Orléans, a descendant of Philippe, brother of Louis XIV and later king of France.

But they committed error after error. They should have striven, first of all, to win over the army, but they did everything in their power to alienate the spirit of the military. They substituted the white cockade for the tricolour cockade so dear to every soldier's heart. They installed in the army too many commanders who had served only in the ranks of the émigrés, as if those who had fought against them better deserved the command of our regiments. The award of the Légion d'Honneur, regarded, until then, with such esteem, was handed out as freely as if the intention was to debase it. The army bitterly resented these abuses. Finally, the princes, even if they meant well, unfortunately lacked the language with which to appeal to the hearts of the soldiers when they stood before them

In the realm of civil administration it seemed that, in every respect, there was a wish to return to the ways of the past. Every victory of the Revolution, even the most justifiable, appeared to be threatened.

If the initial sentiments with which the Bourbons had been welcomed were quickly changed, the blame must lie with the errors of the government and not with the fickleness of the French people. Discontent grew day by day, and needed only some opportunity to erupt.

The return from Elba. The 7th Military Division, to which I belonged, was divided into two commands; the first was at Grenoble under General Marchand and the second at Valence under General Mouton-Duvernet,* who was a good and energetic soldier; the idle General Quiot† was under his command.

During the night of 3/4 March we learned that Napoleon had disembarked in the gulf of Juan near the Antibes and was marching towards Grenoble. The town was in a state of great excitement.

The sentiment of the army, and of the people of Dauphiné, was in favour of the Emperor but, as for me, like all sensible people I deplored this occurrence. I foresaw, and this was not difficult, all the evils that would descend upon France as a result, and the first of them would be civil war.

I understood the situation perfectly. My duty was to remain at my post; my self-interest was to join the Emperor. I had taken my oath to the monarchy so, as long as this government remained the true government of the country, I should continue to serve it.

---

* Mouton Duvernet, General Regis-Barthélemy, Baron (1770–1816). He declared for Napoleon on the latter's return from Elba and was a member of the war council at Lyons that agreed the surrender of Paris in July 1815. He later went into hiding and was made prisoner in March 1816, being shot the following July, a victim of the White Terror.

† General Joachim-Jérôme Quiot du Passage (1775–1849).

The news of the disembarkation had hardly been received when, on 4 May, General Mouton-Duvernet left for Gap by way of Grenoble, in order, with the help of General Marchand, to provide the means by which Napoleon's progress could be halted. He did not go to Gap and by the 6th was back in Valence.

On the 5th Napoleon was in Gap with, at most, a thousand men.

The Emperor entered Grenoble at eight in the evening of the 7th to the acclaim of the garrison and of the population. Colonel Labédoyère,* at the head of the 7th Regiment of the Line, went to meet and join him. The troops sent to oppose him went over to his side.

One hundred and fifty gunners armed with rifles under the command of Major Hurtaux were sent to Die from Valence. In spite of the shouts and the incitement of the population, not a single gunner deserted, and all of them returned to Valence on the 11th.

Generals Mouton-Duvernet and Quiot left in their turn for Die on the 8th. They returned to Valence on the evening of the following day.

While they were away, on the afternoon of the 8th, I received a direct order from General Bertrand† that was passed to me by an officer of the 4th Regiment of Foot Artillery, to go at once, with my regiment, to Grenoble to join the Emperor. At the same time, this officer handed me a packet of proclamations that I threw in the fire without reading them. I arrested the officer and took him before the adjutant-major Servan, who was in command in the absence of the generals, and he was handed over to the police, so that he was not able to communicate with the troops.

The Emperor reached Lyon on the 10th, and, during the night of the 9th/10th, General Mouton-Duvernet and the adjutant-major, Servan, left Valence for Lyon, where they joined the Emperor.

General Debelle‡ arrived in Valence during the morning of the 10th and assumed command of the Drôme department in the name of the Emperor. I was summoned to the hotel where he was staying and there I found the prefect, General Quiot, and other military authorities. We refused to recognise General Debelle and he was placed under the surveillance of the police captain. He was allowed to leave the town on the following day.

On the 11th the gunners began to indicate their wish to join the Emperor and, on the same day, the major of my regiment, Duchand, who had been on leave, returned and expressed the same wish.

---

* Colonel Charles de Labédoyère (1786–1815) was shot following the second Bourbon Restoration for having rallied to Napoleon's cause during the Hundred Days.
† This may be General Henri-Gatien, Count Bertrand (1773–1844) who accompanied Napoleon to his exile on St Helena.
‡ General César-Alexandre Debelle, Baron de La Gachetière (1770–1826).

I was summoned to the prefect on the morning of the 12th. I found the military and civilian authorities gathered there and, in their presence, staff officer Servan, who had just arrived from Lyon, passed an order to me that came from General Mouton-Duvernet to leave at once for Lyon with my regiment. I refused, but I was aware that it was no longer possible to hold the gunners back; I passed the order on to Major Duchand, who was present, and I ended my service until the day on which the proclamation of Louis XVIII became known; this was issued at Lille at the time he left French territory and by doing so absolved the army of its oath of loyalty.

Major Duchand went to the barracks and harangued the soldiers, after which, accompanied by most of the regiment and a good number of officers, he left for Lyon, where the Emperor promoted him to colonel. Duchand, put on half-pay at the Restoration, was made *maréchal de camp** in 1830, and later was promoted to lieutenant general. In 1804 he was an orderly officer to the Emperor and had arrived in the artillery as a *chef d'escadron* in replacement, I believe, for Paul-Louis Courier. Thus, I was under his command in 1804, he was under mine in 1814 and, if I had stayed longer in the service, he would have been my superior in 1830.

When politics begin to disturb the soldier's life and force him to grapple with unforeseen events, when passions and loyalty obscure ideas of duty, it seems to me that an honest man should not consider his own interest or sympathies, but only the good of his country. Heated opinions, the worship of an extraordinary man, should all be forgotten when opposed to the good of the fatherland. When this is recognised and accepted, all reasonably strong and moral government deserves our support when it is based upon social principles sanctioned over the centuries.

When the royal government was the legal government of France, I had taken my oath to support it and so I was bound to remain faithful as long as it did not itself withdraw, and while the country had not chosen another.

General Debelle returned to Valence on the 15th to assume the command of the department. On the 20th Napoleon entered Paris.

This news reached Valence on the 24th together with that of the departure of the king for Belgium. He had abandoned France and sought refuge abroad, and was about to rely upon our enemies to help him to return. It was no longer a civil war with which we were threatened, but an invasion. I could no longer hesitate, my duty was clear and on the 28th I resumed my service.

This was still a critical moment. It was known in Valence that the duc d'Angoulême[†] was raising a force of troops at Pont-Saint-Esprit with the intention of marching on Lyon. He entered Montélimar at ten in the morning of the 29th.

---

* The rank of *général de brigade* reverted to the old Royalist title of *maréchal de camp* at the first Restoration.

† Louis de Bourbon, duc d'Angoulême (1775–1844), a nephew of Louis XVIII.

When he heard this news, General Debelle went to Loriol, taking with him fifty veterans and some of the National Guard from Valence and the surrounding area, and on the 30th attempted an unsuccessful attack on Montélimar. However, fifty chasseurs of the 14th Regiment went over to his side and announced that all their regiment and also the 10th of the line would probably follow their example.

At eight in the evening of the 31st, General Debelle returned to Valence, claiming to be wounded, with his fifty chasseurs and the veterans. He ordered me to leave that night to take command of the troops stationed at Loriol and at Livron and to defend the crossing of the Drôme against the advancing Duc d'Angoulême. I left at once and reached Loriol at dawn on 1 April.

The battle of Loriol. Loriol and Livron were two localities separated by the Drôme. I found there 250 men of the 2nd Battalion of the 39th Regiment of the Line, commanded by Chef de Bataillon Chitry, between twenty and twenty-five mounted honour guards* from Valence, twenty armed gendarmes, and between three and four hundred of the National Guard from nearby villages; there were also some gunners from my regiment.

It was essential, with these few troops, to protect the heights of Loriol and guard the crossing of the Drôme, while preserving my communications with Crest, about four leagues away from Livron. I now understood why General Debelle had disencumbered himself of this part of his command on to me.

As soon as I arrived, I had reconnaissance parties sent towards Montélimar, and despatched urgent orders to all the neighbouring National Guards to come at once to Loriol. My reconnaissance parties reported that the enemy had, that same day, reconnoitred the position at Logis-Neuf and at Tourettes on the road to Montélimar, with a view to taking up positions there on the following day.

Wishing to see the movements of the enemy for myself and to discover his intentions, I left Loriol at five o'clock the following morning, with two hundred men of the 39th Regiment and sixteen police to go to Logis-Neuf; I arrived there at half past seven. I halted the infantry and pushed forward with the police until we saw an immense cloud of dust on the road; we heard shouting and the sound of drums and knew that troops were on the march. Soon the head of the column appeared.

I returned to Logis-Neuf and sent the infantry back, while we carried out our retreat, with the police as rearguard keeping an eye on the enemy.

Contrary to my expectations, the enemy did not stop at Logis-Neuf and continued on his way. His columns continued to arrive on the little plain that stretched between

---

* Ceremonial guards that, from the sixteenth century, had been formed in some French cities to perform escort duties. Some of them were made up of the wealthier citizens and adopted flamboyant uniforms.

Sauze and Logis-Neuf. From that moment it was clear that he intended to attack us that same day at Loriol. In fact he pursued us right up to our advanced posts.

I then reinforced the police with the honour guards, whom I positioned as look-outs. I also put skirmishers on the heights near Loriol and on the right of the plain. I left the remainder of the battalion of the 39th as a reserve just outside the town. The National Guard, with the exception of those from the market town of Étoile, I stationed at the bridge, with my two 8-pounder guns – the only ones I had – placed to the left and right at the edge of the embankment. I positioned the men from Étoile on a hillock near the road behind Loriol to cover the retreat and to ensure that the enemy, who was very much stretched out to the right, could not turn our flank there while we were confronting him outside the town.

According to the reports I had received, the enemy force was at least four thousand men strong; two battalions of the 10th Regiment of the Line, the 4th Chasseurs, two hundred men of the foreign regiment, six heavy guns served by gunners of the 3rd Regiment of foot artillery, with the remainder made up of volunteers and National Guard from the Midi, fanatics and impassioned Royalists. That there was at least this number could be assumed from the depth of the enemy's columns, and the activity on the flanks indicated a determined and serious attack on the bridge.

The lie of the land did not permit me to defend Loriol and the hills around it with the few men I had. It was my view that, to avoid being cut off from the bridge, it would be prudent to cross to the right bank of the Drôme. I carried out this withdrawal, which was performed without haste and in good order. A few moments earlier, several infantrymen of the 10th came over to us; they told us that their entire regiment was only waiting for a favourable opportunity to join our side. Incidents like this took place every day. My belief in their words was strengthened by the fact that some cannon shots, fired at us by the enemy column after we left Loriol, did us no harm although we were only a short distance away. We responded with a hail of bullets.

I could have done a great deal of damage to this column in the position it occupied but, apart from the fact that in the circumstances I was loath to fire on the line, I felt sure, as everyone in my place would have done, that these troops were about to join us and I wanted to avoid an unnecessary blood-letting.

However, before returning across the bridge, the honour guards, without any orders from me, had tried to charge the head of the column. This was a very rash thing to do in view of the enemy's strength, and it proved to be disastrous, as many of them were grievously wounded.

When all the infantry had gathered at the bridge, I ordered them to cross. At that moment I received a despatch from General Debelle for the enemy general. I ordered a cease-fire and sent a trumpeter as negotiator. He blew his trumpet and was answered by gunfire.

It was between midday and one o'clock when we withdrew from the left bank of the Drôme. With the few men under my command, I was unable to occupy a farm near to the bridgehead. It was, above all, essential to protect the bridge itself and the river crossing in the area.

As it would have been possible for the enemy to ford the Drôme anywhere, I positioned the National Guards, as I have said, along the dykes, extending their line as far as possible. I put the only serviceable gun that I had on to the bridge, with gunners from my own regiment armed with muskets. The carriage of my second gun had broken down through old age; it had not been dismounted as it was afterwards said to be. This gun was taken to the rear. The battalion of the 39th formed column on the road.

It was in this position that the fusillade began.

The gunners, under the command of Sergeant* Verdière, held their position on the bridge in spite of the danger and the losses they suffered.

My situation was very bad; for, as the river was fordable, I was liable to be outflanked by a much superior enemy. Nevertheless, always hoping that the 10th Regiment would come over to my side, I held on. But, finally accepting that they would not do so and that the enemy, who were extending their right flank further and further, would certainly force the river crossing, I was about to order a retreat. I was hoping that this could be carried out by an orderly withdrawal on Valence, when suddenly firing stopped and I saw the battalion of the 39th move on to the bridge in front of the 10th and heard, at the same time, a shout of 'They are with us!' I rode forward through the crowd, and when I reached the bridge, the men of the 39th and the 10th, mingling together, surrounded me. I saw the officers embracing each other. But, at the same time, some were shouting, 'Long live the Emperor!' while others cried, 'Long live the King!'

An infantryman of the 10th thrust his bayonet towards me, shouting 'Down with the tricolour cockade!' I took the despatch that I had vainly attempted to send to the enemy commander from the pouch on my saddle and held it out to him, 'Take this to your general,' I said. So I got rid of the man.

Averos, an artillery captain, was with me and I told him: 'We've been betrayed. Safeguard your gun.' But it was already too late, the horses had been seized and the gunners arrested.

The *chef de bataillon* of the 39th, M. Chitry, and quite a large number of the soldiers, the gunners and the National Guardsmen, although they had been surprised by this treachery, still contrived to escape despite being surrounded. The enemy pursued us, but we were able to put a fair distance between them and ourselves, and this gave me hope that we might rally enough men to put up some resistance, so that we could halt the enemy and reach Valence, when a sudden cavalry charge threw us into

---

* *Maréchal des logis.*

disorder. The *chef de batallion* of the 39th was captured. Captain Averos and I found it impossible even to rally thirty men to resist the second charge, which swept away the remainder of the fugitives and in the course of which both of us were wounded and captured. I received a sabre slash across the face. We were already at La Paillasse, two leagues from Valence.

The National Guardsmen had rivalled the bravery of troops of the line, and the honour guards from Valence had behaved perfectly. The conduct of all of them had inspired great confidence; it is certain that, without the treason of the 10th, our retreat would have been carried out in good order. This disloyal breach of our trust cost the lives of a hundred brave soldiers, who were taken prisoner and massacred, not by regular soldiers but by the horde of volunteers from the Midi.

Captain Averos, Sergeant Cassé and the gunners from my regiment were outrageously mutilated, and I should have been subjected to the same fate if, at the moment I was captured, the Count Guiche, an aide de camp of the Duc d'Angoulême, had not arrived and saved me from the violence of the Royalist volunteers.

He took me to the rear, where I met the prince, but he did not speak to me. Lieutenant Bordolle, of my regiment, to whom I had granted leave of absence before these events took place, escorted me to Loriol. I owed my life to this officer on several occasions; every time we met the Royalist volunteers they took aim at me and were only restrained by their officers stepping forward from the line.

Lieutenant Bordolle did even more for me. As orderly officer to the artillery General Berge,[*] he persuaded him to approach the prince to have me returned to Valence. On the following day, 3 April, when I was already on the way to Montélimar with the convoy of prisoners, Lieutenant Bordolle came to fetch me and accompanied me as far as Valence, which we reached on the same day.

When she learned of our defeat at Loriol and of the progress of the Royalist troops, my wife, with all those in authority, had left Valence, to go to Lyon. She was very distressed for there was a rumour that I had been captured and murdered. General Mouton-Duvernet received her very kindly at Lyon.

I went to my apartment at Valence, where the colonel of the 10th Infantry, M. d'Ambrugeac, came to see me; he gave me an orderly corporal, more to protect me from insult than to guard me, for I had not received any orders requiring my confinement.

On the 4th, the same evening as the affair, the Duc d'Angoulême, who had slept at La Paillasse, arrived in Valence. The troops had marched on Romans on the same day and had seized it without encountering any resistance, but they did not cross the Isère.

* General François, Baron Berge (1778–1832). After 8 March 1815 he commanded the troops under the orders of the duc d'Angoulême.

During the afternoon of the 5th, some withdrawal on the part of the Royalists could be discerned. It was predictable. They would most certainly be pushed back by the troops advancing from Lyon.

Cannon fire from the direction of the Isère ferry could be heard on the 6th. At about ten in the evening, the Duc d'Angoulême left Valence with his staff. His army retreated during the night.

The National Guard entered Valence at eight in the morning of the 7th, and was quickly followed by the troops of the line. The town had remained quiet during the occupation of the Royalists and no atrocities were committed.

My family came to join me on the 11th.

As soon as General Piré,* who was in command of the Imperial troops, arrived at Valence, I submitted my report on the battle of Loriol to him.

The Royalist troops withdrew as far as the Montélimar road and, strangely enough, it was to be exactly here, at the crossing of the Drôme, that these same 4th Chasseurs who had charged us abandoned the Royalist cause. The 10th, surrounded by Royalist volunteers did not dare to do the same, but a few days later it came over to the Imperialists, together with the 3rd Foot Artillery – in fact, all those troops of the line who had attacked us at Loriol.

Thoughts on the battle of Loriol. This affair of the bridge over the Drôme had a great impact in the Midi and in the army. In the Midi it encouraged the Royalists, who thought it to be a great victory. In the army, it aroused a feeling of deep resentment. It was considered to be treachery, and the *Moniteur*, in the course of an incomplete account, announced that it was with cries of *'Vive l'Empereur'* and while flying the tricolour flag that the 10th crossed the bridge.

The minister of war ordered an inquiry that Marshal Suchet, who was in command of the Army of the Alps, instructed Staff Colonel Carion-Nizas to carry out. However, as the 10th Regiment came over to our side a few days later, in order to avoid duels and conflicts, an ambiguous note was published in the *Moniteur* in which an attempt was made to explain the affair as the result of a misunderstanding, in which even the wind was involved.

What is quite certain is that the 10th and the other troops who were at Loriol were the only ones in all the army who had fired on the Bonapartists, and that, when they returned to our ranks, the 10th was ostracised in the rest of the army, that many of their officers were dispersed to other regiments and that many of them subsequently entered the royal guard. It is also true that their frame of mind was so suspect that, when the Emperor inspected them at the Tuileries, the officers of his escort, fearing

* General Hippolyte-Marie-Guillaume de Rosnyvinen, Compte de Piré (1778–1850).

213

some attempt upon him, pressed closely around to protect him. Napoleon, finally, addressed harsh words to them, telling them that their flag would not be returned to them until they had earned it by their conduct. This regiment asked to be allowed to be part of the army that was marching into Belgium, and then behaved courageously at Waterloo.

Different accounts of this unhappy affair at Loriol have been given, depending upon the opinions of the various historians concerned.

A former *trompette-major* of the guard, of whom I have no recollection, who later became an officer,* and who had been in command of the twenty-five members of the honour guards of Valence has accused me in his *Souvenirs Militaires* of having connived with the Royalists because I refused to comply with his injunctions to fire on the 10th Infantry Regiment. I have given the reason for this. In the account given by this officer he lays claim to a part that he did not play, and which was one he could not have performed.

According to him, I did not reach Loriol until the 2nd at the moment the engagement began, and at a time when he had already taken up position for an energetic resistance. So my arrival had relieved him of the command of the troops – to his great annoyance.

It was out of the question for the leader of twenty-five mounted honour guards ever to have the right to such a command, for there was already present a *chef de bataillon* at the head of 250 infantrymen; and their commandant, Chitry, was not the man to allow anyone to encroach on his rights. It was he who, not on the 2nd but on 1 April at dawn, had handed the command to me, and all the arrangements for the defence had been made by me.

The honour guards, like the National Guard, behaved most courageously; if their unfortunate first charge had been ordered and carried out by the author of the *Souvenirs Militaires,* then it was of great credit to his courage, but certainly not to his intelligence as a cavalry officer, for it was completely ill-timed.

At that time, everything pointed to the likelihood that Royalists were about to cross over to the Bonapartist side, so that it would have been a very inopportune moment for me to join the Royalists. If I had, indeed, been conniving with them, nothing would have been easier for me than to join them on the bridge, rather than to leave myself open to being wounded, captured, injured and killed, as I so nearly was. Finally, when the second Restoration took place, I should have been rewarded rather than put on half-pay for two years and allowed to remain as a colonel for fifteen.

All of us at this time believed that there had been premeditated and deliberate treason. Now, contemplating these sad matters more coolly, I am able to appreciate

* This may be a reference to *Souvenirs Historiques* of Captain Krettly. Of doubtful accuracy, these were first published in 1839 (Paris, Berlandier, two volumes).

that the conduct of the 10th might not have been premeditated. The soldiers in the army were Bonapartists; the officers were often more divided. Most of those in the 10th were Royalists, since many of them were taken into the Royal Guard on the return of the Bourbons. Every day, when Royalists and Imperialists met, the first often crossed into the camp of the latter, the reverse never occurred. The soldiers followed their officers.

On the 2nd, at Loriol, it is possible that the leading soldiers of the 10th may have intended to join us but that, after their first enthusiasm, and held back either by their officers or by finding that no one followed them, they again turned against us. However, when I was led as a prisoner in front of the ranks of the 10th, I recognised one of the infantrymen who insulted me as one who, on the previous day, had been among those who had come to tell me that all the troops of the line were about to come over to our side.

Champ-de-Mai.[*] My regiment, which was part of the Army of the Alps under Marshal Suchet, left Valence for Grenoble on 10 April. As the *chef de corps*, I was summoned to Paris to be present at the ceremony of the Champ-de-Mai, with a deputation from my regiment. The ceremony of the Champ-de-Mai took place on 1 June.

Deputations from the military, together with state officials and other authorities, occupied enormous terraces that rose as high as the first floor of the buildings around the amphitheatre in front of the military school. A sort of altar was placed opposite this and, behind it, stretching as far back as the Seine, were the ranks of, on one side, the National Guard and, on the other, the troops.

The Emperor made his entry from the first floor of the military school, and took his place on a gilded throne in the midst of the terraces. He was wearing a purple cloak embroidered with gold and trimmed with ermine. On his head was a black cap adorned with plumes held in place by a huge diamond.

Everyone rose to his feet as he entered and acclaimed him. His family were greeted coldly, for they were unpopular, they had cost France too dearly.

At the coronation, I had been part of the detachment from the 1st Horse Artillery; at the Champ-de-Mai I was part of that of the 4th Regiment, of which I was commanding officer. I am able to say that, on 1 June 1815, there was more cheering than on 2 December 1804. It seemed to me that it was less forced and more sincere. A great deal of sympathy had returned to Napoleon.

The Bourbons had made themselves so unpopular that, even though there was a longing for peace, the return of the Emperor was preferred, even with the prospect of war.

---

[*] This was originally intended by Napoleon as an alternative to a parliament. It was to be a big assembly, on the Champ de Mars, of all the electoral colleges in France.

It was known that he had tried by all means to achieve peace and that the allied sovereigns had refused to receive his envoys; this had given rise to feelings of humiliation and anger.

There was a belief that he had sincerely reverted to a more liberal way of thinking. The publication of the Additional Act,* by Bernard Constant, the head of the Constitutional party, the choice of Carnot as minister of the interior, the re-establishment of freedom of the press, together with his moderation and the absence of persecution of his enemies, all seemed to give guarantees for the future. Moreover, he knew very well that attitudes had changed.

Finally, fate had decreed that we were in dispute with all the rest of Europe, and it was felt that only the genius of Napoleon, in the terrible position in which we found ourselves, could give us any chance of success. One might deplore his return; but as France had, once more, chosen its ruler, there was no alternative but to follow him.

When the Emperor had taken his place on the throne, a Mass, followed by a *Te Deum,* was sung. There is nothing so impressive as these ceremonies of the Catholic Church accompanied by all the military pomp. There were present fifty thousand men under arms as well as one hundred cannon. It offered an imposing and austere spectacle.

The faces of those present did not appear to be giving thanks to Heaven, but rather to be imploring it for help. All seemed aware that this would be needed.

An oath to the constitution was sworn on the Gospels and this was followed by an award of eagles to the National Guard and to deputations from the regiments of the army.

The entire ceremony was magnificent. It conferred an imposing grandeur on the situation. The army was to march as soon as the ceremony ended.

However, it went on too long. There were too many speeches to which no one listened. In the circumstances, one might regret that the ceremony had not been simpler and less theatrical. It might have been preferable to see Napoleon in military uniform for it would have been more suitable at that time. His brothers were all dressed in white satin, and old Cambacérès was covered in a blue cloak strewn with golden bees, while the other dignitaries wore costumes of an earlier age. All this would have been rather grotesque if the gathering had been less imposing.

The Emperor's review took place at four o'clock, the deputations left at five, and by eleven o'clock next morning, I was in Grenoble.

The Belgian campaign. In the course of the few days that I had spent in Paris, I was able to ascertain that wonders had been achieved in two months. I was present at the

---

* The Additional Act to the Constitutions of the Empire. published on 22 April 1815, was a compilation by Benjamin Constant of previous constitutions, with additions by various others including Napoleon himself.

siege of Paris in 1814 and if, at that dreadful time, the defences had been as they were in June 1815, it would have been possible to wait for the Emperor to arrive, even in the face of all the coalition armies.

Confidence returned when it was seen that, in such a short time, the army had been reorganised and brought up to strength, the National Guard had been reinforced and well armed, that the *fédérés** (composed of stout workers, many of them old soldiers) were filled with determination, and the defences of Paris were supplied with many well-manned guns. It was hoped that Napoleon, who had often struggled successfully against the united coalition with an exhausted army of seventy thousand men and while Paris was defenceless, would do so again, with even more success, at the head of an army of one hundred and twenty thousand well-rested soldiers. With Paris fortified and his enemies now separated, he would have the freedom to move as he wished against them.

The Imperial Guard and some of the troops marched away on the day following the Champ-de-Mai to undertake the campaign in Belgium against the Prussians and the English. The Emperor joined the army on the 12th.

Alas, the campaign did not last long. Hostilities started on 14 June. Our army enjoyed some success against the Prussians on the 15th and 16th. The battle of Waterloo took place on the 18th. The Emperor abdicated for the second time on the 22nd. The news became known at Grenoble on the 24th and Napoleon left Paris on the 29th.

The Army of the Alps. The siege of Grenoble. These tragic events seemed to put an end to the war, while for us, in the Army of the Alps, it marked the beginning of our campaign.

On 1 July, the depot of my regiment left Grenoble to go to Lyons. General Charbonnel[†] detained me and gave me the command of the school and of the artillery of the town of Grenoble which was threatened by the Piedmontese.

During the early days of the month the Army of the Alps evacuated Montemélian and, in succession, Chambéry and the Mont-Blanc region. It retreated behind the Rhône, put up a weak defence of the gorges of the Échelles and the Grande-Chartreuse. By the 4th the Piedmontese were within five leagues of Grenoble, on the left bank of the Isère.

A negotiator was sent to the town during the night of the 5th to order the place to surrender; on the same day, at five in the morning, they made a reconnaissance that brought them within cannon shot of the suburb of Tréckiutre.

---

* These were volunteers from among that part of the population who had not, in the past, been encouraged to join the National Guard, the expense of the uniform being perhaps beyond their means. Now Napoleon needed to draw in as many as possible to reinforce the National Guard.
† General Joseph-Claude-Marie Charbonnel, Comte de Salès (1775–1846).

The governor, General Motte, refused to capitulate and, at about seven on the morning of the 6th, the enemy attacked the suburbs on the left bank with great energy and daring, reaching the town's glacis. However, artillery fire, in which pupils from the school served two cannon, quickly drove them out of the nearest houses. After several hours of gunfire, during which they lost, on their own admission, between four hundred and five hundred men, they sent in a negotiator to propose a cease-fire, we agreed that this should last from nine in the morning until midday.

During the whole of this attack, the National Guard had behaved very well, acting as boldly as troops of the line. The pupils of the school had, in their operation of the two guns entrusted to them, shown a zeal, skill and courage that were beyond all praise. Many women had been seen carrying ammunition to the batteries and to the troops as well as bringing them food and drink.

The abdication of the Emperor became known on the 24 June. From that time it became clear that the allies would enter Paris, and that agreements would be made with them to decide the fate of the towns. It was, then, very much in the interest of the town of Grenoble and its garrison to accept a cease-fire that would afford enough time to await the outcome. It was hoped that, in view of the circumstances, such a cease-fire would be prolonged, especially as the enemy lacked the supplies of artillery that would be required to mount a formal siege.

Although Grenoble was not in a position to oppose such a siege for very long, its fortifications permitted a certain amount of resistance. The lower town was suitably fortified, having protruding bastions with demi-lunes – except on the two right-hand fronts that were without this protection. This area of the main town was without earthworks or counterscarps or glacis. The moats could easily have been flooded. The right bank was protected, as far as the top of the mountain that dominated the town, by an old entrenchment of stones. On this summit was a sort of small fort that was called the 'Bastille', but the eastern area was weak and could have been overrun and destroyed without difficulty.

The armament of the town included sixty-two cannon.

The cease-fire brought with it a brief respite, and this gave the townspeople time to reflect. They knew of Napoleon's abdication, nearly fifteen days earlier, and it was known that the enemy was at the gates of Paris. This could provide a solution to their difficulties, and the townspeople soon came to the conclusion that, if the town resisted, their persons and their properties would be uselessly exposed to danger. As ever, events had calmed the ardour of the most enthusiastic.

Also, though the shells fired at the town during the attack had done only a small amount of damage, and there had been no fires, it was clear that if there were to be renewed hostilities, the same good fortune could not be relied upon. The National Guard sent a message by way of its commandant, M. Falcon, an officer on half-pay, to the effect that, if there were to be another attack, they would not mount the ramparts. The garrison, with a strength of three thousand men, was able to defend the town without help but, during the few days of the cease-fire, their despondency also increased. The garrison was made up mostly of battalions mobilised in Dauphiné and many of the soldiers had deserted.

If a letter from the mayor, M. Giraud, and passed to us by the defence council was to be believed, groups had formed who would, in the event of an attack, sound the tocsin and open the town gates to the enemy while the garrison was struggling with the besiegers.

The defence council was assembled in the evening of the 8th, when it was established that the garrison, by reason of desertions, found itself reduced to barely a thousand men, a force insufficient to defend a town surrounded by walls of a length such as those around Grenoble.

Unfortunately, the enemy was aware of the situation and refused to grant an extension of the cease-fire; so the town, already invested, was forced to surrender.

On the 9th, the garrison, with its arms and its baggage, left to go to Lyon, halting for the night at Moirans and, at about seven in the evening of the same day, the Piedmontese entered the town. They carried off all the supplies as well as all the equipment in the arsenal, even down to the fire-backs from the fireplaces of the administrative offices. When they had attacked the town for the second time they had undoubtedly known of the fall of Paris, which had taken place on the 3rd and brought the war to an end. Their only objective, then, in seizing Grenoble, had been to steal all the materials, as the allies had invariably tried to do when they attacked our strongpoints after the capitulation of Paris.

I travelled with my family in my coach when I left Grenoble. At Moirans on the 9th I had been quartered in an isolated house and did not hear the summons to leave. As a result I followed the column in the hope of rejoining it quickly. When I reached Rives, I learned that groups of the enemy were rounding up stragglers; I left the road and travelled along a lane, reaching the road to Valence near Tullinse. I arrived at Romans at nine in the evening and found that General Auguste Debelle* had caused consternation there.

The general had been ordered to travel through the Dauphiné to raise the population and threaten the enemy. But, like his brother, he produced more noise than action. He had been at Saint-Marcellin when he learned of the surrender of Grenoble. He left in a hurry and spread alarm all along his route, proclaiming that groups of the enemy had invaded the whole country and that the Austrians were following them. Reaching Romans at about noon on the 10th, he had not dared to sleep there, but went on to Tain. Still not feeling himself to be safe, he went to Tournon on the same evening,

---

* General Auguste-Jean-Baptiste Debelle (1781–1831).

where he cut the ferry cable and left the inhabitants in a state of dismay, as he had done everywhere else.

The news of what had taken place at Romans was given to me by the *sous-préfet* who came to see me at the hotel when I arrived, and where I slept. Yet General Debelle had fifty horse chasseurs with him; he could usefully have employed them to clear the road to Lyon.

From Romans I went towards Tain, where I took a boat across the Rhône, finally reaching Lyon on the 12th. It was on that day that the Army of Paris crossed the Loire after the capitulation.

At Lyon, Marshal Suchet had just made an agreement with the Austrians for the abandonment of the town and a withdrawal across the Loire.

All was in confusion, and the troops were on the point of revolt against the generals. Everyone spoke of treason, and traitors were seen everywhere. There were many desertions. It was at Lyon that I saw the unfortunate General Mouton-Duvernet for the last time.

The artillery of the Grenoble garrison was sent to Valence when it left Lyon. I knew that my regimental depot was at Roanne, so I went there, but found, when I arrived, that it had left for Clermont, where I eventually joined it. The regiment was then sent to Saint-Armand, a little town three leagues from Clermont, where we were kindly received by the townspeople.

We remained at Saint-Armand for a month and at first were in several cantonments in the neighbourhood of Clermont, and then at Limoges, where we were sent, on 9 October, to be disbanded. It was at Limoges that I had the misfortune to lose M. Clément, my lieutenant colonel and companion in promotion at the artillery school. To combat the sleeplessness from which he suffered, he had often had recourse to opium. One night, having sat up very late with his host eating chestnuts, he took his dose of opium and perhaps it was stronger than usual, for in the morning he was found dead in his bed. He was a clever, active and enterprising officer and I feel sure that, if he had lived, he would have been involved in one of the conspiracies that took place during the Restoration.

On 21 October the regiment was not, in fact, disbanded but was reorganised and many men were dismissed. It left for Toulouse on 20 December, arriving there on the 31st.

I was convinced that I should not be able to retain command of my regiment and, unwilling to expose myself to the insults that an officer of the Imperial army might have reason to fear from the over-excited population in the Midi, I asked for leave and remained at Limoges while I waited for it to be granted. In this I only followed the advice of the excellent general, Baron Bouchu, who wrote to me in confidence from Toulouse. He told me that the townspeople of that city, still greatly annoyed at the resistance I had put up at Loriol, were preparing an extremely hostile reception for me. He urged me to apply for leave and did all he could to make sure it was granted by General Pernetty.* I had no alternative but to defer to his opinion. When my leave was granted I left Limoges on 1 January 1816, travelling with my family in my coach. I reached Nancy on the 17th and stayed there until 2 February, when I travelled on to take up residence in Saint-Dié.

* General Joseph-Marie, Vicomte de Pernetty (1766–1856).

Chapter Thirteen

The Years of Peace (1815–1832)

Now I find myself at the end of my recollections of a military life: for, although I remained in the army for another fifteen years, I have little to recount of this peaceful period.

The affair at Loriol, or the events surrounding it, having placed me in opposition to the Duc d'Angoulême himself, did nothing to cause the Restoration government to view me favourably. Because of this, I was placed on half-pay.

As I had been so fully occupied for twenty years, idleness weighed heavily upon me. I loved reading and set about collecting a library. When I had read my books, I bound them. My teacher in this craft was the old recluse of the Madeleine mountain, who, at the beginning of the Revolution, had returned to the town and there pursued the profession of bookbinder.

After two years, and thanks to the repeated intervention of the generals under whom I had served, I was reinstated on the army's active list. On 1 February 1818 I received my appointment, dated from 15 January, as colonel director of artillery at Bayonne.

At Bayonne I met Commandant (Major) Moron again; he was one of my good friends and, as he was the assistant director, he helped me to settle my family at Bayonne and I was able to benefit from his wide acquaintance. Moron enjoyed turning, at which he was a true craftsman. I became his pupil and, while I never became as talented as he was, I achieved a certain skill. My bookbinding workshop was enlarged to contain a lathe and its accessories.

The administration of Bayonne was important and very wide-ranging. I explored all this wonderful countryside in the course of the inspections I made, and found a great deal there to interest me.

Lieutenant General the Marquis d'Autichamp commanded the division. My dealings with him, as well as with several others, led me to conclude that the generals of the Restoration frequently displayed more respect and consideration for the officers of the old army than for those of the Empire who had obtained commands under the new government. In which divisions did the military conspiracies

222

occur? In those commanded by such as Canuel, Donnadieu, Pamphile Lacrois and Rambourt.

After I had been at Bayonne for four years, I learned, at the beginning of 1822, that the command at Neuf-Brisach was about to become vacant. Although I was sad to leave a place where I had made many good friends, Neuf-Brisach would bring me much nearer to my native countryside; so I asked for the change and obtained it. I received my appointment on 25 March.

The ten years I passed at Neuf-Brisach were almost free of incidents. My life flowed calmly and serenely; so calmly, in fact, that the journey made by Charles X to Alsace was one of the most noteworthy occurrences. The king was visiting the eastern provinces and, on 6 September 1828, I went to Strasbourg to be present when he arrived and to take part in the parades and manoeuvres that were to be held during his stay. He made his entry on the 7th at two in the afternoon to the acclamation of the large crowds that had gathered from all parts. From Saverne to Strasbourg, from Strasbourg to Colmar and from Colmar to Mulhouse, it was a triumphal progress. The men in every village had formed processions, while the women crowded into wagons decorated with foliage; all were in national costume.

The king reviewed the troops on the 8th; and there were manoeuvres at the gunnery school; then he went to the arsenal. The king of Württemberg and the grand duke of Baden had come to greet him at Strasbourg, and accompanied him throughout the day. At the arsenal they saw five hundred field guns arranged on blocks in the courtyard, quantities of equipment on gun carriages and wagons and, above all, the two great armouries that contained the supplies with which one hundred and twenty thousand men could be armed. Thanks to the position I occupied, I had free access to the arsenal and I was close enough to the two foreign princes to see how surprised they were at our wealth. They had, no doubt, believed that France was less well provided with material resources, so they would return to their own countries with a completely new concept of our strength and assets. The king was present on the 9th at the opening of a bridge over one of the small branches of the Rhine. He was so pleased with the artillery that he gave two thousand francs to the bridge-builders, one thousand to the work force and twenty francs to each of the gun-layers.

Could anyone, seeing the enthusiastic welcome given to Charles X, have believed that he would fall so soon? Nevertheless, not even two years had passed when he was forced to take the road to exile. The *Gazette de France,* in which the laws of the 25th were published, reached us on the 28th. But we knew no more than that, and we heard nothing on the 29th or the 30th; so it was only on the 31st that there was news of the trouble in Paris. Definite news of the revolution was not learned until 2 August. On the 3rd I received an 'Order of the Day' from division to revert to the tricolour cockade.

On 8 September, when I least expected it, I received my appointment to the 6th Artillery Regiment. This was dated the 6th. I was to replace Colonel Etchegoyen and I was ordered to proceed to Metz, which I did at once. I reached Metz on the 10th and was in my post on the 11th.

The command I had just received was not really suitable for me. I had not been in a section of the service involving personnel since 1815 and, as a result, possessed none of the basic knowledge required by the new organisation of the regiments and the new manoeuvres. Because of this, I did not presume to think that I could carry out my duties, at least without undertaking studies that would be both tedious and difficult, and by doing so condemn myself to enter a branch of the service that no longer appealed to me. I felt more inclined to go back to my last position rather than to retain the command that had been offered to me. However, before coming to a conclusion, I wanted to ascertain that, by placing me in command of a regiment, there had been no generous intention that it was to lead to my promotion. The enquiries I made did not clear the matter up and left me in a state of uncertainty.

I had quite decided not to retain the command of my regiment if there was no hope of my promotion. I had witnessed many promotions, in all ranks, in particular that of my previous lieutenant colonel, Duchand, who was promoted to *maréchal de camp* although he had been in retirement since 1815 and had not been confirmed in his rank of colonel of the Hundred Days. I took the decision to go to Paris at the end of September, before there would have been time to replace me at Neuf-Brisach. As I was unable to learn anything positive, I asked to return to my previous post, and this was agreed on 10 October.

So I returned to the duties that I had carried out for so long. On the 21st March I was made a commander of the Légion d'Honneur. The following June, King Louis-Philippe with his two sons, the dukes of Orléans and Nemours, arrived at Neuf-Brisach at five in the afternoon. They left again at half past six having handed out several decorations to the 17th Light. All the corps commanders had been previously invited to present their recommendations for the Légion d'Honneur, but General Brayer, the commander of the division, had forgotten me. Forewarned ahead of time, I personally presented recommendations to Marshal Soult in favour of several of my subordinates and had the satisfaction of seeing them implemented shortly afterwards. In this way I obtained the officer's cross for my assistant director, Major M. Guéard and that of *chevalier* for Billar, the captain of the 6th Regiment of Artillery and for Fray, artillery guard. These were well-deserved awards.

This was one of the last acts of my military life. The number of generals in the artillery was limited, no vacancy could be anticipated and, although at the head of the list of colonels, I could not hope for promotion. On the other hand, the new law of 11 April 1831 on the subject of retirement, while it had removed an advantage previously enjoyed by officers of specialist branches – i.e. the right to a superior rank on retire-ment after ten years in one grade – had also retained this benefit, under article 34, for those officers conforming to this requirement who applied for retirement within six months of the promulgation of the new law. I was aware, too, that the command at Neuf-Brisach might be abolished quite soon – this, in fact, occurred under my successor – and this would leave me in danger of a posting that might take me very far away.

All these reasons caused me, at the review of 1831, to ask to be allowed to retire. My request was granted and I left the service on 1 June 1831. I established myself at Nancy, where I hoped to end my life, free and independent.

Index

227

Other Napoleonic Greenhill/Chatham books include:

ARTILLERY OF THE NAPOLEONIC WARS
Kevin F. Kiley
ISBN 1-85367-583-0

THE DECLINE AND FALL OF NAPOLEON'S EMPIRE
How the Emperor Self-Destructed
Digby Smith
ISBN 1-85367-597-0

LETTERS FROM THE BATTLE OF WATERLOO
Unpublished Correspondence by Allied Officers from the Siborne Papers
Gareth Glover
ISBN 1-85367-597-0

A SOCIAL HISTORY OF THE NAVY, 1793–1815
Michael Lewis
ISBN 1-86176-232-1

WELLINGTON'S NAVY
Sea Power and the Peninsular War, 1807–1814
Christopher D. Hall
ISBN 1-86176-230-5

FEEDING NELSON'S NAVY
The True Story of Food at Sea in the Georgian Era
Janet Macdonald
ISBN 1-86176-233-X

Greenhill offer a 10 per cent discount on any books ordered directly. In the UK
please call 0208 458 6314 or email sales@greenhillbooks.com.

For more information on our other books, please visit www.greenhillbooks.com.
You can write to us at Park House, 1 Russell Gardens, London NW11 9NN

Greenhill Books